RELIGION AND THE ONE

RELIGION
AND THE ONE

Philosophies East and West

The Gifford Lectures, 1980

 **FREDERICK COPLESTON**

CROSSROAD · NEW YORK

1982
The Crossroad Publishing Company
575 Lexington Avenue, New York, NY 10022

Printed in the United States of America

Library of Congress Cataloging in Publication Data

Copleston, Frederick Charles.
  Religion and the One.

  (Gifford lectures; 1980)
  Includes index.
  1. One (The One in philosophy)—Addresses, essays,
lectures. 2. Many (Philosophy)—Addresses, essays,
lectures. 3. Philosophy, Comparative—Addresses,
essays, lectures. 4. Religion—Philosophy—Addresses, essays, lectures. 5. Mysticism—Addresses,
essays, lectures. I. Title. II. Series.
BD395.C66   291.2   81-5372
ISBN 0-8245-0092-X   AACR2

CONTENTS

AUTHOR'S PREFACE

This book represents the Gifford lectures delivered in the University of Aberdeen during the autumn terms of 1979 and 1980. The author regards it as a great honour to have been invited to give the lectures, and he expresses his gratitude to the University for all the friendliness and generous hospitality which he received during the periods of his residence in this ancient seat of learning. It was a great pleasure to have the opportunity of meeting and learning from colleagues, especially in the departments of divinity and philosophy.

The general theme of the lectures was suggested by two considerations. In the first place the author wished to choose a subject which fell within the area of thought envisaged by Lord Gifford, namely 'natural' or philosophical theology. In the second place the interest which he had developed in advanced years in the philosophical thought of non-western cultures prompted him to stray beyond the confines of Western philosophy. To yield to this prompting may well have been rash. But at any rate the selected theme, religion and the metaphysics of the One, seemed to meet both requirements. It is not only in Christendom, or in what passes as such, that the human mind has developed theories of one ultimate reality. Nor is it only in the West that such theories, or some of them, have had connections with religion.

The written text was prepared before the lectures were actually given. But the lectures did not take the form of simply reading the text aloud. For one thing, it was not possible to use all the material. For another, the lecturer wanted to allow himself room for developing this point rather than that, and also for some measure of spontaneity. Thus the lectures were perhaps a little more lively than the printed text may suggest. As however in the actual lectures some lines of thought were either omitted or touched on only very briefly, it seemed better to publish the text as it stood than to try to make it conform more exactly to what was actually said.

It is hardly necessary to say that after the delivery of the lectures the thought occurred to the lecturer that the text would

1

benefit by extensive rewriting, not so much with a view to brightening it up as to give it a clearer structure and to eliminate what might seem to be inconsistencies. When however a writer is already in his seventies, it is understandable if he is reluctant to postpone publication of a work, already promised to a publisher, until he is completely satisfied with his production. It has been traditional policy to publish sets of Gifford lectures, and in somewhat advanced years it is perhaps unwise to count on retaining sufficient energy for serious literary activity.

CHAPTER 1

INTRODUCTION

It seems desirable at the outset to make a few clarificatory comments about certain ideas expressed in this book.

It may seem to the reader that there are two lines of thought which find expression in the text and which it is difficult to reconcile. On the one hand there is recurrent reference to the need for an activity of synthesis which is wider in its scope than the synthesis achieved by any particular empirical science and which can be described as metaphysical. The author makes clear his agreement with Whitehead's justification of speculative philosophy as an endeavour to form a coherent system of general ideas in terms of which the different kinds of human experience can be interpreted. The implication seems to be that metaphysics possesses cognitive value, that it can increase our knowledge, not indeed of particular empirical facts but of the structure or pattern of human reality as a whole. On the other hand the author sees the activity of synthesis on the metaphysical level as culminating in the idea of the One, and he makes it clear that his confidence in the metaphysician's ability to pin down the ultimate reality in a conceptual web and to describe it is extremely limited. He seems to regard the metaphysics of the One as expressing the movement of the mind towards an elusive goal, this elusiveness being shown in the history of philosophical thought by the succession of systems. Sometimes he even seems to look on the metaphysics of the One as a recurrent attempt to say what cannot be said. In other words, the author may seem to be trying to combine confidence in the cognitive value of metaphysics with serious doubt about its cognitive value. To put the matter in another way, he appears to be trying to combine the basically rationalistic approach of Whitehead with the line of thought which finds expression in the philosophy of Karl Jaspers and which some people would dismiss as mysticism (in spite of Jaspers' criticism of the claims of mystics). But are these two approaches or lines of thought really compatible? To be sure, we can feel confidence at one time and doubt at another

3

time in regard to the same thing, a certain truth-claim for instance. This is a common enough phenomenon, which occurs not only in the sphere of religious belief but also in other areas, in regard to a person's trustworthiness for example. It is also of course possible to experience hesitation, to feel unable to make up one's mind definitely about the reliability of a truth-claim or hypothesis or theory. But should not a philosopher make up his mind, one way or another, before publishing? It is hardly a satisfactory situation if the reader is presented with two conflicting estimates of metaphysics.

According to William of Ockham, the question 'What is the subject-matter of metaphysics?' resembles the question 'Who is king of the whole world?' Each of these questions makes an erroneous assumption. There is no king of the whole world, and the word 'metaphysics' covers a number of different lines of inquiry. Ockham's statement is doubtless open to challenge. That is to say, while we are all aware that there is no king of the whole world, it can be maintained that metaphysics has one definable subject-matter, for example the study of being as being. If however we prescind from recommendations about what metaphysics ought to be, it is clear that metaphysics as it has actually existed in history has been sufficiently variegated for it to be possible, without at any rate being entirely unreasonable, to make such distinctions as that between ontology and natural theology (made by some writers in the seventeenth century and, in particular, by Christian Wolff in the eighteenth century) and the distinctions made in recent years between descriptive and revisionary metaphysics (Professor P. F. Strawson) and between immanent and transcendent metaphysics (Professor W. H. Walsh). It is not the present writer's intention to endorse all these distinctions. But they are not meaningless. And if there are specifiable grounds for making them, we can hardly exclude the possibility that in one area of the territory covered by the general term 'metaphysics' the extent of the knowledge attainable by the human mind should be greater than it is in another area.

Suppose that we regard it as part of the task of metaphysics to try to identify the basic and pervasive categories in terms of which we think the world and which find implicit expression in the concrete utterances of ordinary language. It may be said that this is a matter of conceptual analysis and that it has nothing to do with metaphysics. But metaphysics, as has been pointed out by others, has always included a great deal of what can be described as conceptual analysis. To reduce metaphysics to speculation about the Absolute, for example, is to narrow unduly the scope of metaphysical reflection. There are of course important issues which arise in connection with the idea of laying bare and exhibiting the basic categories by which we think the world. For example, are these categories to be regarded as purely subjective, in the sense that they are thought-forms which the mind projects on a reality which may be quite different from our ideas of it? Or are the categories objective, in the sense that they reflect the ways in which things actually are? Such questions are obviously themes for philosophical discussion. As far, however, as identification of the categories by which we think the world and which find implicit impression in ordinary language is concerned, there seems to be no reason why reflection should not in principle yield positive knowledge, not of course of particular empirical facts but of the categories themselves. If we conceive the categories in an Aristotelian manner, we can say that knowledge of them gives us knowledge of the fundamental ontological structure of the world about us. If we conceive them in a Kantian manner, we can say the same as far as the phenomenal world is concerned, but not of course as far as things in themselves are concerned, if, that is to say, we are prepared to allow that the Kantian concept of the thing in itself is meaningful. In any case identification of basic categories yields knowledge, whether we regard it as the product of reflection on beings or as the product of the mind's transcendental reflection on its own activity.

From the temporal point of view knowledge of basic categories obviously presupposes experience and empirical knowledge. This is the case however we assess the nature of the categories. If we conceive them as objective, in the sense that they are exemplified in the objective world, experience of this world precedes reflection on the categories exemplified in it. If we regard them as subjective, as thought-forms in terms of which we conceive things which, in themselves, are unknowable, iden-

tification of these thought-forms by means of the mind's reflection on its own activity obviously presupposes this activity as
an object of reflection. From the logical point of view however
the basic ontological structure of the world precedes the particular aspects and characteristics of things which are studied
in the empirical sciences. And the basic and all-pervasive
thought-forms are logically prior to particular concepts of more
restricted application.

The area of 'metaphysics' however can also cover the activity
of constructing world-views which presuppose the world as represented in the sciences and also the human being's aesthetic,
moral and religious experience, together with the development
of human society. The cognitive value of world-views in this
sense is a subject which is discussed in the tenth chapter of this
book. In so far as a world-view presupposes and depends on
current science, for example, or the development of contemporary social and political structures, it obviously cannot be regarded as final and definitive, the system to end all systems. For
science undergoes changes, and so do social and political structures. And a superstructure built upon them is also subject to
change. To put the matter in another way, it is historically
conditioned in specifiable ways. It does not necessarily follow
however that there are no criteria at all for assessing the comparative merits or demerits of world-views. But as some possible
criteria are discussed in the final chapter of the book, this topic
can be passed over here. The author's contention is that though
so-called inductive metaphysics is a natural and legitimate mental activity, and though some criteria for evaluating world-views
can be mentioned, we cannot expect to find a final and definitive
philosophy of this kind. In other words, the succession of
world-views is not anything very surprising. What would be
surprising would be to find all philosophers, belonging to different periods, repeating the same world-view, if, that is to say,
we understand by a world-view a superstructure erected on the
basis of, and presupposing, an infrastructure which changes in
important ways.

The construction of a world-view is obviously an activity of
synthesis. If it is allowed that the existence of the Many gives
rise to a problem, synthesis takes the form of a movement of the

mind towards the One, conceived as the source of the Many and as the ultimate reality. To be sure, it is not everyone who would be prepared to admit that the existence of the Many does give rise to a metaphysical problem. But if a philosopher shares the conviction expressed at the close of Plato's *Parmenides* that if there were not a One, there would be nothing at all, the movement of his mind in metaphysics will be towards the One. Though however the One constitutes the goal of the movement, it remains an elusive goal. If there is a metaphenomenal ultimate reality, some statements can indeed be made about what it is not and cannot be, but any positive descriptive term is derived from language developed for use in other areas or contexts, with the result that such descriptive talk strains language and cannot be adequate. The philosopher may try to bring the One more within the field of understanding, perhaps by identifying it with the phenomenal world and endeavouring to eliminate transcendence. But if the elimination is successful and the One is literally identified with the world of plurality, 'the One' becomes simply a collective name for the Many. If the idea of the One as transcending the Many is retained, the ultimate reality remains on the horizon, as it were, outside the area of what can be clearly seen and described. This was recognized by the author of the *Lao Tzu* when he described the Tao as 'nameless', by the Advaita Vedānta philosophers when they asserted that Nirguna-Brahman, the Absolute in itself, transcends the grasp of discursive thought, by the Muslim thinkers who emphasized the Koranic idea of the hidden essence of Allah, and by Moses Maimonides and St Thomas Aquinas when they claimed that we know of God more what he is not than what he is.

As philosophy, including metaphysics, expresses a desire to understand, the concept of an elusive goal can seem highly unsatisfactory and to smack of mysticism. It is therefore not surprising if some philosophers who recognize that metaphysics cannot be simply eliminated or condemned lock, stock and barrel none the less fight shy of what Professor W. H. Walsh has called 'transcendent metaphysics' and emphasize instead the more mundane areas of what Professor P. F. Strawson has called 'descriptive metaphysics' or what Professor Walsh has named 'immanent metaphysics'. According to Professor Walsh, it is often, or generally, the case that the pursuit of transcendent metaphysics has been associated with a religious interest, in the sense that religion will be found to have played an important role in the lives of the relevant philosophers. The author of this book is obviously inclined to agree. While he certainly does not claim that the pursuit of metaphysics in all its forms is sufficient evidence of a religious interest, he clearly thinks that the movement of synthesis in the various versions of the metaphysics of the One has, or can have, a religious significance. It is indeed an obvious historical fact that this kind of metaphysics has often been associated in some way or ways with religion. And the movement of the mind can be seen as one approach, an approach by way of thought, to the divine reality. It is not the same thing as mysticism, which aims at experiential knowledge or knowledge by acquaintance rather than knowledge *that* or knowledge about. But reflection on the phenomenon of mysticism can serve as a counterbalance to a philosophical gnosticism which attempts to take the One by storm. If the author is right in thinking that the movement of the mind in the metaphysics of the One has a religious significance, it follows that when a religious interest is lacking, the metaphysics of the One is likely to be regarded as a dubious mental activity.

The foregoing remarks are not intended to convey the impression that, according to the author, 'metaphysics' is simply a collective name for a set of completely different lines of study or thought. If, for example, we conceive metaphysics in a traditional manner as the study of beings precisely as beings or, as Martin Heidegger would put it, of the meaning of being, there can be a more or less continuous movement of the mind from reflection on finite beings, members of the Many, up to the idea of the One as the ultimate reality. At the same time it is possible, as an empirical fact, to arrest the movement at a given point. A man may have a deep religious interest even if he would not call himself a religious believer, and he can struggle, so to speak, with the problem of the ultimate reality, with, that is to say, what he sincerely believes to be a problem and a matter of real concern. 'Transcendent metaphysics' should not be represented as being simply apologetics on behalf of a particular creed. But if a religious interest is lacking, 'transcendent metaphysics' is likely to appear as futile speculation. It does not follow, however, that this point of view entails a rejection of all metaphysics. Even if the metaphysician of the One judges that metaphysics without the concept of the One as ultimate source of the Many is truncated metaphysics, it is none the less possible to distinguish between several areas of metaphysical reflection. And if this is the case, it is also possible to focus one's attention on one area rather than another.

Philosophers, both in the East and in the West, have given a number of rather different accounts of the ultimate reality. In this book the author discusses some of them. The discussions cannot be anticipated here. But it may be as well to point out in advance that the author's representation of the metaphysics of the One as a movement of the mind towards an elusive goal should not be understood as equivalent to the claim that in this area anything goes and that there are no criteria at all for assessing or evaluating such accounts. For example, it can be argued that the theory that there is only one reality and that the human self is not different from this reality cannot be stated without involving oneself in a contradiction, inasmuch as one cannot state the theory without objectifying the One as an object of thought, over against oneself as subject. Though, however, the author has no intention of denying that there can be rational discussion of theories of the One, he certainly lays emphasis on the limitations of metaphysics when it is a matter of trying to pin down the ultimate reality in a conceptual web. His sympathies are clearly with thinkers such as Maurice Blondel and Karl Jaspers.

It is argued in this book that recognition of the limitations of metaphysics can contribute to diminishing the hostility shown to this subject by those theologians who see in metaphysics a rival and a creator of idols and who welcome what they regard as its downfall in modern times. The more that the metaphysics of the One is looked on as the movement of the mind towards an elusive goal, so much the more is the way left clear for the theologian's ideas of divine self-disclosure and the response of faith. To be sure, the critical mind can raise awkward questions in regard to the theologian's claims. But the author omits any discussion of them as falling outside his selected subject-matter.

His aim was partly to show that though he regards the metaphysics of the One as having a religious significance and as
tending to be religiously oriented, he does not look on it as 'a
religion', even if it can express a religious interest. It can of
course be closely associated with a religion, as in the case of the
Advaita Vedānta, which can be seen as an esoteric form of
Hinduism. Taken by itself, however, the metaphysics of the One
is, in the author's opinion, a movement of the mind towards an
elusive goal which cannot be taken by storm, though 'decipher-
ings', to borrow a term from Jaspers, have of course been made,
sometimes under the clear influence of a certain religion. It is
not a question of limiting the scope of metaphysics simply in
the interests of theologians. In the author's view philosophy,
exercising its critical function, limits itself. If at times it tries to
embrace everything in its scope, it soon criticizes its own
pretensions.

This, it may be said, is clearly the point of view of a religious
believer whose study of the history of philosophy has convinced
him that all systems are historically conditioned in specifiable
ways but who at the same time sees a religious significance in
the various forms assumed by the metaphysics of the One, at
any rate when the One is conceived as the ultimate reality and
not simply as a collective name for the Many. Given the idea of
the metaphysics of the One as being, in essence, a movement of
the mind towards an elusive goal, it is open to him to maintain
that the complement, so to speak, of this movement is a self-
disclosure on the part of the One. In other words, the religious
believer can find room for the concept of revelation. This position has its advantages. For example, it enables the philosopher
to claim that the problem of evil is a theological rather than a
philosophical problem. That is to say, it arises when the One is
conceived in a certain way, in terms of a certain religious
language-game, as a loving Father for instance, whereas it
hardly arises if the One is conceived simply as an elusive goal,
its nature being left undetermined as far as the metaphysician
is concerned. As for those theologians who are inclined to look
on metaphysics as a dangerous rival, the position in question
provides them with additional ground for claiming that the God
of the philosophers is an idol. Though however the position has

certain advantages, any philosopher who accepts it is faced with some awkward questions. For example, what does he understand by the movement of the mind which he claims to find expressed in the metaphysics of the One? If he is not referring to some mystical intuition or to a desire but to a real movement of the mind, this movement must surely take the form of an inference. The question then arises whether the inference is valid. Further, the existence of a One can hardly be inferred, unless the One is conceptualized, unless it is conceived as having a certain nature. After all, this is what we find in Taoism, in the Vedānta schools, in Islamic metaphysics and in the relevant western philosophies. Or is it a question of inferring the existence of an 'I-know-not-what', of a Kantian unknowable thing in itself? If this is the case, can the metaphysics of the One, as conceived by the author, have any cognitive value at all?

As the author explains in the first chapter, what he understands by the movement of the mind in question is a movement of synthesis which is involved in obtaining conceptual mastery over a plurality and which is exemplified in various areas of thought. In metaphysics he sees it as a movement towards the One as the source of the Many. He does not deny that inference has a part to play in this process, and in the sixth chapter he raises and discusses a problem relating to arguments claiming to prove the existence of a One. He is of course aware that one cannot claim to prove the existence of anything without having some concept of it. But he argues that as the One is metaphenomenal, the concept is formed by way of negating characteristics which would imply that the One is a member of the class of the Many, and that the One in itself eludes the grasp of the mind which is dependent for its ideas on sense-perception. It is indeed natural that the mind should try to comprehend the ultimate reality and pin it down in a conceptual web. But the various pictures or mental constructions are vulnerable to critical analysis. It is the author's contention that the succession of metaphysical systems contributes to illustrating the limitations of metaphysics.

If we consider the Christian religion or the religious language-game of the Christian community, we find the use of analogies, such as that of a loving Father, acceptance of which as governing one's attitude to God and to one's fellow human beings depends on the authority of Christ as recorded in the gospels, not on metaphysics. Unless we propose to push the theory of autonomous language-games to an extent which the author would find unacceptable, we cannot deny to the philosopher the right to raise questions and difficulties in regard to the relevant use of language. But the person best qualified to attempt to deal with such questions and difficulties is the thinker who speaks and writes as a member of the community which plays the language-game in question, the Christian theologian in other words. He is the spokesman of the Christian community, and it is up to him to explain how Christian statements about the One should be understood. It is up to him to clarify the content of Christian faith.

This doubtless sounds as though the author looks on metaphysics from the point of view of a Christian apologist, the apologetics in question being more akin to the thought of the French philosopher Maurice Blondel than to the religious apologetics of the eighteenth century. It would not however represent the mind of the author if he were depicted as attempting to set limits to metaphysics simply from the outside, so to speak, and in the interests of a certain religion. For he is convinced that though philosophy is and should be constructive, it is also, and should be, radically critical, and that it is philosophy itself which calls in question its own pretensions to grasp the ultimate reality. In the author's opinion, it is not a question of metaphysics bringing one to a point at which Christian faith becomes a logical conclusion. It is rather a question of metaphysics bringing one to a point at which there is a parting of the ways. If the One remains an elusive goal, it is possible to doubt or to deny its existence. There is also the possibility of faith. Philosophy cannot compel the assent of faith, the response to what is believed to be a divine self-disclosure. It is true that some theologians, while wishing to maintain the freedom of the act of faith, demand of metaphysics more than the author regards as lying within its competence. But we are not living in medieval society, with its presuppositions. And what metaphysics can or cannot achieve is hardly a matter for dictation from outside.

There is a further point which it is appropriate to make in

this introductory chapter. The title given to this set of Gifford lectures was 'Religion and the Metaphysics of the One'. Perhaps something like 'Religious Aspects of the Metaphysics of the One' would have been more suitable, as indicating more clearly the fact that the author was concerned not with religion in general but with the religious significance or relevance, if any, of the metaphysics of the One. This means that in the case of metaphysical theories which emerged and developed within a given religion the author confines his attention to these theories, or some of them, without intending to imply that adherence to the relevant religion involved acceptance, or even knowledge, of the theories in question. For example, reference is made in the text to certain Buddhist philosophies, such as the Middle Way of Nāgārjuna and his followers. These philosophical schools emerged within Buddhism, and Nāgārjuna certainly thought of himself as presenting genuine Buddhist thought. There is no good reason why one should not reflect on the religious significance, if any, of the concept of Emptiness or the Void as found in the Middle Way philosophy. But it by no means follows that this abstract concept played an important role in the religious life of ordinary Buddhists. For the matter of that, it cannot be simply taken for granted that because a certain doctrine is a basic element in Buddhism, it exercises an effective influence on the lives of all those who profess Buddhism. It has been maintained, for instance, that very many lay Buddhists are chiefly concerned with meriting a more desirable personal life in their next rebirth than with striving to attain Nirvāna, not indeed in the sense that they deny the doctrine of Nirvāna but in the sense that the idea of attaining this goal is not an effective influence in their lives. In other words, they are led by the desire to attain a better state of personal existence rather than by the ideal of liberation from personal existence.[1] Again, whereas the original Buddhist doctrine is that salvation depends on the individual's actions (or intentions) and not on any external sa-

[1]As far as Theravada Buddhism in a particular country is concerned, an interesting example of empirical inquiry is *Buddhism and Society: A Great Tradition and Its Burmese Vicissitudes* by Melford E. Spiro (New York, 1970). As a result of his empirical inquiry into what practising Burmese Buddhists actually believe the author draws conclusions about the way in which common human nature reacts to and triumphs over certain 'normative doctrines'.

viour, the idea of a saviour became prominent in some forms of Mahāyāna Buddhism, such as Pure Land Buddhism. Popular Buddhism, that is to say, is often rather different from what is described as Buddhism in brief summaries. It is not of course simply a question of Buddhism. Though the Advaita Vedānta can be described as a form of esoteric Hinduism, and though it became the most influential school in Hindu intellectual circles, it would obviously be a great mistake to imagine that the philosophy of Śaṁkara could be equated with Hindu or Vedic religion as a whole. In this book however the author is not concerned with popular Buddhism or popular Hinduism or with Taoism as an organized religion. He is concerned with a much more restricted theme, namely with certain theories of the One and with their religious significance or relevance.

It must be admitted that though the subject-matter of the book is limited in the sense indicated, it is none the less extensive. This may well be an advantage in the case of public lectures, open to a general educated public. But from the point of view of a professional philosopher it is a distinct disadvantage. That is to say, the wider the coverage of the historical or expository part of a volume, so much the more difficult is it to discuss the philosophical questions or problems arising in anything approaching an adequate manner. The author was conscious of this when delivering the second set of lectures, represented by the second half of the book. He decided however that he could not do much to remedy this defect, unless the size of the volume was to be greatly increased.

This introduction may read like a review by the author of his own work. It is not however intended to be an evaluation of the contents of the book. It is intended to provide a general idea of the author's line of thought, which probably tends to be obscured by the variety of topics treated in successive chapters. The author is not blind to all objections which can be brought against his general line of thought. He is not fully satisfied with it himself, and he can understand that others may be even less satisfied. But some preliminary account of it seemed to be desirable. Some ideas have indeed already found expression in other writings by the author. But in this work he covers a wider field.

CHAPTER 2

THE METAPHYSICS OF THE ONE
AND THE MANY

*The theme of this book – the contention that the metaphysics of
the One and the Many belongs to a pre-scientific phase of thought
– comments on this contention – philosophies of the One and the
Many and religion – the philosophy of the One and escapism –
concepts of the One and the reality of the Many – discriminating
between philosophies of the One*

I

After having been engaged for a considerable number of years
in lecturing and writing about the history of western philosophy,
I have become interested in the comparative study of the philosophical traditions of different cultures, in the similarities and
dissimilarities between approaches to and treatment of problems
and themes, and in the different ways of thought which find
expression in the philosophies of different cultures and which
are doubtless more long-lasting than individual systems. For
example, we can say (though the general statement stands in
need of qualification) that philosophical thought in China
tended to centre round the human being in this world, round
man as a moral agent in a social context, whereas the classical
philosophies of India, with the exception of the materialist
school, gave (or, in some cases, came to give) prominence to the
idea of liberation from bondage, not only in the moral sense of
freedom from the slavery of the passions and from egoism but
also in the sense of liberation from the world of change, time
and rebirth. Or we can say that while in Indian thought the
search for the inner self, the true self, was a prominent feature,[1]
in China and Japan the human being was seen in terms of his
social relations, in the family and the State. To be sure, this
generalization too is open to criticism. Social relations were not

---

[1]One can see this not only in the Advaita but also, for example, in the
Sāmkhya system, though in a different way.

simply passed over in Indian thought, and in Japan the search
for the true self is conspicuous in Zen Buddhism. But the two
generalizations can none the less stand as statements of general
tendencies or as illustrating distinguishable placings of
emphasis.

An interest in comparative philosophy, considered by itself,
does not need any special justification. No sensible person would
object to the attempt to broaden one's horizon and to understand different philosophical traditions, especially in a world in
which people of different cultural backgrounds are becoming
more and more inter-dependent in a variety of ways. It may
indeed be objected that what we ordinarily think of as Indian,
Chinese or Islamic philosophy belongs to the past, that it is
becoming less and less representative of present-day thought in
the relevant countries, and that it thus possesses only an historical interest. Past philosophy, however, can perfectly well form
a point of departure for and a stimulus to philosophical reflection
in the present. Plato and Aristotle lived many centuries ago, but
it is hardly necessary to say that their thought can still act as
a stimulus. Indeed, it is arguable that one mark of an outstand-
ing thinker is precisely his or her ability to speak meaningfully
to people of a later age, perhaps even of another culture. Further,
as I have already suggested, there can be general lines of thought
which outlive individual systems of philosophy. For example,
the present official ideology of the People's Republic of China
is of western origin and obviously differs in specific ways from
Confucianism, which was the official ideology of imperial China
from 136 B.C. until A.D. 1905. But it is equally obvious that
both centre round the thought of the human being in society,
man as an historical being. The change to Marxism involves
less of a clash with the past than would be involved by an
analogous change either in India or in Islam. Confucianism and
Marxism are different philosophies; but there is more similarity
between them than there is between the religiously oriented
philosophy of India and Marxism.

It is one thing to become personally interested in the comparative study of philosophical traditions and another thing to
undertake to speak or write about the subject. The field of study
is vast. If one cannot be a specialist in all phases of the philo-

sophical thought of one culture, how can one hope to acquire a real knowledge of the philosophies of all cultures in which philosophical thought is known to have developed, especially when one is already advanced in years? To understand the thought of a culture other than one's own is no easy task in any case. It is made no easier if one is ignorant of the relevant language or languages. Whatever view we take of the precise nature of the relationship between thought and language, it is a close relationship. It is only too easy to give to a word or statement translated from a language which one does not know the meaning which it would probably have in Western thought, even when its actual significance is somewhat different. Although, however, there are specialists in this or that phase of oriental thought, the general comparative study of philosophical traditions is a relatively recent development, and there may be room for contributions even by those who lack the ideal qualifications for the task, contributions which are clearly of an exploratory and tentative nature. It does not require, for example, expert linguistic knowledge to understand the importance of context in assessing similarities and dissimilarities. There is an obvious similarity, for instance, between Buddhist analysis of the self and the phenomenalistic analysis expounded by David Hume. The contexts, however, are very different. Hume was concerned with the limits of knowledge, and if he had a practical end in view it was to undermine dogmatism and to deprive certain beliefs of their basis. The Buddhist aim however was to show the non-substantiality of all things with a view to the attainment of enlightenment, of Nirvāna. It does not require a knowledge of Pali or of Sanskrit to grasp this fact.

One of the main questions which originally attracted my attention was whether or not it was possible to discern in the philosophies of different cultures a common recurrent pattern of development. I have already expressed in print some reflections on this subject, giving reasons for doubting whether one can reach any well grounded and definitive conclusion.[2] I looked, therefore, for a more limited theme and decided to discuss certain selected theories in which the world of plurality is conceived

---

[2]*Philosophies and Cultures*, ch. 8 (O.U.P., 1980).

as related to one ultimate reality, whether the relationship is conceived in terms of appearance or self-manifestation or causation. Theories of this kind can be found in both western and eastern thought. They are similar to the extent that in all of them the Many are related to a One conceived as being in some sense the ultimate reality. But they also differ very considerably among themselves, ranging from identification of the One with the self-transforming universe to the conception of the One as transcendent and distinct from the Many. What I wish to do is to examine the similarities and dissimilarities between some of these theories.

My initial approach will be primarily that of the historian of philosophy. That is to say, I shall not be concerned with expounding and defending a particular philosophy in the way in which F. H. Bradley set out, in his work *Appearance and Reality*, to expound his own version of absolute idealism. At the same time some critical discussion will not be excluded. In the later chapters I propose to discuss some of the factors which seem to me to have been influential in stimulating people to think in the ways which find expression in the theories examined in the earlier chapters.

It is hardly necessary to say that I am aware of the fact that the theme which I have chosen is not fashionable in contemporary philosophy. One reason, however, for selecting it is that the metaphysics of the One and the Many has often been associated or connected with religion. I am not prepared to claim that there is a necessary connection. But it is simply an empirical fact that the kind of metaphysics in question has often been related to a religious interest. The connection or relationship has not been uniform; it has taken several distinguishable forms. But the historical occurrence of such connections makes it reasonable to regard the general theme as falling within the area of natural theology, which Lord Gifford envisaged as constituting the subject-matter of the lectures which he established. It might, I suppose, be objected that Lord Gifford referred to promoting and diffusing the knowledge of God, and that, given ordinary linguistic usage, it would be misleading to describe the One, as conceived in some metaphysical systems, as God. But Lord Gifford also referred to natural theology as understood 'in the widest possible sense'. And the theme which I have selected seems to me to exemplify this broad concept.

II

A good many people might feel inclined to comment that this kind of metaphysics is obsolete, belonging to a pre-scientific phase of thought. It is not a question of claiming that metaphysical theories are, by their very nature, meaningless. Rather is it a question of claiming that such theories exemplify an activity of synthesis, that the function of synthesis has been taken over by science, and that the metaphysics of the One and the Many has therefore become superfluous. It is perfectly understandable that philosophers in the past tried to construct overall coherent interpretations of reality. In the history of philosophical thought emphasis has been differently placed at different times, sometimes on synthesis, sometimes on critical analysis. Both, however, are features of philosophical thinking. In other words, no sensible person would condemn philosophers of the past for having practised synthesis. For this is involved in man's attempt to obtain conceptual mastery over his environment. At the same time it is arguable that the work of synthesis has passed into the hands of scientists. By the coordination of phenomena under what we call laws, by the subsumption of more particular under more general laws, and by the construction of scientific theories science clearly pursues an activity of synthesis, the ideal term of the process being knowledge of the universe as one intelligible system. To be sure, this goal may never be reached in any final and definitive form. It is a limiting concept or, to use a Kantian phrase, a regulative idea. But recognition of this fact is a decided improvement on the metaphysician's tendency to dogmatism. It is indeed true that science lacks a conspicuous feature of traditional metaphysics. Even if science is explanatory and not, as some would claim, purely descriptive, it does not explain the existence of the world by postulating an ultimate reality, a One, beyond the phenomenal world. But why should it be supposed that the world needs to be explained in this sense? Can we not argue that even if science lacks a conspicuous feature of traditional metaphysics, this is simply the price which has to be paid, if we wish to advance to positive knowledge of reality?

The matter can be put in this way. Even on the level not only of pre-scientific but also of pre-philosophical thought there can be a vague idea of the Many as being 'in a world', of being, in some undefined sense, manifestations of a One. Philosophy in the past has made this idea explicit by forming a variety of theories of the One and the Many. In some philosophies, such as Taoism, the One has been conceived as the self-transforming universe, considered as logically prior to its changing and transient forms or manifestations. It has been conceived, we might say, as the universal which exists in and through its particulars. This idea of the One as the self-transforming universe can be seen as a preliminary view or vision, to which science, in the cause of its development, proceeds to give body or articulate form and structure. That is to say, science can be seen as moving towards this goal not so much as a conscious and deliberate policy as in virtue of what it actually does. In this sense the metaphysics of the One and the Many belongs to a pre-scientific phase of thought, though it can of course still be of historical interest.

If this point of view is accepted, what becomes of philosophy? A number of answers have been given. One answer is that philosophy becomes a second-order discipline or set of disciplines, taking the form of philosophy of science, philosophy of history, or philosophy of art, the relevant enquiries being meta-scientific, meta-historical, or meta-aesthetic in nature. The idea of philosophy as providing us with positive first-order knowledge of reality then drops out.

This sort of conception of philosophy is generally thought of as a result of reflection on the development of the empirical sciences. Rightly, of course. When Kant conceived the metaphysics of the future as the mind's transcendental reflection on its own activity, he was influenced by the conviction that metaphysics, considered as a source of positive knowledge of the world, had been supplanted by natural science. Another relevant fact, however, was his critique of metaphysical assumptions and arguments, a critique which could have been developed independently, even if in fact it was largely prompted by reflection on the advance of physical science. Indeed we can find examples of a thorough-going criticism of metaphysics even in periods which preceded the historical development of empirical science. One such example is the thought of Nāgārjuna, the Indian philosopher who lived (probably) in the second century A.D. and was the chief representative of the Mādhyamika or Middle Way school of Mahāyāna Buddhism. By means of a series of *reductio ad absurdum* arguments Nāgārjuna criticized all metaphysical systems known to him, whether non-Buddhist or Buddhist, without however proposing any alternative metaphysics of his own. To be sure, Nāgārjuna envisaged his dialectic as facilitating or preparing the way for enlightenment, for an intuitive apprehension of Emptiness or the Void, a concept which will be discussed in the next chapter.[3] In other words, the context of Nāgārjuna's thought differed from that of most modern critics of metaphysics. At the same time it is clear that Nāgārjuna looked on philosophy as having the function not of expounding and defending a particular theory of the One and the Many but of showing the futility of all such theories. (Enlightenment was not, for him, a theory, a construction of the discursive reason.) When, therefore, in a work on the Mādhyamika system – the Middle Way philosophy of Mahāyāna Buddhism – a modern scholar suggests what seem to him to be the implications of Nāgārjuna's thought in regard to the relation between metaphysics and science, we can hardly describe his point of view as extravagant or altogether unreasonable, even though Nāgārjuna lived long before the development of modern science. I am referring to T. R. V. Murti's book, *The Central Philosophy of Buddhism: A Study of the Mādhyamika system.*[4] The author argues that, on Nāgārjuna's premises, if metaphysics tries to compete with science as a means of attaining positive knowledge of reality, it inevitably finds itself eventually pushed out of the way as superfluous or otiose. In the Mādhyamika system philosophy becomes purely critical. If, therefore, we presuppose the development of science, we can say that on the level of discursive thought (and philosophy is the work of discursive thought) science has taken the place of traditional

[3]Pp. 52–55.
[4]London, 1955 (2nd edition, 1960).

metaphysics as a way of obtaining positive knowledge of reality. Obviously, recognition of an intuitive apprehension or insight transcending the subject-object distinction is hardly in accordance with the spirit of western positivism. Nor does Professor Murti imagine that it is. It remains true, however, that in Nāgārjuna's thought we find an oriental philosopher who undertakes to expose the futility of all metaphysical theories of the One and the Many. And it is reasonable to argue, as Murti does, that in a modern context the implication would be that the task of synthesis has passed into the hands of science, as far as discursive thought is concerned. In the historical context of Nāgārjuna's thought it is more a question of metaphysical theory having been pushed aside in favour of an intuitive apprehension, the content of which cannot be described. But the Buddhist philosopher did not of course claim that discursive thought had no function in human life. And in a later historical context he might well have sympathized with the thought of Kant, with whom Professor Murti likes to compare him, even though his idea of an intuition transcending discursive thought would have been quite unacceptable to Kant.

In making such comparisons one obviously runs the risk of anachronism. My main point, however, is that criticism of the metaphysics of the One and the Many is not an exclusively western phenomenon. Not all oriental philosophers were what Kant would describe as dogmatists.

III

The contention that the task of synthesis has passed into the hands of science can be presented in a persuasive manner. But it is also possible to argue persuasively against it. It is not of course a question of denying that science performs a work of synthesis. For it obviously does. Even if a subjectivist interpretation of science were defended, it would still have to be admitted that its theoretical construction exemplifies synthesis (as well as analysis). It is a question of denying or at any rate casting doubt upon the claim that, apart from futile speculation, the task of synthesis has passed without residue into the hands of science.

Science takes the form of particular scientific disciplines, natural and social, the number of which tends to multiply. Thus there are several sciences, such as physiology, psychology, anthropology and the social sciences which treat the human being under different aspects and which have, as the Scholastics would put it, different formal objects. Further, these particular sciences tend to undergo fragmentation or internal division into distinct disciplines or sub-disciplines. For example, there are different branches of psychology, experimental, abnormal, educational, industrial, and there is an increasing number of social sciences. It can therefore be reasonably argued that there is not only room but also a need for a philosophical anthropology, for a more general interpretation of the human being, which would counterbalance the tendency to fragmentation. It would be incorrect to speak of a philosophical anthropology as trying to compete with the particular sciences. It could presuppose them.[5]

To be sure, a philosophical anthropology is not the same thing as a metaphysical theory of the One and the Many. But I am suggesting one reason for claiming that there is still a need for philosophical synthesis, in spite of the development of science. It might be asked, I suppose, why a synthesis of this kind should be described as philosophical. One answer might be that it would be meta-scientific, if science is understood as consisting of distinct sciences with increasingly particularized functions.

Let us take a further step. In William Golding's novel *Free Fall* one of the characters asserts that between the scientific conception of the world and the ethico-religious view of reality there is no bridge. It is not asserted that the real world is coterminous with the world as represented by physical science, and that the moral and religious conceptions are a madman's dream. On the contrary, both worlds are said, by the speaker, to be real. What is asserted is that they are different, and that there is no bridge between them. It can be argued, however, that it is one of the jobs of philosophy to try to construct a

---

[5]Some philosophers might maintain that philosophical anthropology should proceed in an *a priori* manner, independently of the relevant particular sciences. Even so, it would presumably have to take note of relevant scientific theories. In any case I am primarily concerned with making the point that the fragmentation of science renders the need for synthesis more acute, and that the task cannot be performed by one of the particular sciences in question.

bridge. Immanuel Kant made a notable attempt to do this. So
have some other philosophers. It is easy to say that the task of
synthesis has passed into the hands of science. If the scientific
conception of the world is itself one of the elements requiring
synthesis, this can hardly be the case. Whatever we may think
of Kant's way of going about his task, his problem was a real
one. It has not disappeared simply because science has developed since his time and the social sciences have come into being.
For example, if Kant was right in claiming that recognition of
moral obligation implies freedom, this claim needs to be har-
monized with the perhaps inevitable methodological determinism of the relevant sciences.[6]

By philosophical synthesis I do not mean the construction of
an encyclopaedia. An example of the sort of thing which I have
in mind is provided by A. N. Whitehead, who attempted to
identify a set of basic categories in terms of which different types
of human experience and different aspects of the world can be
coordinated and their interrelations exhibited.[7] Some philosophers might maintain that this cannot be done, that, as William
Golding's character in *Free Fall* put it, there is no bridge. But
an attempt at synthesis at any rate should precede any such
statement. Whether a synthesis of this kind can be achieved
once and for all, in a definitive manner, is another question. In
any case, I am not concerned here with claiming that there can
be a system to end all systems. I am simply claiming that the
idea of a wider synthesis than that which can be achieved by
any particular science, or indeed by the particular sciences taken
together, cannot justifiably be regarded as belonging to an outmoded pre-scientific phase of thought. For the idea is prompted
by a need which persists.

The matter can be approached in another way, in terms of
the neo-Wittgensteinian theory of language-games. Wittgenstein
himself seems to have understood language-games primarily in
the sense of distinct linguistic operations such as asserting, com-

---

[6]I distinguish between methodological determinism and a dogmatic determinism which seems to be a philosophical thesis rather than a scientific
hypothesis or a guiding rule of procedure.
[7]*Process and Reality* represented Whitehead's Gifford lectures delivered in the
University of Edinburgh.

manding, questioning and praying. But they have also been understood in the sense of the language of science, religious language and the language of morals. Language-games in this sense are said, by Wittgenstein himself, to be grounded in 'forms of life'. In spite, however, of the neo-Wittgensteinian theory of autonomous language-games, all of them are played by human beings; and all 'forms of life' are forms of human life, having a common basis in human nature. This suggests not only the possibility but also the desirability of exploring the interrelations between them in the light of reflection on man in his historical development. We thus arrive once more at the idea of a philosophical anthropology.

This idea need not be unacceptable to analytic philosophers. After all, Gilbert Ryle's book *The Concept of Mind*[8] exemplifies synthesis as well as analysis, even if the latter is more prominent than the former. For Ryle conveys a general picture of the human being, as one organism. Again, though one naturally tends to think of the emotive theory of ethics as a kind of by-product of logical positivism, the theory suggests to the mind one way of coping with the question which arises out of the statement in William Golding's novel, namely, that there is no bridge between the scientific and ethical conceptions of the world. For the emotive theory of moral and aesthetic judgements suggests that a bridge can be found in human nature, which has its emotive as well as its cognitive aspects. By saying this I do not intend to express my personal adherence to the emotive theory of ethics. I am illustrating what I believe to be the case, that analysis and synthesis are complementary, each requiring the other.

It can indeed be objected that anthropology, whether philosophical or otherwise, is not the same thing as the metaphysics of the One and the Many. This is doubtless true. At the same time reflection on language-games can give rise to ontological questions. For example, first-order religious language, in some of the forms which it takes, implies that the world and all that is in it depends on the creative and sustaining power of God. And it is natural that in some minds at least the question should

[8]London, 1949.

arise whether belief in the truth of their implication can be
justified. It may be that some neo-Wittgensteinians would protest that a language-game does not need, and indeed cannot be
given, any justification of the sort that I probably have in mind.
If it expresses an existing form of life, it is *ipso facto* justified. We
cannot, however, enter here upon a discussion of the claim that
every language-game is completely autonomous.[9] My point is
simply that reflection on language-games naturally gives rise in
the mind to questions of a metaphysical nature.

Even if it is admitted that the questions arise, it by no means
follows, someone may urge, that they can be answered. Human
beings and their language-games constitute empirical data for
reflection. An invisible One, however, whether it is called God,
Allah, Brahman, the Tao or the Void, is not an empirical datum.
We cannot point to it in the way in which we can point to a
mountain and say 'that is Mont Blanc' or 'that is Mount Ev-
erest'. If it is possible to know that an invisible One exists, its
existence has to be inferred. But though arguments have been
advanced in the past, the extent to which they are accepted has
increasingly diminished. To many philosophers it seems that
there is no way of proving the existence of a One, and that there
is no adequate way of showing that any particular theory of the
One is true. We can indeed appeal to criteria such as internal
coherence. And by the application of such criteria it may be
possible to rule out certain theories, at any rate as they stand.
But a theory might be internally coherent and yet not represent
reality. In fine, it is the cognitive value of the metaphysics of
the One and the Many which is in doubt, not the legitimacy of
synthesis as a mental activity. And it is for this reason that we
can describe the metaphysics of the One and the Many as
belonging to a pre-scientific phase of thought. To be sure, bold
speculation has a role to play in science, speculation which
outruns any possibility of immediate verification or empirical
testing. To deny this would be to condemn science to sterility.
But scientists do at any rate try to confirm, or hope to confirm,
their hypotheses or theories, directly or indirectly as the case

[9]In *Philosophers and Philosophies*, ch. IV (London and New York, 1976) I have
discussed some aspects of the theory of autonomous language-games, in regard
to religious language.

may be. Metaphysicians, however, are inclined to tell us what *must* be the case, though their arguments win scant acceptance. It was not without reason that the German philosopher Karl Jaspers spoke of the One as the object of philosophical 'faith'.

If we are acquainted with the history of European metaphysics and with Kant's criticism of what he called 'dogmatic metaphysics', it is natural for us to think of those philosophers who asserted the existence of a One of which the Many are an appearance or on which they depend ontologically as trying to prove the existence of the One by explicit argument. Obviously some may be convinced that this or that philosopher succeeded in proving what he intended to prove, while others may be convinced that all the philosophers failed to accomplish what they undertook to accomplish. Both parties, however, may agree in assuming that metaphysicians of the One and the Many have in fact tried to prove the existence of a One.

This assumption, however, is not universally verified. For example Śaṁkara, the ninth-century philosopher and representative thinker of the Advaita Vedānta school, maintained that the existence of Brahman as the sole reality, with which the inner self (*ātman*) was one, could not be known by inference. For Śaṁkara, the truth was known in the first instance from the testimony of the Hindu sacred texts and was confirmable by direct intuitive or mystical experience, rather than by reasoning. The philosopher could of course submit rival theories to critical analysis, and he could argue that the philosophy of non-dualism was internally coherent and did not contradict experience. But any positive knowledge of Brahman was the fruit of scriptural revelation and suprasensory experience. As philosophy was an activity of discursive thought, and as discursive thought involved or presupposed the subject-object distinction, it could not grasp a reality transcending all distinctions and relations.

This should not be understood as meaning that questions about the cognitive value of metaphysics are unimportant. For one thing, such questions arise out of reflection on what I have just said about Śaṁkara. For example, what, if any, is the cognitive value of mystical experience? My point is not that the questions are unimportant, but rather that discussion of them is best postponed until we have examined a number of examples

of the metaphysics of the One and the Many and ascertained
on what grounds they asserted the existence of a One. It would
be a mistake to suppose that they all set out to prove the
existence of a One by the sort of argument which we find, for
instance, in the writings of St Thomas Aquinas or even that
they all thought that this could be done in principle.

IV

Reference has been made above to Jaspers' concept of 'philosophical faith'. As further reference will be made to Jaspers,[10] I
do not wish to discuss here precisely how the phrase 'philosophical faith' should be understood. Use of the word 'faith',
however, naturally suggests the idea of an association between
the metaphysics of the One and the Many and religion. It is my
conviction that there has often been an association of this kind.
And though this subject forms the main theme of this book,
some preliminary remarks are appropriate here.

There are some obvious examples of a relation between the
metaphysics of the One and religion. Śaṁkara's philosophy of
non-dualism is a case in point. It has to be seen in a religious
context, in a line of thought oriented to enlightenment and
liberation; and its connection with Hindu sacred texts, especially
the *Upanishads*, is abundantly clear. Analogously, Sufi-inspired
philosophy, such as developed in Persia, with its emphasis on
spiritual illumination, has to be seen in the context of Islamic
religion. It was in fact esoteric Islam, even if some Muslims
have considered a good deal of it as unorthodox.

Mention of Śaṁkara and of Sufi-inspired philosophy may
give the impression that, when I refer to a relationship between
the philosophy of the One and religion, I have in mind simply
a relation between philosophy and mysticism, a connection
which we probably conceive as characteristic more of oriental
than of western thought, even if there are some examples in the
West. But I do not in fact conceive the connection exclusively
in this way. Consider St Thomas Aquinas's proofs of God's
existence. They can indeed be considered simply by themselves,

[10]In Chapter 6, pp. 141–44.

and for the purpose of critical examination this is how they are generally treated. Although, however, they naturally appear to us as free from the subjectivity which characterizes any line of thought which concentrates on the idea of the inner self and is preoccupied with the goal of enlightenment and final liberation, the proofs were none the less developed in a religious context. They can be seen as the result of a Christian theologian's reflection on the presuppositions and implications of Christian faith. They can also be seen as representing, for Aquinas, a stage in the human mind's progress from ignorance of God to the vision of God in heaven, not indeed as a stage through which every mind must pass but as a stage in a logical pattern of advance from ignorance to vision. In other words, in spite of their impersonal and objective character, the proofs are related in specifiable ways to the Christian religion. The fact that they incorporate lines of thought found in Aristotle, Maimonides and other thinkers does not obliterate this relation.

A natural comment on what I have been saying is that while nobody denies that the philosophy of the One and the Many has often been connected with religion, philosophy has developed in such a way that it has separated itself from the religious background and affiliations which it often had in the past. To call for a return to the past would be an obscurantist policy. In particular, a fusion of philosophy and mysticism would be most undesirable. As for Aquinas's proofs of the existence of God, it is true that they were developed in a religious context. The relevant question, however, is whether they can stand on their own feet. The majority of philosophers think that they cannot, even if they much prefer St Thomas's way of reasoning to appeals to mystical experience.

This sort of comment is understandable. But it may express a misunderstanding. Śaṁkara, for example, did not regard mystical experience as philosophy. He reflected, however, on the significance of a certain type of experience. It is of course arguable that his interpretation was questionable and that it was determined by his reading of Hindu sacred texts. But there is nothing obscurantist in reflection on mystical experience as such. It pertains to reflection on the religious forms of life which find expression in the varieties of religious language.

As for the general connection between philosophies of the One
and religion, it has been stated by an eminent writer on the
history of religion that 'all authentic religious experience implies
a desperate effort to penetrate to the root of things, the ultimate
reality'.[11] There are various objections which might be brought
against this general statement. None the less, we can regard
some philosophies of the One and the Many as closely associated
with the sort of effort of which Eliade speaks, the philosophizing
being an attempt to reach the ultimate reality by thought, even
if in the end the philosopher finds himself compelled to recognize
the limitations of discursive thinking. But some other philosophies of the One and Many may have little or no connection
with religious experience and be simply the product of a synthesizing activity which goes beyond what any particular science
can accomplish. Again, even when there is a connection between
a philosophy of the One and mysticism, the relationship need
not be uniform, exclusively of one kind.

V

If it is asserted that philosophies of the One and the Many have
often been associated in some way with a religious interest and
that they have sometimes included a belief in the cognitive value
of mystical experience, the statements are not likely to meet
with much, if any, opposition. For they seem to be pretty obviously true. It may, however, be argued that the kind of religion
with which philosophies of the One have been particularly associated has been a world-fleeing mystical religion which involves depreciation of the world of plurality and an aspiration
to realize a state of oneness with a metaphenomenal ultimate
reality. For example, in Plotinus's often quoted phrase 'the flight
of the alone to the Alone'[12] the word 'flight' is clearly used in a
metaphorical sense, but the selection of this term is none the
less significant. For it indicates a turning away from the empirical world. Again, in the Advaita Vedānta the ideal is in the
inner self's liberation not only from the wheel of rebirth and the

[11]*The Two and the One*, by Mircea Eliade, translated by J. M. Cohen, p. 192
(London, 1962).
[12]*Enneads*, 771b (vi, 9, 11).

world of time and change but also from the illusion of individuality, of the ego-consciousness. Taoism did not encourage active participation in political life with its attendant ambitions, anxieties and insecurity. It encouraged withdrawal by the sage rather than social commitment. As for Buddhism, one of the objections which the Confucianists brought, whether fairly or not, against Buddhism in China was that it tended to divert people from their social and political obligations to a self-centred search for Nirvāna.

The critic of the metaphysics of the One and the Many can also draw attention to the fact that in some philosophies of the One moral distinctions were regarded as being purely relative or as belonging to the sphere of appearance. Thus for the Taoist philosophers moral distinctions and rules were man-made and should not be attributed, as Confucius and his followers attributed them, to Heaven. From the Taoist point of view Confucianism first attributed man-made moral distinctions and precepts to the will of Heaven and then pretended to derive or receive them from Heaven. Again, in the Advaita Vedānta philosophy Brahman, the Absolute, was regarded as transcending morality. True, Śaṁkara and the other Advaita thinkers had an ethics and insisted on moral purification as a prerequisite for realization of oneness with Brahman. But, it has been argued, this ethics was oriented to the goal of liberation by absorption in the Absolute, rather than to action in this World and the betterment of society.

Obviously, these lines of thought do not prove the falsity of any of the relevant philosophical systems. It is more a question of evaluation. That is to say, if we attach great value to social activism, we shall naturally tend to adopt a negative attitude to any metaphysics which encourages or seems to encourage escapism or an anti-social policy. We are likely to judge, for example, that talk about Brahman and about transcending the empirical self are not what is required in modern India, and that Plotinus's 'flight of the alone to the Alone' is not a suitable ideal for modern Europe or America.

This attitude may lend itself to caricature, as though it were simply an expression of materialism and of a blindness to spiritual values. But it can equally well express the point of view of someone with high ideals of human conduct. It is obviously possible to maintain that though we can understand the attraction of, say, the Advaita Vedānta or Taoism or Mādhyamika Buddhism in their historical contexts, man's realization that he can, within limits, control his physical environment has been followed by the realization that he can also influence his social environment and its structures, and that it would be undesirable to divert him from social commitment by resuscitating escapist philosophies of a past age.

As this line of thought is not uncommon, and as it has some basis in fact, I propose to discuss it later (in Chapter 10). For the moment I restrict myself to suggesting two considerations. In the first place we should avoid sweeping generalizations and pay attention to the different features or characteristics of distinct philosophies. For example, at first sight at any rate there is a considerable difference between a philosophy in which empirical reality is described as the transient appearance of a suprapersonal and changeless One or Absolute in which individual souls seek to be absorbed, and a philosophy in which the world is conceived as created by a personal God for a purpose in the utilization of which human beings are called upon to cooperate. In a philosophy of this second kind there may indeed be an emphasis on the soul's ascent to union with God, but there is likely also to be a counterbalancing emphasis on human activity in the world. In Islamic thought, for example, the Sufi thinkers did indeed emphasize the mystical aspect of religion, but there was also an emphasis on the creation of Islamic society. To be sure, the kind of society envisaged was not the kind of society which the modern European or American is likely to consider acceptable. At the same time we could hardly describe Islamic thought as expressing simply a spirit of escapism. Again, to mention a very different line of thought, the early Taoist sages did indeed exhort the wise man to preserve peace of mind by avoiding, as far as possible, the vicissitudes of political life. Further, Taoism was in fact associated with an aesthetic attitude towards Nature and with what might be described as a cosmic emotion more than with promotion of social activism. It is arguable, however, that Taoism was potentially a philosophy of social change, inasmuch as the One was conceived as the self-developing universe, and that it could consistently have encouraged a less conservative attitude to social structures than we find in Confucianism. If it did not do so in fact, this may have been due partly to the cyclical theory of history which dominated Chinese thought in general for many centuries.

In the second place we have to bear in mind the possibility of the influence of factors other than the nature of a given philosophical system or set of systems. For example, the hardening of the early class distinctions in India according to ability and social function into a caste system based on birth, a transformation which has not encouraged social progress, cannot be laid at the door of the Advaita Vedānta philosophers, nor of course at that of the Buddhists.

Apart from any particular critical comments which might be made about what I have been discussing, some might wish to argue, in a general way, that as far as man's awareness of his ability to shape his environment, whether physical or social, is concerned, it has increased in proportion to the degree in which belief in a One of any kind has been abandoned. We can recall Nietzsche's contention in *Fröhliche Wissenchaft*[13] that, with the death of God (more precisely, the death of belief in God), there lies before man an open horizon and an unchartered sea on which he can adventurously set sail. The idea that belief in God entails the view that human beings are simply his instruments is doubtless relevant to this contention. That is to say, the death of God means the liberation of the human being. But I cannot pursue the theme any further here. The main point which I wish to make is the perhaps obvious one that when reflecting on any general statement about the metaphysics of the One and the Many we should consider individual forms assumed by this metaphysics.

VI

This point, obvious though it may be, is relevant to the impression, where it exists, that philosophies of the One do not merit

---

[13]Section 343. In the translation of Nietzsche's works edited by Dr O. Levy (London, 1909–13) this book is entitled *Joyful Wisdom*. In America the work is generally referred to as *The Gay Science*.

any serious consideration, inasmuch as they contradict or are incompatible with both our ordinary view of the world, based on sense-perception and self-consciousness, and the view of the world presented by science. We ordinarily think of the world as comprising many things and a plurality of distinct persons. And as far as plurality as such is concerned, science does not upset this view. To postulate atoms, electrons and so on is not to imply that plurality is an illusion. Nor does increased astronomical knowledge do anything to show that our natural belief in a plurality of entities is false. The relation between the account of an object such as a table in atomic physics and the account which would be given of it by a person innocent of scientific knowledge is a theme which need not detain us here. Even if someone claims, somewhat misleadingly in my opinion, that the table is not really a solid object but a vast number of whirling particles, he or she is clearly not denying plurality. Whatever we may think of Émile Meyerson's statement that science is 'only a prolongation of common sense',[14] it confirms rather than negates our belief in plurality. The philosophy of the One, however, so it may be said, asserts that all things are really one reality, an assertion which runs counter both to ordinary experience and to science. A philosopher might wish to add that the metaphysician who asserts this implicitly contradicts himself. For to think in this way and make his assertion he employs discursive thought, which involves at any rate the subject-object distinction. He objectifies the universe as an object of thought and thus distinguishes between himself as subject and the object of his thought. He cannot help making distinctions. The alternative is silence.

This account of the metaphysics of the One is far too sweeping. Let us suppose that the One is conceived as transcendent, the one reality on which all other things depend ontologically. The plurality of dependent things and persons is not thereby asserted to be illusory. It is indeed possible to object that if the transcendent One is said to be infinite, it should be regarded as

---

[14]*Identity and Reality*, p. 384 (London and New York, 1930). In the original *Identité et réalité* (Paris, 1908) the passage occurs on p. 439. Meyerson meant that science presupposes and has its point of departure in 'common sense', and that it continues to employ concepts such as that of causality.

containing everything within its own being, and that the concept of God needs to be transformed into that of the Absolute. This was a line of argument defended by, for example, F. H. Bradley. The fact remains, however, that theism does not entail denial of plurality.

Or let us suppose that the One is identified with the self-transforming universe, in the sense that the Many are regarded as transient forms assumed by the One in its process of self-development. It is not unreasonable at any rate to interpret Taoism in this way. If the One is conceived as real, so too are the Many. The fact that they are transient does not, by itself, entail the conclusion that they must be regarded as unreal or illusory. After all, the ordinary man is perfectly well aware that there are many things, plants and animals and human beings, which come into being and pass away. But he does not on this account regard them as unreal or illusory. Even if they are described as appearances of the One, this does not necessarily imply that they are unreal. For they could be real appearances, real forms really taken by the One in its dynamic process of self-transformation.

It must be admitted that the situation is different if the One is conceived not only as unchanging but also as the sole reality. In this case it seems that the Many must be relegated to the sphere of appearance, when the word 'appearance' suggests something illusory or deceptive. It is perfectly understandable that critics of the Advaita Vedānta philosophy have argued that it is at variance with ordinary experience and with science. One might perhaps retort, 'So much the worse for ordinary experience and science'. But if the world of plurality is appearance, it must presumably appear to someone. Hannah Arendt argued in her Gifford Lectures at the University of Aberdeen that the word 'appear' is a relative term, in the sense that nothing can properly be said to appear except in relation to some subject.[15] In this case to describe the empirical world as appearance is to employ the subject-object distinction and thus to imply an acceptance of plurality, or at any rate of duality. In

---

[15]*The Life of the Mind*, 2 vols., edited by Mary McCarthy, vol. 1, p. 19 (London, 1978).

other words, there seems to be a difficulty in even stating a theory of pure monism.

In fairness to Śaṁkara it should be explained that he did not assert that the world of plurality was unreal in the sense of being non-existent. He tried to harmonize the existence of our ordinary view of reality (which, on its own level, he regarded as valid) with belief in Brahman as the sole ultimate reality by means of a theory of degrees of knowledge and degrees of reality. Moreover, he spoke of phenomena as effects or products of Brahman, thus enabling Radhakrishnan to claim that Śaṁkara admitted 'the factual nature of the pluralistic world'.[16] But as we shall be concerned with Śaṁkara's philosophy in the fourth chapter of this book, I do not wish to discuss the subject any further here. I have been simply trying, with the aid of a few examples, to illustrate the fact that not all philosophies of the One denied the real existence of the Many, and that even in the case of a system (the Advaita Vedānta) which may appear to do so, a serious attempt was made, whether successfully or not, to allow for and accommodate our ordinary view of the world and, by implication, accounts given by science.

VII

I have already emphasized the fact that there have been different philosophies of the One and the Many, and that the various types have to be considered separately. If I have written, as in fact I have, about 'the metaphysics of the One and the Many', I was simply referring in a global manner to philosophies in which the idea of one ultimate reality has been prominent. I did not intend to imply that there is only one such philosophy.

The plurality of such philosophies is an historical fact. It is, however, a fact which can give rise to doubts about the cognitive value of any philosophy of the One. For if there has been a succession of very different conceptions of the One, in both eastern and western thought, the question arises, how can we decide between the relevant truth-claims? Whitehead remarked

[16]*The Brahma Sūtra: The Philosophy of the Spiritual Life*, translated with an introduction and notes by S. Radhakrishnan, p. 137 (London, 1960; New York, 1968).

that if the history of European philosophy is littered with discarded metaphysical systems, 'abandoned and unreconciled',[17] so can the history of science be represented as littered with discarded hypotheses, though we do not on this account dismiss science as devoid of cognitive value or as unworthy of serious consideration. This is doubtless true. But we are accustomed to think that there are, in principle and often in practice, recognized ways of deciding between scientific hypotheses, whereas it is difficult to see how we can decide between the truth-claims made on behalf of theories relating to an alleged invisible reality, especially when this reality is said to transcend the grasp of conceptual thought.

As the final chapter of this book is concerned with 'The Succession of Systems and Truth', I do not wish to pursue the subject at present. It may, however, be worth pointing out in advance that our inability to decide between different philosophies of the One can be exaggerated. Let me take an example. Within the Vedānta school or tradition as a whole there were at any rate three distinguishable lines of thought, which we can associate with the names of Śaṁkara, Rāmānuja and Madhva. Madhva attacked the Advaita Vedānta philosophy of Śaṁkara, one of his main contentions being that its monism was incompatible with experience, the experience which is presupposed by all philosophizing. Śaṁkara would not indeed have agreed. If, however, we accept the assumptions that a theory which contradicts ordinary experience cannot be true and that Śaṁkara's theory of Brahman does in fact contradict ordinary experience, then, on these assumptions, we have a good reason for asserting that the theory cannot be true. Obviously, it does not follow that we are thereby committed to accepting Madhva's own theistic conception of the One. But before we say that no decision about its truth or falsity can be arrived at, we ought first to inquire whether he gives any arguments in favour of his belief and, if he does, to evaluate the arguments. Similarly, if a philosopher identifies the One with the phenomenal world, we need not remain speechless or say that we are entirely unable to know whether what he asserts to be the case is true or false. For we

[17]*Process and Reality*, p. 18 (London, 1929).

can at any rate consider whether there are sufficient reasons for claiming that the phenomenal world is in some sense one, a unity. If we come to a negative conclusion, we can hardly accept the philosopher's theory.

Perhaps we can sum up the matter in this way. If we assume that a theory of reality which is self-contradictory cannot be true, we can exclude any theory in so far as it is self-contradictory. There may be people who would not be prepared to accept the assumption, but I think that most people would. It is also possible to dispose of a theory by means of *reductio ad absurdum* arguments, a policy which was pursued by Nāgārjuna in regard to all metaphysical theories of the One and the Many. But if a philosopher advances arguments in support of his theory and we consider the arguments invalid or insufficient, this, by itself, entitles us to conclude only that he has not shown that his theory is true. It might none the less be true, even if he had not proved that it was true. If therefore someone regards all arguments to prove the existence of a meta-phenomenal reality as invalid, he will doubtless maintain that we can never know that any theory of an invisible One or ultimate reality is true. This position, however, does not necessarily commit the person to denying that it may be possible to show that certain theories cannot be true, on the ground that they are self-contradictory or that they entail absurd conclusions. In this sense at any rate we can discriminate between theories.

The situation is rather different of course if in defence of his theory of the One a philosopher appeals not to any formal argument but simply and solely to an intuitive or mystical experience. In this case of course there are no formal arguments offered by the philosopher which we can evaluate. At the same time it is assumed that there can be an intuitive or mystical experience which possesses cognitive value. And this is an assumption which we can examine. Besides, if the philosopher asserts a positive view of reality, allegedly grounded on mystical experience, we can consider whether or not it satisfies certain criteria, such as internal coherence. If the philosopher maintains that discursive thought can make no contribution at all, inasmuch as the One and the mystical experience on which belief in the One is based transcend thought, we can consider whether in this case his theory of the One can even be stated. Must we not exclude all theorizing, all philosophy, and relapse into unbroken silence? If we speak, what we say is subject to critical examination.

These remarks may perhaps seem to express a degree of scepticism which does not fit in with what are presumably my religious beliefs. The remarks were intended, however, simply to indicate that it is an exaggeration to claim that in regard to the metaphysics of the One and the Many our verdict can only be, 'Take it or leave it'. We can justifiably adopt a more discriminating attitude. When, however, an interest is shown in this kind of metaphysics, it is generally fostered by a religious interest, as has already been suggested. In the absence of any religious interest, the philosophies of the One, whether in East or West, are apt to be regarded as historical curiosities. It is indeed true that a religious interest may engender a hostile attitude to the metaphysics of the One, such as we find with some Christian theologians. But hostility is obviously not the same thing as indifference.

CHAPTER 3

THE ONE IN TAOISM AND
BUDDHISM

Confucianism and Taoism – the Taoist theory of the One – its
religious significance – the Mādhyamika system – Zen Buddhism
and the Absolute – some comments on Zen – concluding remarks

I

When we think of philosophy in ancient China, it is probably
Confucianism which comes first to mind. For one thing, Confucianism was made the official state philosophy or ideology of
imperial China in 136 B.C. under the Emperor Wu of the Han
dynasty. And in the course of time it became the basis of ex-
aminations for the imperial civil service, retaining this favoured
position until A.D. 1905, when the traditional civil service ex-
aminations were abolished. It is hardly necessary to say that the
elevation of a philosophy to the privileged position of official
state philosophy is unlikely in the long run to promote vigour
and originality of thought, even if, as was the case in China,
other systems of thought were not banned or proscribed. But
this does not alter the fact that Confucianism was for centuries
a powerful educative instrument. Further, Confucianism, centering round the thought of the human being as a moral agent
in a social context, gave expression to the practical orientation
of the Chinese mind and its strong sense of family ties and social
obligations. It was an expression of Chinese life and of an
important aspect of the Chinese outlook, which in time it helped
to mould.

Confucianism was not, indeed, simply an ethical system in a
narrow or restricted sense. Confucius himself, in the sixth century B.C., conceived the moral law as representing, in an admittedly ill-defined sense, the will of Heaven, the word 'Heaven'
(*T'ien*) apparently retaining for him something at any rate of the
meaning attached to the concept of the 'Lord on high'. The idea
of God never occupied the same place in Confucianism as it did

in the relatively short-lived Mohist philosophy, the creation of Mo Tse in the fifth century B.C. At the same time the moral law, for Confucianists, was rooted in some sense in the universe. Further, as the idea of the universe as a harmony was prominent in Confucianism, the need for a cosmology naturally made itself felt. Thus the ancient Chinese theories of the two complementary cosmic principles or forces, *yin* and *yang*, and of the five elements (earth, wood, water, fire and metal) were incorporated into Confucianism at an early date. And in what is known as neo-Confucianism, which developed during the Sung (A.D. 960–1279) and Ming (1368–1644) dynasties, metaphysical theories were elaborated, to some extent under the influence of Taoism, which culminated in the concept of the Great Ultimate, uniting all principles (*li*) within itself. In some respects the Great Ultimate might be described as a One.

Basically, however, Confucianism was and remained an ethical and social philosophy. Any tendency to emphasize theory at the expense of practice evoked a reaction. Thus the neo-Confucianist Wang Yang-ming (1472–1529) insisted on the unity of theory and practice, knowledge and action, representing ideas, in a manner which anticipated the thought of Josiah Royce, as incipient actions.[1] Confucianism had its speculative minds, such as Chu Hsi (1130–1200), but when cosmological theory seemed to be becoming too prominent, the result was a kind of 'back to Confucius' movement. In *What Is To Be Done?* Leo Tolstoy states that the elucidation of moral truths is not only the chief but ought to be the sole business of man. Confucianists would tend to agree.

Since the Chinese were a predominantly agricultural community, a community of farmers and peasants, there was a very strong emphasis on family life and family ties, an emphasis which was reflected in Confucianism. It also meant that the Chinese stood close to nature, and advertence to interrelations

[1]For Wang Yang-ming's teaching on this method see the 'Record of Discourses' as given in *The Philosophy of Wang Yang-ming*, translated from the Chinese by F. G. Henke, with an introduction by J. F. Tufts (2nd edition, New York, 1964). As for Royce, in *The World and the Individual* (2 vols., New York, 1900–1), representing his Gifford Lectures, he described what he called the internal meaning of an idea as 'the partial fulfilment of a purpose' (Vol. 1, p. 25).

in nature led reflective minds to conceive an underlying all-pervasive unity, one power operating in a multitude of ways. With the Confucianists the Tao or Way was understood in a moral sense and was regarded as the Way of Heaven. With the Taoist sages the term 'Tao', though it continued to be used in the sense of Way, also came to be used for the ultimate reality itself, the One, conceived as the source of Heaven and Earth and of the 'myriad things'.

There are two points about this which should be noted in advance. In the first place I am concerned here with Taoist philosophy as presented, for example, in the *Lao Tzu* or *Tao Te Ching*, not with what is commonly described as religious Taoism or Taoism as an organized religion. The relationship between the two is a disputed matter. Some scholars have objected to Taoism as a religion being described as a corruption of Taoist philosophy instead of a justifiable development of the latter.[2] Others have insisted on the difference between the two and have regarded Taoism as a religion as having unjustifiably claimed for itself a venerable name.[3] For my own part, I think that a distinction can reasonably be made between Taoist philosophy and Taoism as a religion with its preoccupation with means of increasing longevity and even of attaining physical immortality. I am not, of course, suggesting that Taoist philosophy was irreligious. I simply claim that it should be distinguished from the popular religious Taoism which still exists in Taiwan, if not in mainland China.

In the second place references to works such as the *Lao Tzu*, the *Chuang Tzu* and the *Lieh Tzu* are simply to these compilations as they have come down to us. When referring, for instance, to the *Lao Tzu*, I do not commit myself to the thesis that the work was composed by one man, still less to the belief that the author was an older contemporary of Confucius named Lao Tzu. The work in question is generally thought to be an anthology, which did not assume its present form until a date which was perhaps later than that of the death of Chuang Tzu in the third century

[2]This point of view was expressed by Henri Maspero in his book *Le Taoisme* (Paris, 1950).
[3]See the first chapter of Professor H. G. Creel's *What is Taoism?* (Chicago and London, 1970).

B.C. This does not, however, preclude the possibility that some parts of the work go back to a much earlier period. Indeed, there are some scholars who are not prepared to assert, as some have, that the Lao Tzu of tradition did not exist. As for the *Chuang Tzu*, the so-called 'inner chapters' (the first seven) may have been composed by the sage Chuang Tzu, while the rest are additions. The *Lieh Tzu*, traditionally ascribed to Lieh Yu-k'ao (c. 450–375 B.C.), seems to be a compilation by a neo-Taoist writer of the third century A.D., even if some parts are of an earlier date. Anyway, the three works can be used as expressions of Taoist thought or, in the case of parts of the *Lieh Tzu*, of neo-Taoist ideas.

II

The *Lao Tzu* is doubtless best known for its statements about the ultimate reality, the Tao. To be sure, on reading the work we can hardly fail to notice that a large part of it is devoted to what might be described as political theory, of an embryonic kind. Indeed, Professor H. G. Creel makes a sharp distinction between 'purposive' Taoism, as exemplified in the *Lao Tzu*, and 'contemplative' Taoism, as exemplified in the *Chuang Tzu*.[4] While, however, the distinction is certainly based on fact, the political policy advocated in the *Lao Tzu* can be seen as a practical application of the theory of the ultimate reality. Just as the One or Tao allows things to be themselves, to follow their natures, so should the ruler interfere as little as possible with the activities of the citizens, letting them develop spontaneously in a natural manner. This policy of governmental inaction was obviously different from the Confucianist idea of the morally educative function of the ruler and his ministers. It was even more sharply opposed to the programme of the so-called Legalists, who emphasized the rule of positive law, backed by strictly applied sanctions. We cannot, however, discuss the political aspects of Taoism here. We are concerned primarily with the Taoist philosophy of the One and the Many.

In the *Lao Tzu* all determinate beings, all things of which we

[4]*What is Taoism?*, p. 45.

can say that they are this rather than that, x rather than y, are regarded as products of an ultimate reality which is not itself a determinate being and which is therefore indescribable or nameless. 'The nameless was the beginning of heaven and earth.'[5] This reality, which never came into being but exists everlastingly, is compared to an 'uncarved block'[6] which has been given no determinate form or shape. (Obviously, even an uncarved block of marble has a shape. But it is here regarded as formless relatively to the finished statue.) As the Tao is indescribable, it is for the human mind void, 'empty'.[7] It can even be referred to as 'not-being'.[8] But this does not mean that it is literally nothing at all. For it is also said to be 'the mother' of all that can be named or described.[9] To say that it is not-being is to say that it is not a member of the class of determinate beings. It is their matrix, their (in itself) indeterminate source.

It may be objected that it is obviously inconsistent to claim that the ultimate reality is nameless and indescribable and at the same time to refer to it as the One, the mother of all determinate beings, and so on. If it is really nameless, would not silence be the only consistent policy? Perhaps so. But at any rate the Taoist sages were not altogether unaware of this possible objection. This is evident from the statement, 'I know not its name; so I call it the Way'[10] and from the fact that though the Tao is referred to as the One, it is said to transcend number.[11] That is to say, the terms used to refer to the Tao are regarded as makeshifts, as means of referring to what is dimly discerned as underlying and unifying all the things of which it can be said that they are of this nature rather than that. The words are expedients for making people see things against a background which eludes clear vision and descriptive language.

We cannot of course justifiably expect to find in the writings of the early Taoist sages a systematically developed metaphysical system, characterized by formal argument and precision of

---

[5]*Lao Tzu*, 1, 1. The work was divided by editors into two books or parts.
[6]*Ibid.*, 1, 32 and 37.
[7]*Ibid.*, 1, 25.
[8]*Ibid.*, 2, 40.
[9]*Ibid.*, 1, 1.
[10]*Ibid.*, 1, 25.
[11]*Ibid.*, 2, 42.

thought and expression. We find assertion rather than argument, and an intuitive and imaginative approach rather than the sort of argumentation which we find in, say, the philosophy of Spinoza. If we wish to make comparisons with western thought, there is more resemblance to the pre-Socratics, such as Heraclitus, than to later western metaphysical systems. At the same time the statements made about the Tao were clearly intended to have some meaning, even if the ultimate reality was said to be indescribable. We are therefore entitled to imagine what sort of conception of the ultimate reality emerges from or is suggested by these statements.

In the first place the Tao is conceived as transcending the Many, in the sense that it cannot be identified with the sum total of the Many as existing at any particular time. This is clear from the fact that it is regarded as the source of all determinate things, past, present and future. In the second place the Tao is also conceived as being immanent in all things. We can recall the well-known passage in the *Chuang Tzu*, where the sage asserts that the Tao is present in everything, even in urine and excrement.[12] If, however, we seek a more precise account of the relation between the One and the Many, we find ourselves confronted by sets of statements which have different implications.

Some statements suggest that the Tao is the transcendent source of all things in the sense that while determinate things change, the Tao itself does not.[13] It is that from which all things proceed, but it is not itself subject to birth or death, increase or diminution, or any kind of alteration. There is indeed no good reason for claiming that the Taoist One was regarded as a personal deity. But those who wish to assimilate the Tao to the concept of God are obviously inclined to emphasize the passages in which it is represented, or seems to be represented, as the transcendent source of Heaven and Earth and the myriad things.

Other passages, however, suggest that the One is the formless material out of which all determinate things emerge and to which they eventually return. For example, the relation between

[12]*Chuang Tzu*, ch. 7.
[13]*Lao Tzu*, 1, 25.

the One and the Many is said to be analogous to that between
a river or a sea on the one hand and rivulets on the other.[14]
Again, the Tao is said to move by 'turning back',[15] a statement
which suggests that the One is the universe, which pursues a
cyclic course, producing the Many in a process of self-transformation, absorbing them into itself, and then reproducing them
once more. It is natural to think of Aristotle's concept of 'first
matter'. But the two ideas are not of course the same. Aristotle's
'first matter' was not the universe but a component of the
universe. Nor did Aristotle think of 'first matter' as being present
in all beings. Further, the Tao was conceived as dynamic, as
the active source of all determinate beings, whereas Aristotle's
'first matter' was not, in itself, an active principle.

There seems to be no doubt that the Tao was in fact regarded
as the self-transforming Universe, in which the relative distinctions made by human beings between up and down, left and
right, far and near, good and evil, are transcended or lose
their meaning. As Chuang Tzu puts it, 'the Tao identifies
them all as one'.[16] The One can be conceived as the unity of
opposites.

In this case what are we to make of the statements which
imply that the Tao is unchanging? As we have noted, we cannot
expect to find in early Taoist thought a neat and systematically
developed philosophical system. At the same time, to reconcile
the two sets of passages it is reasonable to employ a distinction
which played a prominent role in later Chinese thought. This
is the distinction between substance and function. In terms of
this distinction the Tao as substance is the One considered
abstractly in itself, as the source or 'mother' of the changing
Many. As function the Tao is the One considered in its self-
manifestation in the Many. This should not be understood as
implying that there was ever a time when the One existed in
splendid isolation, apart from any self-manifestation or self-
transformation. For this reason I have suggested that the Tao
as unchanging, timeless substance is the One considered
abstractly. An analogy can be found perhaps in the philosophy

---

[14]*Ibid.*, 1, 32.
[15]*Ibid.*, 2, 40.
[16]*Chuang Tzu*, ch. 7.

of Hegel. Obviously, from our point of view any comparison between Taoism and Hegelianism is anachronistic. Provided, however, that we do not interpret Hegel in a theistic sense, there is at any rate a similarity in regard to one point. For the Absolute of Hegel can be regarded abstractly, purely in itself, as it is in the *Logic*. It is then considered as transcending time. But it does not follow that the Absolute was regarded by Hegel as ever having existed apart from its self-manifestation in the world. When Hegel talks about God in himself before the creation of the world, he is using, as he not infrequently does, theological language, which conveys the truth, but in pictorial form. Needless to say, there are many important differences, both in historical context and in content, between Taoism and Hegelianism. For one thing, Hegel defines the Absolute as Spirit (*Geist*), whereas the One of Taoism is more naturally conceived as Nature with a capital letter, nature conceived as a totality. In regard, however, to the point mentioned there seems to be some resemblance between the two philosophies.

This way of harmonizing sets of statements with conflicting implications may seem to be too sophisticated. But if they are to be reconciled at all, some such distinction as that between substance and function is required. Moreover, the distinction emerged in Chinese thought because it was felt to be needed in order to be able to cope with situations such as the one in question. It is the kind of distinction which is likely to be made when the One or Absolute is conceived as the universe, while at the same time there is the desire to avoid reducing the One to the Many. I have alluded to Hegel. One might also refer to Spinoza's distinction between *Natura naturans* and *Natura naturata* between infinite substance considered in itself and its self-manifestation in the system of modes.

III

What, if any, is the religious significance of the Taoist theory of the One? Generally speaking, writers on Taoism have associated the thought of the early Taoist sages with mysticism, in the sense of a feeling or intuitive awareness of unity with the ultimate reality and with all determinate beings as phenomena[17] or manifestations of the One. They are doubtless justified in doing so. To be sure, the *Lao Tzu* does lay emphasis on the political implications of the philosophy of the Tao and illustrates what Professor Creel describes as 'purposive Taoism'. But the statements about the nameless and indescribable One are likely to seem to most people to smack of mysticism, and we find the assertion that the man who knows does not speak, whereas the man who speaks does not know.[18] At the same time what Professor Creel calls 'contemplative Taoism' is found more in the *Chuang Tzu*. 'All things and I are one,'[19] says the sage. This unity is not an object of sense-perception. It is evidently regarded as being grasped intuitively, in an experience which many people would have no hesitation as describing as mystical.

Although Taoism, however, as presented in the writings of the early Taoist philosophers, certainly has a mystical aspect, the question arises whether the kind of mysticism with which it is associated can properly be described as religious. Obviously, this is a question about the use of a descriptive term, not about the occurrence of the relevant impression or experience. There is no good reason for denying, or even doubting, that from the subjective point of view at any rate there can be a feeling or experience of oneness with nature. We can find expressions of it in, for example, *The Story of My Heart* by Richard Jefferies, as well as with certain poets. R. C. Zaehner cites a number of examples.[20] Indeed, a good many people probably experience something of the sort at some time in their lives. Nor is this surprising. We can of course objectify the world or nature, in the sense that we can make it an object of thought, thus turning the subject into 'a limit of the world', to borrow a phrase from Wittgenstein.[21] But this does not alter the fact that before any such objectification we are in the world, members, so to speak,

[17]By describing a being as 'phenomenal' in this context, I mean simply that it appears or can appear to sense-perception, whereas the Tao in itself transcends sense-perception. The term 'phenomenal', as used here, is not intended to imply unreality.

[18]*Lao Tzu*, 2, 56.

[19]*Chuang Tzu*, ch. 2.

[20]See *Mysticism, Sacred and Profane*, chapter 3 (Oxford, 1957).

[21]*Tractatus Logico-Philosophicus*, 5. 632.

of nature. The experience of oneness with nature and with all other phenomenal beings can be regarded as a lively awareness of this situation. It is not necessarily a question of awareness of plurality being entirely obliterated. We can interpret the statement of the *Chuang Tzu* that 'all things and I are one' in the sense not that the self and other things are unreal illusions but in the sense that they are all united in and through the all-pervasive One, on which they are all dependent, of which they are all transient manifestations, and to which they all return. An intuitive grasp of this unity can certainly occur, at any rate as a subjective experience. But is there sufficient reason for describing the experience as religious, especially if the concept of the Tao is interpreted as equivalent to the concept of nature or of the self-transforming world? Might it not perhaps be more appropriate to speak of a 'cosmic feeling' or a 'cosmic emotion' than to bring in religion?

Reference will have to be made later to drug-induced experiences; but one can, however, raise the following question in passing. If we had firm ground for supposing that an experience of unity in multiplicity could be produced by certain drugs, would we be justified in describing the experience as religious? If not, would the same sort of experience be religious when it was not produced by drugs and not religious when it was produced by a drug? If this is our view, how do we propose to defend it? I return to this question in Chapter 9.

It may seem that the obvious way of approaching the question whether Taoist mysticism can properly be defined as religious is first to define such terms as 'mysticism' and 'religion' and then to apply the definitions. To define these terms is indeed a notoriously difficult task, and any proposed definition is likely to be open to criticism on some ground, for example that the definition is too broad or too narrow. I do not feel inclined to add to the number of definitions already proposed by others. Yet if we do not proceed in this way, how are we going to proceed? How can we possibly decide whether a given phenomenon can or cannot reasonably be described as religious without presupposing some idea of religion? We may not formulate an explicit definition, but can the matter be discussed at all without implicit definitions being presupposed? At any rate no decision can be arrived at unless we have some idea of what we mean by religion.

We need not, however, formulate definitions of our own. We can make use of other people's definitions and enunciate conditional statements. For example, if we were to accept Schleiermacher's definition of religion in terms of the feeling of dependence on an ultimate reality,[22] we would seem to have no good reason for refusing to describe Taoist mysticism as religion. But if we defined religion in such a way that no world-view could count as religious unless it involved belief in a personal God, Taoism would not qualify for being described as religious. For there is no good reason for thinking that in the *Lao Tzu* or the *Chuang Tzu* the Tao was regarded as a personal deity. Both definitions, however, are open to challenge. Schleiermacher's definition can be objected to on the ground that it is too broad, while the second definition can be challenged on the ground that it is too narrow and would exclude the Advaita Vedānta from being considered as a religious philosophy, in spite of the fact that it can reasonably be regarded as a form of esoteric Hinduism.

There are of course other possible procedures. Some might wish to argue that in Taoist mysticism there was a genuine religious element but that the ultimate reality was incorrectly located. To argue in this way is to argue in terms of a pre-existing belief. And even if the belief is in fact true, it is not accepted by everyone. It may therefore seem much more appropriate to appeal to ordinary language. But though there are doubtless limits to what ordinary language would allow us to describe as religious, the limits are ill defined and vague.

In order to avoid raising questions and then making no attempt to answer them, I had better express my own opinion. The Tao of the *Lao Tzu* and the *Chuang Tzu* can be regarded as the self-developing universe, as one reality which produces all phenomenal beings out of itself, pervades them all, unifying them in and through itself, and to which they all eventually return, production, reabsorption and reproduction being a cyclic process. It is possible to argue that, though there are certainly

[22]See *Werke*, 111, p. 72 (edited by O. Braun and J. Bauer, 4 vols., Leipzig, 1911–13).

phenomenal beings, there is no One to be found. The so-called nameless and indescribable is not-being. It does not exist as a distinct reality. The Tao or the One is simply a collective name for the Many. This line of thought seems to have been pursued by Kuo Hsiang, a neo-Taoist whose date of death is said to have been A.D. 312. In his commentary on the *Chuang Tzu* he maintained that Nature is simply the general name for all things. In other words, the concept of the One was submitted to reductive analysis, the One being reduced to the sum total of the Many. I would not myself describe this rationalistic version of Taoism as a religious world-view. It also seems to me that the association between Taoism, as so interpreted, and mysticism would tend to disappear. Instead we might expect a development of scientific inquiry, even if this did not in fact occur.

It is, however, clear that in the writings of the early Taoist philosophers the One is not regarded as reducible to the Many, inasmuch as it is the dynamic source of the Many. There is therefore a place for mystical experience, if by this we understand a feeling or experience of unity with an ultimate reality and with other phenomenal beings in and through this all-pervasive reality. For my own part, I am prepared to describe this kind of mysticism as religious, especially as it is supposed to influence human life. Even if the ultimate reality is conceived as the universe or as Nature with a capital letter, we can recall that in his account of the development of religion Hegel found a place for the religion of Nature. Further, though mysticism obviously requires that the reality with which oneness is experienced should be accessible, it none the less acts as a support to belief in the transcendence of the One, in the sense, that is to say, that it resists the reduction of the One to the Many. In other words, mysticism and the Taoism of the *Lao Tzu* and the *Chuang Tzu* are interrelated.

IV

Taoism, like Confucianism, was a native Chinese philosophy. Buddhism was an importation from India, effectively introduced into China in the first century A.D., even if there was perhaps some slight knowledge of it before this time. When Buddhist thought became known, Taoist scholars came to see in some of the doctrines of Mahāyāna Buddhism an affinity with their own conception of the Tao, while in the process of commending Buddhism to the Chinese and adapting it to its new cultural environment some Buddhist scholars began to use Taoist terms to express their own beliefs. During the period of disunity which followed the collapse of the Han dynasty in A.D. 220, and which lasted until the reunification of China under the Sui dynasty (A.D. 589–618), there was discussion between Taoist and Buddhist thinkers in southern China. As, however, Buddhism developed and became influential, it naturally aroused hostility, ranging from verbal polemics, especially on the part of Confucianists (who saw in Buddhist monasticism an anti-social force) to occasional repressive measures taken by the political authorities. Thus in A.D. 845 the political authorities, egged on, so it is said, by representatives both of Confucianism and of religious Taoism, ordered the destruction of a large number of Buddhist monasteries and temples, the confiscation of lands held by Buddhist communities, and the return of the monks to secular life. The main reason for this repression seems to have been the accumulation of untaxed property and wealth by Buddhist communities and the increasing political influence of the monks, rather than any ideological consideration.

One of the schools of Mahāyāna Buddhism which aroused the interest of Taoist scholars was the Mādhyamika or Middle Way school. Introduced into China by Kumārajīva in the fourth century A.D., it became known as the Three-Treatises school. This name was due to the fact that three basic texts, two by Nāgārjuna and one by his disciple Deva, had been translated into Chinese by Kumārajīva. It may well be true that the doctrine of the school proved to be too abstract for the Chinese mind, but Taoist adherents of what was known as 'the dark learning' understandably saw a likeness between the Mādhyamika idea of Emptiness or the Void and their own conception of the Tao as 'not-being'.

Denial of the existence of a permanent substantial self, underlying all passing psychical states or mental phenomena, goes back to the beginning of Buddhism. The adherents of the

Mādhyamika school insisted that all things, both the mind and external things, were insubstantial, not in the sense that they were absolutely non-existent or unreal, but in the sense that there was no abiding substance or core in any of them. In other words, they applied a phenomenalistic analysis to all things. This view was expressed by saying that all things, including selves or minds, were 'empty'. They were not only causally dependent but also essentially changing and transient, devoid of any permanent substantial core or self-nature. They were all manifestations of emptiness.

This view, taken by itself, did not of course entail the hypostatization of Emptiness or the Void as an all-pervasive reality. One might assert that all things are causally dependent, changing and transient, and at the same time deny that there is any reality beyond these causally dependent and changing things. But Buddhism is essentially a spiritual path, a path to Nirvāna. And if Emptiness or the Void is simply a collective name for the changing Many, considered in regard to certain characteristics, it seems to follow that Nirvāna, which involves transcending the world of time and change, is equivalent to annihilation. This was indeed what some Buddhists believed that it was. Others, however, regarded Nirvāna as a positive state of bliss, not indeed describable or even conceivable, but none the less not equivalent in an absolute sense to non-existence. Given this point of view, there was naturally a tendency in the Mādhyamika school to refer to Emptiness or the Void as though it were the Absolute, the One. For Nāgārjuna, the great Mādhyamika philosopher, it was incorrect to say that Emptiness did not exist. It was equally incorrect to say that it existed. It was also incorrect to say both that it existed and that it did not exist. Finally, it was incorrect to say that it neither existed nor did not exist. In other words, one could really say nothing at all. As we noted in the first chapter, Nāgārjuna developed an elaborate dialectic to expose the fallacies in all positive metaphysical systems and made no claim to expound a metaphysical system of his own. This clearing away, so to speak, of metaphysics was thought of as facilitating or preparing the way for an intuitive apprehension of Emptiness. This intuition can hardly be interpreted simply as an assent to the conclusion of an agreement, namely the conclusion that all things are insubstantial. For this conclusion can be established philosophically, according to the Buddhist thinkers. The intuition might perhaps be interpreted as a more lively awareness of what is already known, as a personal realization of the emptiness of all things which goes beyond mere intellectual assent to the conclusion of an argument and which influences conduct, promoting detachment for an example. At the same time the idea of philosophical reasoning as a preparation for an intuition of Emptiness naturally tends to suggest that Emptiness or the Void is the Absolute, the ultimate reality which is called 'Emptiness' because it transcends conceptual thought and all description. This appears to have been the view of a Buddhist abbot who said to me, 'We must remember that Emptiness is also a Fullness.' His statement may have been paradoxical, but it presumably expressed a belief in an Absolute, though the speaker would doubtless insist that the Absolute was immanent, not transcendent.

Some scholars are sharply opposed to any such interpretation. In their opinion terms such as 'Emptiness' and the 'Void' do not refer to any ultimate reality. They do not refer even to the inner reality of phenomena. They have no inner reality. We should not allow ourselves to be misled by the use of nouns and proceed to assimilate the philosophy of Nāgārjuna to that of Śaṁkara. The Mādhyamika system is simply a faithful development of the teaching of the Buddha, who did not postulate any metaphysical reality. It is true that in the *Udāna*, a Pali text, the Buddha is represented as telling his monks that there is an unborn, a not become, a not made, an uncompounded, and that if there were not this Unborn, there would be no escape from the born, the become, the compound.[23] Though, however, if this passage were taken in isolation, it would be natural to understand the adjectives as referring to some such noun as 'reality', the context suggests that the reference is to Nirvāna

---

[23]The Pali text of the *Udāna*, edited by P. Steinthal, has been published by the Pali Text Society (London, 1948). English translations (somewhat different ones) of the relevant passage can be found in, for example, *Some Sayings of the Buddha According to the Pali Canon*, edited and translated by F. I. Woodward, p. 220 (Oxford, 1973; first published, 1925) and *Buddhist Texts Through the Ages*, edited by E. Conze, I. B. Horner, D. Snellgrove and A. Waley, p. 95 (Oxford, 1954).

as a state, as contrasted with *samsāra* (the state of becoming, the life of transmigration).

It must be admitted that terms such as 'Emptiness' should not be understood as referring to a reality distinct from the phenomenal world. Candrakīrti, commenting on a work by Nāgārjuna, asserted that there was no distinction between Nirvāna and *samsāra*.[24] This is a hard saying, but at any rate it implies a rejection of a two-world theory. And it can be argued that we should not think of Emptiness even as the reality of phenomena, as such a way of talking implies a distinction between the inner reality and the external phenomenon. At the same time, if Nāgārjuna does not permit us to say that Emptiness exists, neither does he permit us to say that it does not exist. And even if Professor Murti is perhaps too keen to assimilate Nāgārjuna to Kant, I find it difficult not to agree when he says that, in the Mādhyamika system, phenomena, devoid of the falsifying thought-forms which we impose on them, are the Absolute.[25] In this case the Absolute cannot be thought, as all our categories or thought-forms distort or falsify. But it is not nothing at all, and there can be an intuitive apprehension of it. Hence it is easy to understand how, whether Nāgārjuna would have approved or not, there was a tendency in Mahāyāna Buddhism to postulate an Absolute, a One, transcending the subject-object distinction. After all, though the Buddha abstained, as far as possible, from any metaphysical pronouncements, a practice which Nāgārjuna doubtless tried to follow, it does not seem that he denied there was any ultimate reality.

What, if any, is the connection between Buddhist philosophy and religion? Some writers, including, for example, Professor Fung Yu-lan, the historian of Chinese philosophy, have claimed that a clear distinction should be made between the two. The claim is doubtless justified, if we are thinking of popular Buddhism with its introduction of various deities and its devotional

[24] *Candrakīrti Prasannapadā Madhyamakavrtti*, edited by J. May, p. 535 (Pius, 1959). See *Early Mādhyamika in India and China*, by Richard H. Robinson, p. 40 (Madison, Milwaukee and London, 1967).
[25] *The Central Philosophy of Buddhism. A Study of the Mādhyamika System*, by T. R. V. Murti, p. 251 (2nd edition, London, 1960).

practices. It seems to me, however, that Buddhist philosophy can be regarded as an attempt, or set of attempts, to penetrate the significance and develop the implications of the Buddha's teaching. In this case, provided that we are prepared to see in the Buddha's teaching religious as well as purely ethical aspects, it follows that Buddhist philosophy is internal to Buddhism as a religion. To be sure, it is possible to consider theories or doctrines expounded by Buddhist thinkers in themselves, abstracted from their context, and to compare these theories with theories in western thought. For example, we can compare the Buddhist analysis of the self with Hume's. But the respective contexts are both different and important. Hume was primarily concerned with the limits of what we can be said to know. The Buddhist analysis of the self, though doubtless meant seriously, was also intended to promote detachment, detachment in this case from the ego or self, and detachment was oriented to the attainment of Nirvāna, to what can fairly be described as salvation, even if salvation, in a system such as the Mādhyamika, was to be attained by one's own efforts rather than, as in Pure Land Buddhism, through faith in and the grace of the Eternal Buddha. Indeed, the view has been expressed that Buddhist doctrines should be judged simply in regard to their pragmatic significance or function, in regard, that is to say, to their contribution to the attainment of what was believed to be the goal of human life, rather than in regard to their truth or falsity as philosophical theories. This view may be an exaggeration, but it expresses an understanding of the fact that even the sometimes pretty obscure theories of Buddhist philosophers are oriented to the attainment of Nirvāna. Some Buddhist philosophical theories, considered purely in themselves, have no immediately evident connection with religion. Considered, however, in their context, they have such a connection, being subordinated to the attainment of a religious goal.

There are two further points which I wish to make. The first is this. Though I am doubtful about the validity of a purely pragmatic interpretation of Buddhist philosophical theory, it may very well help those who accept it to cope with apparent discrepancies between different doctrines. For example, if the self is reduced to a succession of causally linked momentary states, the question arises, what is it then that enters Nirvāna? If Nirvāna is regarded as annihilation, as total cessation of the series of states, this question does not arise. But if Nirvāna is regarded as a positive state of bliss, the question certainly does arise. The phenomenalistic analysis of the self and the view of Nirvāna as a positive state are difficult to reconcile. But the difficulty is greatly diminished if each theory is looked on as having a purely pragmatic function, if, that is to say, the phenomenalistic analysis of the self is regarded simply as an instrument for promoting detachment and the positive conception of Nirvāna as a means of encouraging the leading of a certain sort of life in this world. However, I remain doubtful about the interpretation of Buddhist thought purely on 'As if' lines.

The second point relates to my description of the attainment of Nirvāna as a religious goal. Let us call to mind the Bodhisattva ideal in Mahāyāna Buddhism, the ideal of the holy man who postpones his own final entry into Nirvāna until all have been saved. It is difficult to suppose that the salvation in question was regarded as total annihilation. And if it was regarded as a state of positive bliss, somehow enjoyed when the ego-consciousness had been laid aside, it presumably involved fusion with the Absolute. In this case the goal can reasonably be described as religious. The alternative, it seems to me, is to interpret the relevant doctrines in a purely pragmatic way.

V

The only other Buddhist school or sect about which I intend to make some remarks is Ch'an Buddhism, known in Japan as Zen. According to tradition, the first patriarch of the sect was Bodhidarma, who came to China from India early in the sixth century A.D. and taught the way of meditation. Two schools or sub-schools developed, the northern, represented by Shen-hsiu (c. 605–706) and the southern, represented by Hui-neng (638–713). Ch'an Buddhism survived the repression of A.D. 845, and in the twelfth century it was introduced into Japan, Eisai (1141–1215) being the originator of the Rinzai sect, while Dōgen (1200–1253) introduced the Sōtō sect in the thirteenth century.

When Ch'an Buddhism took root in Japan, it naturally assumed some local characteristics. But we cannot concern ourselves here either with differences between Ch'an and Zen or with differences between the sub-schools. As the name Zen is made more familiar to westerners than Ch'an, it will be employed here, unless the context demands 'Ch'an'.

Zen Buddhism may indeed seem to be a very unpromising subject for discussion in the present context, namely the metaphysics of the One and the Many. For if we asked a Zen teacher 'what is Zen's theory of the One and the Many?' he might well reply, 'There is no such theory'. Zen lays emphasis on immediate experience and discourages theorizing as an obstacle to enlightenment. It is true that the word 'meditation', which is commonly used as a translation for *Zazen* (the Japanese equivalent of the Sanskrit *dyhāna*), suggests the idea of thinking about some particular theme. Thus a Christian might say, 'I was meditating on the parable of the prodigal son.' In point of fact, however, *Zazen* is not discursive thinking. It involves the discarding of discursive thought. It is intuitive experience and is conceived not so much as a preparation for enlightenment (*satori*) as enlightenment itself.

One might express the point in this way, by comparing Zen with the thought of Nāgārjuna. As we have seen, Nāgārjuna developed an elaborate dialectic, designed to expose the antinomies arising out of all positive conceptual representations of reality and thus to prepare the way for an intuitive experience of Emptiness. In Zen, however, the dialectic tends to disappear. Instead, Zen teachers have been noted for taking what we might describe as a short cut, using shock tactics to shatter the mind's domination by categories of thought presupposing the subject-object distinction. Because of his critical dialectic Nāgārjuna appears to us as recognizably a philosopher, whereas Zen masters are naturally conceived as spiritual teachers and guides rather than as philosophers.

If, therefore, one tries to talk about Zen from an external point of view, one lays oneself open to the objection that Zen is essentially a way of experience and that it can be understood only by participation in the relevant form of life. At the same time it is an historical phenomenon and, as such, it can be discussed. To be sure, we cannot talk about it without employing concepts and discursive thought. But this applies also to those Zen masters who undertake, as some of them have done, to provide some explanation for interested westerners. Further, Zen practice implies some presuppositions. And it is difficult to see why a philosopher should not reflect on them. After all, some Zen teachers have not hesitated to make doctrinal assertions. Dōgen is an example.

We can describe Zen as aiming at the realization of one's true or original nature, which is identified with the Buddha-nature or Buddha-mind or Dharma-nature, these terms having the same reference. To speak of Zen as aiming at the realization of one's true nature may seem entirely inappropriate inasmuch as Zen is a form of Buddhism and Buddhism rejects the idea of a substantial inner self. The Buddha-mind, however, is not the particular mind of this person or that. Nor is it the mind of the individual man Siddartha Gautama. The Buddha-mind, said to be present in all sentient beings, is really the ultimate reality which is called 'mind' to indicate its spiritual nature. To say, however, that it is present in all sentient beings, and therefore in oneself, is misleading. Strictly speaking, it is not present 'in' anything. The human being *is* the Buddha-mind, as the wave *is* water. Hence realizing the Buddha-nature or Buddha-mind does not mean bringing into being what was not there before. It means becoming aware, through enlightenment, of what one really is all the time, and thus becoming aware of one's unity with others, and indeed with everything else. As the fourteenth-century Zen teacher Bassui expressed the matter in a sermon, 'Your own mind is itself Buddha, the Void-universe.'[26] Again, in a poem attributed to Seng-t'san, the third Ch'an Patriarch, we read, 'One in All, All in One'.[27]

The identity of the Absolute and the phenomenal world is expressed by Dōgen in his main literary work, the *Shōbō-gen-*

[26]Quoted from *Three Pillars of Zen: Teaching, Practice and Enlightenment*, edited with translations, introductions and notes by Philip Kapleau, p. 170 (revised and expanded edition, London, 1980).

[27]Quoted from 'The Seal of the Believing Mind' as given in *A History of Zen Buddhism* by H. Dumoulin, translated by P. Peachey, pp. 76–77 (New York, 1963).

zō,[28] by claiming that being and time are the same, and that impermanence is the Buddha-nature. We must not therefore conceive the Absolute as an unchanging reality, distinct from or even inside changing phenomena. The Absolute is itself becoming, and though it is described as mind, it comprises all phenomena, including those which would be ordinarily conceived as external objects of mind. It cannot be said to exist. For this statement would suggest that the Buddha-mind is a permanent reality, distinct from transient phenomena. At the same time it is wrong to say that it does not exist. Like the phenomena with which it is one, it neither exists nor not exists. It is the identity of being and not-being. It is in fact equivalent to Emptiness in the Mādhyamika system.

If being and becoming coincide, there cannot be a permanent state of the self transcending the world of becoming. Some Ch'an teachers seem to have envisaged such a state. But the Zen teacher Dōgen at any rate did not hesitate to assert that 'birth and death are in themselves Nirvāna'.[29] Nirvāna is not a reality different from the life of becoming, of transmigration. At the same time, if there is no Nirvāna to be desired, there are no birth and death to be hated.[30] The enlightened person sees all as one.

What does the enlightened person see which the unenlightened person does not see? The Zen teacher can answer, 'Nothing at all'. After enlightenment, as before, a person sees rivers, lakes, mountains, human beings. At the same time enlightenment is said to transform a person's view of the world. Thus a modern Zen master says that 'each thing *just as it is* takes on an entirely new significance or worth. Miraculously, everything is radically transformed though remaining as it is.'[31]

[28]Dōgen writes about this matter in the *Uji* section of the *Shōbō-genzō*. As I owe my knowledge of the relevant passages to translations kindly shown me by a scholar who was preparing a work for publication, I have avoided quotation.
[29]*Zen Master Dōgen. An Introduction with Selected Writings*, by Yūhō Yokoi, with the assistance of Daizen Victoria, p. 58 (New York and Tokyo, 1976). The quotation is from Dōgen's *Shushō-gi*.
[30]*Ibid.*
[31]Quoted from P. Kapleau's translation of lectures by Yasutani-roshi in *The Three Pillars of Zen*, p. 85. (See Note 26.)

Every phenomenon presumably, even a blade of grass or a leaf of a tree or a snowflake, takes on a profound meaning as a manifestation of the Buddha-mind, though the meaning cannot be verbally expressed. It is largely because of this emphasis on the value and significance of every phenomenon that Zen Buddhism was able to exercise a strong influence on Japanese art.

It is worth adding that if the enlightened person does not see anything which he did not see before enlightenment, no more does he necessarily do anything different from what he did before. To be sure, some Zen teachers, including Dōgen, laid emphasis on the monastic life and on the difficulty experienced by the laity in attaining to enlightenment. Generally speaking, however, the Zen view was that enlightenment was attainable by all, even in the midst of secular life. Normally of course the seeker after enlightenment would put himself under the direction of a qualified guide or director, a monk teacher. But after enlightenment he could perfectly well carry on with his ordinary occupation, provided that it was morally reputable. He would perform the same actions as before, though he would perform them in a different spirit, with detachment for example. It is well known that samurai practised Zen. Merchants, civil servants, artisans and farmers could do the same. In spite of monasticism, there was really no distinction in Zen between sacred and profane, though Zen Buddhists were of course expected to follow the Buddha's moral teaching.

VI

To return to the Zen conception of ultimate reality. The thought may very well occur to the reader that if the identity of the One and the phenomenal world is seriously asserted, the use of terms such as Buddha-mind and Buddha-nature becomes so much superfluous mystification. In an essay on pantheism Arthur Schopenhauer remarked that if God and the world are identified, the word 'God' is a superfluous label.[32] The statement 'the world

---

[32]The essay is contained in *Parerga and Paralipomena*. In Julius Frauenstädt's edition of the Works (*Werke*, Leipzig, 1877) of Schopenhauer it is given in volume VI, pp. 104–7.

is God' is equivalent to 'the world is the world'. Similarly, it might be urged, if the phenomenal world and the Buddha-nature are identical, 'Buddha-nature' is no more than a label for the world. To be sure, just as calling the world 'God' may express and tend to evoke a certain emotive attitude to the world, so may the description of the phenomenal world as the Buddha-mind or Buddha-nature express and evoke an emotive attitude. But there is nothing more, so to speak, in the Buddha-nature than there is in the world. If we talk about the 'phenomenal' world, this may suggest that there is a meta-phenomenal reality, a reality of which the world is an appearance. But to describe something as phenomenal can mean no more than that it appears or can appear to a sentient subject. It need not imply that what is called phenomenal is an appearance of something else. Indeed, if the world and the Buddha-nature are identical, it obviously cannot mean that the world is an appearance of a meta-phenomenal reality. If 'Buddha and sentient beings are no different',[33] are we not entitled to draw the conclusion that 'Buddha' is a collective name for sentient beings?

This line of thought occurs naturally to the critical, analytic mind. It may be said that it does not fit in with, for example, Bassui's statement that after enlightenment one will feel like a man come back from the dead.[34] But one might, I suppose, interpret him as meaning that one has seen that the world *is* the ultimate reality and that the problem of reality is solved by the vanishing of the problem.[35] The nature of reality becomes clear, and problems about it disappear. Though, however, Bassui does indeed seem to mean something of this sort, Zen teachers are given to emphasizing the inexpressibility of the content of enlightenment and the fact that the Buddha-mind or Buddha-nature transcends conceptualization, so that any mental representation of it is bound to be wrong.[36] The Buddha-nature is not indeed a supernatural reality, but it seems to be like the Tao in

[33] *The Blue Cliff Record*, translated by T. and J. C. Chang, Vol. 1, p. 244 (Boulder, Colorado, and London, 1977).

[34] *Three Pillars of Zen*, p. 172.

[35] Cf. what Wittgenstein says about 'the problem of life', *Tractatus Logico-Philosophicus*, 6. 521.

[36] See, for example, the translations from Yasutani-roshi's lectures in *The Three Pillars of Zen*, in particular p. 79.

the sense that it is irreducible simply to the sum total of phenomena, inasmuch as it is the dynamic One which exists in and through phenomena. It is true that, on Zen premises, this statement, like all other statements about the Buddha-nature, is incorrect. We cannot say, for example, that it exists or that it does not exist, that it is being or that it is not-being. In this case of course to say that 'Buddha-nature' is simply a collective name for phenomena must also be incorrect, even if to say that it is not a collective name for phenomena is again incorrect. We are in the sphere of mysticism, of the inexpressible. And if rationalist metaphysics falls short, so does logical analysis.

All this obscurity, it may be suggested, can be avoided, if we adopt a different approach to Zen. Let us take it that Zen involves a resolute and persistent attempt to discover one's true nature. As we have noted, this cannot be understood as a search for a permanent, substantial, individual self, the existence of which is denied by Buddhists. It is evident, however, that in Zen there is an attempt to get behind the discriminating mind to a prediscriminating or pre-reflective state. This involves going behind or beneath the ego-consciousness with its subject-object distinction. And it is understandable if the mind which is arrived at is regarded as a kind of universal mind, the Buddha-mind. But does not this pre-discriminating mind correspond to what Jung called the collective unconscious? Dr. D. T. Suzuki, possibly writing under the influence of William James, has described *satori* as 'an insight into the Unconscious'.[37] If this descent into the unconscious or infra-conscious is attained, mind and body, as some Zen teachers have put it, fall away, as far as consciousness is concerned that is to say. In other words, if we interpret Zen in psychological terms, we can understand what is meant by penetrating behind discursive thought to what has been called one's 'original face', 'one's face before one's parents were born'. The so-called Buddha-mind can be interpreted simply as the unconscious, mind in a state anterior to emergence of the subject-object distinction. It may be the case that temporary release from the discriminating mind and from discursive thought has a beneficial therapeutic effect. But even if it has,

[37]*Essays in Zen Buddhism*, 11, p. 31 (London, 1933).

the release has no necessary connection with metaphysical theories, whether religiously oriented or not.

There is certainly a good deal to be said for a purely psychological interpretation of Zen. After all, Zen is essentially the practice of *Zazen*, and *Zazen*, identified by Dōgen with enlightenment, is an experience or a state of mind. But there are certain points to bear in mind. In the first place the external observer is not in a good position to claim that his interpretation of *Zazen* is correct. It is true that attempts have been made to study *Zazen* empirically, by recording, for example, its effects on breathing and the heart. But there may be aspects of *Zazen* which elude the relevant machines. If we dismiss this possibility out of hand, we lay ourselves open to the accusation of having embraced a dogmatic behaviourism and of seeing everything in the light of this position. In the second place the fact remains that, whether we like it or not, there are certain doctrines in Zen Buddhism, notably that ultimate reality and the phenomenal world, the One and the Many, are not different.

If we do interpret Zen practice as our attempt to penetrate to the level of what William James called 'pure experience',[38] and if we accept his view that 'pure experience' is nothing 'but another name for feeling or sensation',[39] it is natural to ask whether *Zazen*, as so interpreted, has any religious significance at all. For the matter of that, if we take it that enlightenment is a vivid awareness that this phenomenal world of time and change is the only reality, could one reasonably regard enlightenment as a religious phenomenon, except perhaps in the sense that it would solve (or dissolve) a problem to which belief in God or in an unchanging Absolute constitutes an answer, a false one according to Zen Buddhism? If the Buddha-mind and sentient beings are said to be one, this presumably implies that non-sentient objects are mind-dependent, as in Yogācāra Buddhism, the Indian school which in China became the Weih-shih or Consciousness-only school. But it is by no means evident that idealism of this kind can properly be described as having a religious significance, unless of course the mind on

[38]*Essays in Radical Empiricism*, p. 117 (New York and London, 1912).
[39]*Ibid.*, p. 94.

which things are said to be dependent is conceived as the divine mind.

It is difficult to see how one can give unconditional answers to such questions. On condition that we are prepared to regard a unifying vision of reality as religious, provided at any rate that the One is regarded as spiritual rather than as material, the Zen Buddhist's vision of the world seems to qualify for being described as religious. Zen not only provides a unifying vision of the world but it also unifies a person's life, not so much in the sense, as we have noted above, that after enlightenment a person performs a different set of actions from those which he or she performed before enlightenment, as in the sense that daily actions are performed in a different spirit. If, however, we take a narrower view of religion and demand belief in a transcendent reality, whether it is described as personal or as suprapersonal, the Zen conception of reality would not count as religious.

At the same time the last statement may stand in need of qualification. If we go simply by Zen disclaimers of belief in any transcendent reality, the statement can stand. But some Zen teachers, in spite of their, so to speak, official identification of the One with the phenomenal world, seem pretty clearly to regard the Buddha-mind with a reverence which can be described as religious and which suggests that their inner attitude transgresses the limits set by any statement that there is no reality transcending the phenomenal world. After all, though Zen is a simplified form of Mahāyāna Buddhism, it is none the less Buddhism. And if we are prepared to look on Buddhism as a religion, this presumably applies to Zen.

VII

Let me risk a generalization or two. In Taoism the approach to the idea of the ultimate reality, the *Tao*, was by way of reflection on nature rather than through a retreat into the self. In Zen Buddhism the approach to a vision of reality is through a penetration beneath the discriminating and reflective mind to one's 'original face'. In the first instance, that is to say, attention is directed inwards rather than outwards. Despite this difference, however, Taoism and Zen are at one in rejecting the idea of a transcendent ultimate reality, entirely distinct from the phenomenal world.

In a book entitled *The Tao of Physics*[40] the author, Frithof Capra, argues that oriental mysticism presents us with the vision of a cosmos in which all things are interrelated, and that this idea has been emerging centuries later in modern physical science. He does not of course claim that oriental mysticism and modern science are the same thing. His thesis is that by different paths they converge towards the conception of the cosmos as one reality in which all things are interrelated.

It seems to me that the concept of mysticism can be overemphasized. When Chuang Tzu asserted that words such as 'up' and 'down', 'far' and 'near', 'great' and 'small', are relative terms, we can doubtless regard his assertion as confirmed or supported by modern relativity theory. But the assertion was surely the product of reflection, not of mystical experience as such. I do not deny that Taoism was associated with mysticism. My point is simply that Taoist expression of the view of the world as a unity is perhaps better ascribed to oriental thought, to a certain oriental philosophy, than to mysticism as such. I notice that Werner Heisenberg, one of the eminent scientists who is quoted by Capra in support of his thesis of an affinity between oriental mysticism and modern science, refers explicitly to 'philosophical ideas in the tradition of the Far East'.[41]

However this may be, let us assume that Frithof Capra's thesis is substantially correct, and that there is an affinity between some oriental philosophies and modern physics, as far as a general view of the world is concerned. One can then raise the following question. If modern science is regarded as standing on its own feet and as having no religious significance, in the sense, that is to say, that it can coexist either with religious belief or without it, is there any good reason for looking on the anticipatory vision of the world in oriental thought as possessing religious significance? If it does possess a religious significance

[40]By Frithof Capra (Shambala Publications, Boulder, Colorado, 1976: Bantam Books, New York, 1977).

[41]*Ibid.*, p. 4. The author quotes from Heisenberg's *Physics and Philosophy*, p. 125 (New York, 1958).

which modern scientific theory does not possess, what is this significance?

In the first place we can point to differences in context. In Taoism the vision of the unity of all things in and through the Tao was regarded as influencing the human being's attitude to others and one's conduct in the face of vicissitudes. In other words, Taoism was a philosophy of life. As for Buddhist conceptions of reality, they were developed within the Buddhist religion and were subordinated to the fulfilment of a spiritual programme culminating in the attainment of Nirvāna. The context of modern science is very different. Science is of course compatible with both ethics and religion. Further, by those who believe in God scientific inquiry into the divine creation can of course be regarded as having a spiritual value. At the same time it is obvious that modern science is not part of a programme of spiritual life in the sense in which Buddhist philosophies were directed to the attainment of a spiritual goal. To say this is not to say anything against science. It is simply to note a difference between oriental thought and modern physics.

In the second place, even when in oriental philosophy the ultimate reality was said to be not different from the phenomenal world, it seems to have been conceived, except by some reductionist philosophers, as more than the sum total of the Many. In other words, in the concept of the One there was an element of transcendence, which was associated with mysticism. I doubt whether the One, as so conceived, has a place in modern science. It is not, of course, a question of claiming that it should have a place. It is a question of noting differences.[42]

[42]See below, pages 140–41.

CHAPTER 4

THE ADVAITA VEDĀNTA AND ITS CRITICS

Introductory remarks – the philosophy of Śaṁkara – some points made by its critics – the Advaita Vedānta and religion

I

People who have only a very vague idea of Indian philosophy are inclined to equate it with monism. In point of fact the majority of Indian philosophical schools, Vedic as well as non-Vedic, had a pluralist conception of the world. The impression that Indian philosophy as a whole was monist is indeed understandable. For one thing, the Advaita Vedānta, the philosophy of non-dualism, became influential in intellectual circles in India. For another thing, in writings devoted to commending the wisdom of the East and oriental mysticism emphasis is likely to be laid on such famous statements of the Upanishads as 'That thou art' and on the system of thought developed on the basis of such statements. None the less, the notion that Indian philosophy in general was monist is incorrect. It is not true even of the Vedānta school as a whole.

Another common impression is that Indian philosophy as a whole was deeply religious and other-worldly. If we except the materialists, the Cārvāka or Lokāyata school, which was neither religious nor other-worldly, we can say that the impression is correct or incorrect according to the meaning we give to the words 'religion' and 'religious'. If we understand religion as involving belief in a personal being whom Jews, Christians and Muslims would recognize as God or as approximating to the idea of God, the statement that Indian philosophy was religious is incorrect. Of the non-Vedic schools the materialists did not believe in any spiritual reality. As for Jainism, popular Jainism accommodated belief in some Indian deities, but Jain philosophy did not include belief in any divine creator and can be described as atheist. In Buddhist philosophy there was no tran-

scendent, personal deity, though it is true that in certain forms
of Buddhism the concept of the Eternal Buddha, as object of
faith and invocation and as bestower of grace, came to play an
important role. Of the Vedic schools some seem to have had
originally no belief in God, even if in the course of time they
came to adopt this belief or at any rate to postulate a relatively
supreme being. The Nyāya and Vaiśesika schools are examples. It is true that the *bhakti* movement, the tradition of religious
devotion of which the Bhavagad-Gītā is a magnificent literary
expression, came to influence philosophical thought. We can see
this in the development of the Vedānta school, in which Śamkara's monism was followed by a theistic reaction. If, however,
we equate religion with Jewish, Christian and Muslim belief in
a personal divine creator, it is incorrect to say that Indian
philosophy as a whole was religious.

In another sense of 'religion', however, Indian philosophy,
with the exception of the materialist school, was, or in some
cases became, deeply religious. For the non-materialist schools,
Vedic and non-Vedic, were or became concerned with the salvation of the human being. That is to say, they were or became
oriented to the idea of the human spirit's enlightenment and
liberation from the world of time, change and rebirth. The
degree of emphasis placed on liberation and the interpretation
of its nature varied from school to school. But, with the exception
of Cārvāka, all the schools accepted or came to accept the idea
of liberation, and it is in this sense that they were other-worldly.
The Jains, for example, envisaged enlightened and liberated
souls as joining the Jain sages in a higher state of existence. It
does not follow, of course, that the schools were engaged in
never-ending talk about liberation. The Nyāya school, for example, developed an elaborate logic, and the Sāmkhya school
was interested in cosmological questions. Again, epistemology
or theory of knowledge was widely cultivated. My point is simply
that there is a sense in which Indian philosophy as a whole,
with the exception of the materialist school, was or became
religiously oriented.

Having made these general remarks about Indian philosophy,
I shall now confine my attention to the Vedānta tradition, to
the non-dualism of Śamkara in the first instance and then to its

critics in the Vedānta school. This school was one of the Vedic
schools, so called because they accepted the authority of the
Vedas as a source of truth, though the extent to which they
derived their doctrines from the sacred texts varied from school
to school. As far as the Vedānta school is concerned, the point
of departure was provided chiefly by the earlier Upanishads,
which formed the 'end of the Veda' or Vedānta, the most
significant texts being those which referred to the ultimate reality, Brahman.

In the Upanishads we find a variety of different lines of
thought, some of which were doubtless chronologically more
ancient than others. To try to identify the different strata and
to determine their origins, in so far as this is possible, is a task
for specialists. It is, however, clear that the Upanishads are
compilations, and that they do not present one uniform view of
reality. Anthologies which are confined to a selection of the more
sublime passages may provide excellent texts for the purpose of
religious meditation, but they can give a misleading impression
of the Upanishadic literature as a whole. For the Upanishads
contain not only doctrine relating to an ultimate spiritual reality
but also a good deal of primitive speculation about the stuff of
which things are made and about the formation of the world, as
well as directions relating to sacrifices. It is a mistake to make
a rigid distinction between the Brāhmanas and the Upanishads,
as though the former contained no philosophical speculation at
all whereas the latter were concerned solely with the Absolute.
It is true that we can see the idea of a One beginning in the
Vedic hymns and becoming much more prominent in the Upanishads. We can also see expressions in the Upanishads themselves of the progressive spiritualization of the concept of the
One. It remains true, however, that it is possible to appeal to
the Upanishads in support of different philosophical systems.
For example, the Sāmkhya philosophers were able to appeal to
the sacred texts.

Obviously, a philosopher could select one particular aspect of
Upanishadic teaching and try to interpret the rest in such a way
as to fit in with his emphasis on the aspect in question. But this
procedure involved a presupposition about the truth, a presupposition which required support on independent grounds. In

other words, appeals by Indian thinkers to the sacred texts should not be understood as meaning that they relied simply on scriptural authority and employed no philosophical reflection or reasoning. When, however, as with the Advaita Vedānta philosophers, the ultimate reality was said to transcend discursive thought and conceptualization, the appeal to scriptural authority naturally became a prominent feature, though the relevant texts were regarded as expressing insights enjoyed by sages of old, insights which were in principle repeatable and, as such, serving as confirmation of the doctrine. The Advaita thinkers were indeed perfectly justified in claiming that their doctrine of Brahman was present in the Upanishads. But, as has been noted, it was not the only doctrine, even if it can be regarded as the culmination of a process of search for the ultimate reality. There was no ready-made uniform philosophical system in the Upanishads. It is more a case of the sacred texts together (Vedas, Brāhmanas and Upanishads) forming a point of departure for various lines of thought. Thus the Vedānta school, as its name implies, derived inspiration mainly from the Upanishads, whereas the Mīmāmsā school had a conspicuous connection with the Brāhmanas. (By the Mīmāmsā school I mean the Pūrva Mīmāmsā school, as distinct from the Uttara Mīmāmsā or Vedānta school. It is in these two schools, Pūrva Mīmāmsā and Vedānta, that the influence of sacred texts is most evident.)

It is not possible to determine the precise dates of the foundation of the Vedic schools, though Sāmkhya seems to have been the oldest of them. The formation of definite schools, however, was preceded by the composition of a number of texts, some of which were ascribed to reputed founders of schools. A basic text for the Vedānta school was the *Brahma-sūtra* or *Vedānta-sūtra*, an often cryptic and obscure exposition of the doctrine of the Upanishads, which was composed by Bādarāyana in perhaps the second century B.C.[1] (The dates of early Indian philosophers are generally uncertain and difficult to determine.) This text was made the subject of commentaries by

[1]See *The Brahma Sūtra. The Philosophy of the Spiritual Life*, translated with an Introduction and Notes by S. Radhakrishnan (London, 1960; New York, 1968).

leading thinkers of the Vedānta school, such as Śaṁkara, Rāmānuja and Madhva. The Advaita or non-dualist philosophy is commonly said to have originated with Gaudapāda's commentary on the Māndukya Upanishad, composed about A.D. 780. Tradition has it that one of Gaudapāda's disciples, Govinda, was Śaṁkara's teacher. Śaṁkara, therefore, whose dates are generally given as A.D. 788–820, was not the originator of the Advaita philosophy. At the same time he is its most famous representative. His thought is not exactly synonymous with the Advaita philosophy, as there were some differences between his views and those of other Advaitins. But for our present purposes we shall have to confine our attention to Śaṁkara.

II

The impression has often been given that according to Śaṁkara the world of plurality, the world which we know through sense-experience and influence, is unreal, mere appearance, illusory. This impression, however, stands in need of a good deal of qualification. Śaṁkara has no intention of denying that for the purposes of everyday life the Many are real enough. The world of waking consciousness, the world of many things and persons, related to one another in various ways, is a public world, and in comparison with the world of dreams it is the real world. Even on Śaṁkara's premises it is perfectly reasonable to say that on waking from my private world of dream-images I awake to reality. Further, within the world of waking consciousness we can distinguish between what appears to be the case and what is really the case. To take an example used by Indian thinkers and by Śaṁkara himself, a coiled rope may appear to someone to be a snake. But his error is corrigible.

The rope is not, for Śaṁkara, a mere idea of a subject, an unreal projection. On the contrary, it is a datum, a perceived object which is irreducible to the subject. That is to say, on the level of experience characterized by the subject-object distinction the object can no more be reduced to the subject than the subject to the object. In this sense Śaṁkara is a realist. To be sure, if there is a level of experience transcending the subject-object distinction, both terms are sublated. But this does not alter the fact that subject and object are correlative terms, and that we cannot retain the subject and at the same time reduce the object to the subject. Śaṁkara had little use for idealist tendencies as found in one line of Buddhist thought.

To mention science in connection with Śaṁkara's thought may seem anachronistic, inasmuch as he lived centuries before the development of science as we know it. But it is worth noting that scientific knowledge could be accommodated within the framework of his philosophy. He could not indeed regard science as the only way of obtaining knowledge about the world. Further, given his interest in and emphasis on the liberation of the human spirit from the sphere of time and change, he obviously would not attach the same value to science as was given it by, for example, Auguste Comte. Again, there are doubtless many scientific theories, acceptance of which would require abandonment or revision of views stated in his writings, views about, for example, the formation of kinds of things. At the same time he could quite recognize the pragmatic value of science not only in regard to its technological application but also in regard to the conceptual mastery which it provides over the world of plurality. After all, Śaṁkara did not need to be told that until liberation everyone lives in a world of plurality. He knew this by his own experience. And it would be possible for him to recognize the role of science within this world, without thereby being compelled to abandon his metaphysics.

Accepting the world of plurality as a datum, Śaṁkara argues that the existence of an ordered world provides evidence of the existence of an intelligent, indeed omniscient creator. All members of the Many must have a source, which can be neither a material body nor a human soul. This cosmic cause and sustainer of the world is Īśvara, the Lord, also named Vishnu and Nārāyana. The creator is not only the efficient cause of the world but also its material cause. On this matter Śaṁkara can appeal, for example, to the Taittirīya Upanishad which asserts the existence of a being from which all other beings have come, by which they all live, and to which they all return.[2] The picture

[2] 3, 1–6. See, for example, *The Thirteen Principal Upanishads*, translated by R. E. Hume, pp. 290–1 (2nd edition, Oxford, 1931, paperback 1971).

is that of a reality from which all finite things issue and into which they are periodically reabsorbed. According to Śaṁkara, 'the omniscient Lord of all is the cause of the origin of this world in the same way as clay is the material cause of jars and gold of golden ornaments'.[3] 'There is no other substance from which the world could originate.'[4]

The reader who is aware of Śaṁkara's theory of non-dualism may feel inclined to protest that I have been trying to represent the Indian philosopher as a theist, so far as this is possible in the case of someone who described the supreme Lord as the material as well as the efficient cause of the world. Did not Śaṁkara believe that the ultimate reality, Brahman, was suprapersonal and that the human spirit was identical with Brahman?

The reply is that, for Śaṁkara, the concept of Iśvara or a personal creator is the form in which the Absolute appears to discursive thought, operating with the subject-object distinction. If we try to think of the Absolute, we unavoidably objectify it as distinct from ourselves and the things around us and as the object of religious devotion. The objectified Absolute, endowed with attributes or qualities, is God, Saguna-Brahman. To say that God does not exist would be false. For God *is* Brahman, Brahman as appearing to or conceived by discursive thought. And as religious devotion, *bhakti*, involves the subject-object distinction, another way of expressing the matter is to say that God is the Absolute as appearing to the religious consciousness. In worshipping God, whether he is called Iśvara, Vishnu, Śiva or by any other name, the devout believer is not worshipping nothing. In point of fact devotional religion was by no means alien to Śaṁkara himself. To see this one has only to look at the hymns attributed to him. It is also recorded of him that he founded four monasteries, in different parts of India, and several religious orders.

To the mind operating within the framework of the subject-object distinction the highest reality is the supreme Lord,

[3]From Śaṁkara's commentary on the Vedānta- or Brahma-sūtra, 2, 1, 1. (In such references to commentaries as the *Brahma-sūtra* the first number refers to the Adhyāya, the second to the Pāda, and the third to the section within the relevant *Pāda*.) *The Sacred Books of the East*, edited by Max Müller, vol. XXXIV, part 1, translated by G. Thibaut, p. 290 (Oxford, 1890).

[4]*Ibid.*, 1, 4, 23. Thibaut, p. 286 (see preceding note.)

Iśvara. The Upanishads, however, at any rate as interpreted by Śaṁkara, teach that the inner self (*ātman*) of the human being is one with Brahman. The Upanishads, as we have noted, do not present us with one uniform doctrine. But there are of course passages which assert the oneness of the human spirit with the Absolute. The best known, 'That thou art', occurs several times in the Chāndogya Upanishad.[5] It is on such passages that Śaṁkara bases his doctrine that *ātman* is not different from Brahman. In this context Brahman means Nirguna-Brahman, the suprapersonal Absolute, transcending all distinctions and the sole true reality.

A modern philosopher is obviously unlikely to be convinced of the truth of this doctrine by an appeal to the testimony of the Hindu sacred texts. He would demand an independent proof of the truth of the doctrine. But this is precisely what Śaṁkara cannot give and does not claim to be able to give. For philosophical proof is the work of the discursive reason, and the Absolute eludes the grasp of discursive and conceptual reason. The existence and nature of Brahman could not be proved without Brahman being objectified. But Brahman objectified is an appearance of the Absolute, not Nirguna-Brahman itself. Śaṁkara does indeed argue that rival theories, theories, that is to say, which are incompatible with non-dualism, cannot stand up to criticism and give rise to insoluble antimonies. He is also prepared to argue that his own theory does not contradict experience and is internally coherent. But the fact that the human spirit is one with the Absolute is known only by the testimony of the sacred texts and by a suprasensory intuitive experience. This experience is not of course enjoyed by everyone, but for the person who has the experience it acts as an experiential confirmation of the teaching of the Upanishads.

Śaṁkara's position bears an obvious resemblance to that of the Buddhist thinker Nāgārjuna. Both men developed a critical dialectic exposing what they believed to be fallacies in other people's theories. And both men postulated a suprasensory intuitive experience. One difference between them, however, is that whereas Nāgārjuna referred to the object (if one may so

[5]6, 8–616. Hume, pp. 246–50. (See Note 2.)

describe it) of suprasensory experience simply as Emptiness or the Void, Śaṁkara did not hesitate to assert that Brahman is pure consciousness or intelligence and bliss (*ānanda*) or joy. A disciple of Nāgārjuna would doubtless contend that the Buddhist thinker was the more consistent of the two. And in view of Śaṁkara's belief that the Absolute transcends conceptual thought, the contention appears to be justified. But when Śaṁkara applied positive epithets to Brahman, he was simply following the practice of the Upanishads. Nāgārjuna, being a Buddhist, did not accept the authority of the Hindu sacred texts.

We can also note a point of resemblance between Śaṁkara and the western philosopher Spinoza. It would be a mistake to think that for Śaṁkara the oneness of the human spirit with Brahman was something to be brought about or achieved in an ontological sense. *Ātman* is one with Brahman, whether one is aware of the fact or not. What is required is an advance from ignorance to knowledge of an already existing fact. Similarly, for Spinoza it was not a question of the human mind becoming a mode of infinite substance, as though it had not been a mode before. It was a question of coming to know an already existing ontological fact. With both philosophers, therefore, we find theories of degrees of knowledge. Whether Śaṁkara's intuitive experience of oneness with Brahman can properly be described as knowledge is another matter, to which we shall return in the context of criticism of the Advaita philosophy by later Vedānta philosophers. My point here is simply that Śaṁkara's metaphysics clearly demands an emphasis on theory of knowledge.

Let me expand a little the bare assertion that for Śaṁkara the inner self is one with Brahman. In the introduction to his commentary on the *Brahma-sūtra* Śaṁkara asserts that 'everyone is conscious of the existence of (his) self and never thinks "I am not." '[6] The existence of the self cannot be seriously doubted, inasmuch as to doubt whether one exists implicitly affirms one's existence. The nature of the self, however, is not immediately clear. The materialists give one account of it, the Sāmkhya school another, the Buddhists yet another. According to Śaṁkara, the empirical self, the self which can be made the

<hr />

[6] 1, 1, 1. Thibaut, p. 14. (See Note 3.)

object of introspection, the changing self which is bound up with a particular body, belongs to the sphere of appearance. There is, however, an inner, substantial and unchanging self (*ātman*), which is, so to speak, really real, the true self.

Up to this point Śaṁkara's theory of the self is not peculiar either to himself or to the Advaita school as a whole. The materialists did not of course accept the idea of a spiritual and substantial self. Nor did the Buddhists believe in a permanent and substantial self, though they were certainly not materialists. The Vedic philosophers, however, asserted the existence of a permanent self, which provides continuity in successive terrestrial lives and which can attain final liberation. This self is really the self as pure subject, which cannot be turned into an object. It is 'the witness', corresponding more or less to what in western philosophy has been called the transcendental ego, and which F. H. Bradley described rather caustically as a miserable, metaphysical point.[7]

Whereas, however, the Śaṁkara philosophy was pluralist and envisaged the self, at liberation, as entering into a state of splendid isolation, freed from all entanglement with the material world, Śaṁkara asserted that *ātman* was not different from Brahman and therefore not different from other selves. It was this claim which was peculiar to the Advaita philosophy. And it was the truth of the claim which was believed to be grasped in mystical intuition.

Śaṁkara's view of the relation between the inner self and the Absolute has often been described as the theory that *ātman* and Brahman are identical. And it must be admitted that there are statements in the Upanishads which warrant use of the word 'identity'. If, however, we take the statement of identity literally, it seems to follow that one can say, 'I am the sole reality'. I suppose that on Śaṁkara's premises this can be said, provided of course that the pronoun 'I' is not understood as referring to the empirical ego. At the same time it seems to me that Śaṁkara's attitude would be better expressed by saying, 'Brahman is the sole reality, and the permanent element in you is not-different from Brahman'. In a prayer to Vishnu Śaṁkara as-

---

[7] *Appearance and Reality*, p. 87 (2nd edition, London, 1897).

serted that 'the wave belongs to the ocean, and not the ocean
to the wave.'[8] The wave can be said to be not different from the
ocean, but the wave would be mistaken if it thought that it was
the whole ocean. It may indeed be objected that what Śaṁkara
said in a prayer to God, under the name of Vishnu, cannot
legitimately be taken as evidence of what he would say in regard
to the relation between *ātman* and Nirguna-Brahman. If asked,
however, Śaṁkara might very well remark that at final liberation, when appearance ceases, it is the wave which is absorbed
in the ocean, not the ocean into the wave. In any case, Śaṁkara
should not be represented as a solipsist, certainly not as far as
his intentions are concerned.

If in mystical experience the subject-object distinction is transcended, then within the experience itself all consciousness of
plurality disappears. And at final liberation all consciousness of
a world of plurality finally disappears. For the self absorbed in
Brahman there is no consciousness either of itself as a distinct
entity nor of the world of finite objects. As far as understanding
the psychological state of absorption is concerned, there does
not seem to be any great difficulty. But it is one thing to say
that awareness of X disappears and another thing to say that X
ceases to exist. Let us assume that all inner selves are really one
with Brahman and thus one with one another. And let us suppose that one self attains liberation. Does the world of appearance, the world of plurality, cease to exist? If so, must it not
cease to exist for other selves too, if they are all one self? But
this does not appear to be the case. It may be said that the
world of plurality does not cease to exist for selves still in the
grip of ignorance. But if all selves are one self, it is difficult to
see how 'some selves' and not others are affected by ignorance.
And in any case does it make sense to talk about the world of
plurality existing and not existing at the same time?

It might be urged in reply that problems of this sort can be
raised only in a language in which no answers can be given.
Our language belongs to the world of appearance. In this world
there are indeed many selves, and we can of course talk about
them. But they are empirical selves, individual selves. If we

[8]Quoted from Radhakrishnan's edition of the *Brahma-sūtra*, p. 38. (See Note
1.)

refer not to empirical selves but to the inner self which is one with Brahman, we cannot talk meaningfully about 'other selves'. And any problem which depends on our ability to do so is a pseudo-problem.

However this may be, some writers have in fact raised the problem and have tried to answer it, if I understand them correctly, in terms of the following distinction. From the psychological point of view the world of plurality ceases to exist as an object of consciousness for anyone who enjoys mystical experience of oneness with Brahman. But it does not cease to exist in a definitive sense until all have been finally liberated, until, as one might put it, the end of time, when Brahman will be all in all.

In any case the philosophy of non-dualism does not commit the Advaitin to holding that the world does not exist in any sense. For one thing, it is the appearance or self-manifestation of Brahman, and it exists as appearance. For another thing, it is the effect of Brahman as its cause. But we may very well want to ask why and how Brahman comes to appear under the guise of plurality. As for the question 'Why?', the Advaitin suggestion that the world was created simply in play or sport and not for any end seems to me equivalent to saying that no answer can be given. As for the question 'How?', the answer given by Śaṁkara is, as we have seen, in terms of causality, efficient and material. We can, of course, go on to ask how the unchangeable suprarelational Absolute can exercise causality of any kind. But Śaṁkara could reply that no answer can be given except by the discursive reason, for which Brahman appears as creator.

It is at any rate clear that for the Advaitin the world of plurality can be seen as the appearance of the Absolute only from a higher point of view than that of everyday life. Let us suppose that in the state of dreaming the dream-world is the only reality which is envisaged. On awakening we can judge that the dream-world was less real than the public world of the waking consciousness; but we cannot do this within the dream-world itself.[9] We have first to wake up. Analogously, for

----

[9]Objection might be taken to the phrase 'less real', on the ground that dreams really occur (that is, people really dream), and that they are as real as anything else. But I prescind from such objections here.

very many people the world of plurality, of time and change, is the only reality that there is. It cannot be seen as the appearance of the Absolute except from a higher level of knowledge. This higher knowledge is derived, as we have noted, from the testimony of the sacred texts, which is experientially confirmed by mystical experience. This enables us to see the world of plurality as the appearance of the Absolute. But it leaves empirical reality intact, so to speak, on its own level. The Advaitin therefore feels justified in claiming that the philosophy of non-dualism does not contradict ordinary experience, though it asserts a higher point of view or level of knowledge. The world is empirically real, but from the transcendental point of view it is appearance.

III

In the opinion of Madhva, who lived in the thirteenth century A.D. and was the chief exponent of the Dvaita or dualist Vedānta philosophy,[10] the contention that the philosophy of non-dualism did not contradict experience was simply invalid. On the contrary, the Advaita system was contradicted by an experience which could not reasonably be doubted, namely the experience of plurality. The basic (though not the only) form of experience is sense-experience, sense-perception. And though we can certainly make mistakes sometimes in our judgments of perception, no sane person can really doubt that in perception the subject apprehends an object or datum distinct from itself. Further, memory, which for Madhva is a source of knowledge, bears witness to the distinction between a given self and all other selves. My memories are mine and not yours, and they are known or experienced as mine. Indeed, the self as 'witness', as the reflective subject, is aware that all its knowledge is its own. We can say that it experiences its knowledge as its own. That is to say, it is aware of itself knowing, 'itself' being this individual.

[10]The word 'dualist' refers to the distinction made by Madhva and his followers between the human spirit and God. Inasmuch, however, as the Dvaita philosophers asserted the existence of a plurality of selves and things, 'pluralist' would also be an appropriate descriptive epithet.

The Advaitin would doubtless retort that Madhva's thesis is naive. The Advaitin does not deny that there is such a phenomenon as an experience of plurality. What he maintains is that just as the dream-world is sublated by waking consciousness, so is the experience of plurality sublated at a higher level of experience. That there is such a higher level of experience is known in the first instance from the testimony of the sacred texts, but this testimony is confined by *ātman*'s intuitive experience of its oneness with Brahman and so with all other inner selves.

This line of thought did not convince Madhva. In his opinion, all the knowledge which we can obtain without 'revelation', apart from scriptural authority, is based on experience. Inference is indeed a source of knowledge, but it is based on experience. To deny the witness of experience in the name of a philosophical theory would be equivalent to cutting through the branch on which one was sitting. As for scriptural authority, this was of course recognized by Madhva, a devout Vedānta philosopher; but he considered it a matter of common sense to prefer an interpretation which was compatible with what everyone knew to be true to one which was incompatible with known truth. To be sure, Madhva was quite well aware that his appeal to experience was unlikely to convince the Advaitins. And in his last work, the fourth of his commentaries on the Brahma-sūtra, he remarked sarcastically that there was really nothing to be said to the person who claimed that the phrase 'the other' had no application, and that some blows with a stick might be more efficacious.[11]

The Advaitin would naturally reply that to represent him as denying the evidence of experience was unjustified. In the first place he did not reject the testimony of sense-experience on its own level. In the second place it was precisely to experience, the intuitive experience of oneness with Brahman, that he appealed in confirmation of his interpretation of the sacred texts. As for the relation between the testimony of sense-perception and that of suprasensory perception, the Advaitin would claim that there was no contradiction. It was a matter of degrees of truth. In comparison with the testimony of suprasensory or

[11]*Anuvyākhyana*, 1, 4, 108.

mystical perception, the truth of the testimony of sense-perception was relative, relative to the purposes of everyday life and scientific inquiry.

Madhva, however, was not prepared to accept the theory of degrees of truth. For him, a proposition was either true or false, and that was that. The statement that there is a plurality of selves and the statement that there is no plurality of selves cannot both be true. If one of them is true, the other is false. And it would be absurd, in Madhva's opinion, to reject the evidence of sense-perception and self-consciousness in favour of a theory which flatly contradicts them. As for consciousness of identity with Brahman, there can be no such consciousness. For consciousness by its very nature involves the subject-object distinction. It is true that in self-consciousness the self as subject and the self as object are not different entities. 'Though there is generally a difference between the agent and the object of the action, non-difference is also possible.'[12] But this does not alter the fact that one cannot be conscious of oneself without introducing an epistemological distinction between subject and object.

There were other Indian thinkers who defended much the same view as Madhva's. For example, Rāmānuja had already said 'nor is there any consciousness devoid of objects, for nothing of the kind is ever known'.[13] We can therefore claim that Madhva and the other Indian thinkers who thought in the same way would have agreed with the doctrine of intentionality as defended by modern phenomenologists, the doctrine, that is to say, that consciousness is by its very nature intentional, consciousness of an object. At the same time the contexts are different. Brentano, the Austrian philosopher (1838–1917), wished to find a feature distinguishing mental acts from all other acts, and he found it in intentionality of consciousness, i.e. that all consciousness is essentially consciousness *of* (an object). Madhva however was interested not so much in distinguishing mental from physical acts as in attacking the Advaitin claim that there could be a state of consciousness in which the identity

[12]*Ibid.*, 1, 2, 3.
[13]See Rāmānuja's commentary on the *Brahma-sūtra*, 1, 1, 1. Quoted from *The Sacred Books of the East*, Vol. XLVIII (translator G. Thibaut), Part III, p. 52 (Oxford, 1904).

of the human spirit with Brahman was known. His line of argument is that there cannot be consciousness of identity with Brahman, inasmuch as consciousness involves a distantiation of the subject from the object of consciousness. In other words, he is attacking the idea of 'pure consciousness', in which the subject-object distinction is said to be transcended. If it were urged in reply that there might be an ecstatic mystical state in which the distinction between subject and object disappeared, Madhva would presumably retort that to describe this state as consciousness would be to misdescribe it, and that no ontological conclusion could be drawn from its occurrence about the identity of *ātman* and Brahman.

It might perhaps be objected that to say that consciousness is always consciousness *of* is simply to illustrate one use of the word 'consciousness'. Words such as 'consciousness' and 'conscious' have various uses in ordinary language, and we can hardly assert *a priori* that the word 'consciousness' cannot justifiably be applied to the sort of state which the Advaitins had in mind. After all, one might equally well claim that all experience is experience *of* (an object), and that therefore there can be no experience transcending the subject-object distinction. Yet if a state of ecstatic union with one ultimate reality occurs, how else can we describe it but as an experience? If this is a legitimate description, it is surely a case of sheer dogmatism if we refuse to admit that there can be such a thing as 'pure consciousness'.

How Madhva would reply to this line of thought is obviously a matter for conjecture. But if he stuck to his view that consciousness by its very nature involves the subject-object distinction, he would presumably claim that if the word 'consciousness' is applied to the state in question, it is thereby deprived of meaning and so misapplied. However this may be, he gives other arguments to show that the human self cannot be identical with Brahman. For example, in an early commentary on the *Brahma-sūtra*, his *Brahma-sūtra-bhāsya*, he remarks that 'there exist the attributes of absolute independence, wisdom, and so on, which differentiate Brahman from the soul'.[14] In other words,

[14]Quoted from *The Vedānta-sūtras with the Commentary of Sri Madhvacharya* (Madhva), translated by S. Subba Rau, p. 93 (Madras, 1904). The reference is to 2, 1, 14. (See Note 3). Madhva is actually quoting, but with approval.

Brahman is conceived as possessing attributes which the human soul certainly does not possess. Brahman, for example, depends on nothing at all outside itself, and it is said to be absolute knowledge, omniscience. Such attributes cannot be predicated of the human soul without absurdity.

An Advaitin might, I suppose, reply that when he asserts the non-difference between *ātman* and Brahman, he is not talking about the human soul in the sense intended by Madhva. What he is saying is that the One is present in the human being as that being's innermost core, as what some western mystics have described as the citadel of the soul or as the divine spark in man. The rest is appearance.

In this case, Madhva might retort, to say that *ātman* is not different from Brahman is really equivalent to saying that Brahman is not different from Brahman. But the teaching of the Advaita school about the need for moral purification, for detachment from selfish passions, and for the advance from ignorance to knowledge presupposes that it is in fact the human being who is being urged to turn to the One. It is the human being, not Brahman, who is called upon to recognize his or her relationship with the One. If the Advaitin really means that the human being must disappear altogether, he should say so in an unambiguous manner and not give the impression that *ātman* is the human being. Further, if the human being is appearance, to whom does the appearance appear? To Brahman? If so, the Absolute presumably misleads itself, though why and how remains obscure.

The foregoing remarks may perhaps give the impression of tiresome polemics directed against an impressive and venerable philosophical system. They can, however, be regarded as illustrating the difficulty which is bound to be encountered if a philosopher tries to give verbal expression to the content of an experience which is conceived as transcending discursive thought. The Advaita philosophy cannot be expounded except in terms of the categories of discursive thinking, thinking which involves the subject-object distinction. Discursive thought however belongs, on Advaitin premises, to the sphere of appearance. It follows that the philosophy of non-dualism belongs to the sphere of appearance. Indeed, though Śaṁkara believed that the Hindu scriptures had Brahman for their source and mirrored Brahman's omniscience, does it not follow, from the doctrine that this world is appearance, that the sacred texts, as existing in the world, must also be appearance, together with all interpretations given to them?[15] In fine, even if we grant that there can be an experience of reality, as distinct from appearance, the nature and content of the experience can be expressed only in ways which are inevitably inadequate.

The point can be made in this way. When people awake from sleep and remember a dream, they can accommodate the dream-state within their mental history, within the general framework of reference of the waking consciousness. But if we postulate a further awakening to a state in which plurality is transcended, there seems to be nobody left to accommodate the experience of the working consciousness. Any such accommodation has to be made on the level of the waking consciousness. It can therefore hardly be anything else but an inadequate and distorting account. As we have already noted, an adherent of the Mādhyamika school of Buddhism would doubtless comment that Nāgārjuna was wise to disclaim any intention of developing a positive metaphysics of his own and to avoid predicating any positive attributes of Emptiness or the Void.[16]

In view of the fact that on Advaitin premises discursive thought, and therefore the philosophy of non-dualism, must belong to the sphere of appearance, it is tempting to represent this philosophy as a kind of ladder leading upwards to mystical experience, a ladder which in the end can be kicked away as an instrument which is no longer needed. Though however there may be something in this idea, Śaṁkara was of course a serious philosopher who believed in the truth of what he was saying. He certainly regarded his philosophy as having an instrumentalist value. For the Indian philosophical schools were more than groups of thinkers who happened to think on more or less the same lines. In their vigorous days at any rate they were

[15]To meet this sort of difficulty it was held that the scriptures are eternal. I find this thesis perplexing.

[16]According to Madhva, there was really no difference between the Advaitin Nirguna-Brahman, the qualityless Absolute, and the Buddhist concept of Emptiness. He did not however intend this assertion as a compliment to the Advaitins.

schools for life, theory not being divorced from practice. But it
does not follow that Śaṁkara made no truth-claims on behalf
of the philosophy of non-dualism, nor that, if he did make such
claims, truth was conceived in a pragmatist fashion. Śaṁkara
may have thought that truth worked, so to speak; but it worked
because it was true. I do not believe therefore that criticism
levelled at the Advaita philosophy, whether by its Vedānta
critics, such as Madhva, or by anyone else, can legitimately be
regarded as beside the point in principle. Śaṁkara did not, for
example, deny the principle of non-contradiction as an irrele-
vancy. On the contrary, he was careful to argue that his philosophy was internally coherent and that it did not contradict
experience. If anyone disagrees with these contentions, he is
entitled to say so and explain his reasons. For example, perception was recognized as a source of knowledge (a *pramāna*) by all
Indian schools of philosophy, including the materialists on the
one hand and the Advaitins on the other. Hence Madhva was
fully entitled to examine critically the way in which the Advaitins tried to reconcile their acceptance of perception as a source
of knowledge with a metaphysics which, at first sight at least,
seemed to be incompatible with the testimony of sense-perception and of self-consciousness.

At the same time it is clear that Madhva's marked hostility
to the Advaita Vedānta was not due simply to his conviction
that it was incompatible with experience. It was also due to his
conviction that the philosophy of non-dualism was potentially
destructive of religion. It was not a question of accusing Śaṁkara himself of having been an irreligious man or of intending
to undermine or destroy religion. It was a question of the implications of non-dualism.

IV

Although Madhva was probably the most outspoken representative of the religiously inspired reaction within the Vedānta
school to the Advānta philosophy, there were other philosophers who shared his view that monism was potentially destructive of religion, religion being conceived in terms of loving
service of God. These thinkers were strongly influenced by the

bhakti movement, which had found expression in the Bhavagad-Gītā, and which they saw as threatened by the theories of a suprapersonal Absolute and of the identity of *ātman* and Brahman.

The most famous representative of this line of thought within the Vedānta school is Rāmānuja, who died in A.D. 1127 some seventy years before Madhva's birth, and who insisted on the personal nature of Brahman, on the identity, that is to say, of Brahman and Iśvara, the Lord and creator. Śorīkantha[17] too maintained that the ultimate reality was personal. So did Nimbārka, who probably lived in the second half of the thirteenth century, as well as Vallabha in the fifteenth century and Baladeva at the beginning of the eighteenth century. The Advaita philosophy may indeed have come to be the most influential system of thought in intellectual circles; but the reaction inspired by the *bhakti* movement was not a passing phenomenon. Further, it is clear that some Hindu teachers and philosophers who accepted the Advaita philosophy or who were heavily indebted to it, interpreted it in such a way as to leave room for religious devotion and the ideal of loving service of God. Thus the famous Hindu mystic and teacher Rāmakrishna (1834–1886) accepted the Advaita philosophy; but it is clear from his life and words that he was inspired by a genuine love of God. Again, Sir Sarvepalli Radhakrishnan (1888–1975), who adhered to the Advaita tradition, none the less interpreted it as teaching not that the personal God was simply an appearance of Brahman but rather that the personal God is Brahman, though in his relationship as lord and creator to the world, which, for Radhakrishnan, was real and not illusory. In other words, even if the Advaita Vedānta can be regarded as having triumphed over the Dvaita Vedānta of Madhva, as far as influence is concerned, the modification which it has received at the hands of prominent adherents bears witness to the relevance of criticism levelled against it in the name of religion.

Some of the earlier thinkers named above stood closer than others to the position of Śaṁkara. For example, though Rāmā-

[17]Śorīkantha's dates are uncertain. Some writers have regarded him as a contemporary of Rāmānuja, while others believe that he lived at a somewhat later date, in the thirteenth century.

nuja emphasized the personal nature of the One, he had no intention of making a complete break with non-dualism. His philosophy has generally been described as qualified non-dualism, though Radhakrishnan claimed that it would be more properly described as 'the non-dualism of the differenced'.[18] According to Rāmānuja, the world is the body of God. We know from the sacred texts that Brahman is 'the highest Person, or Nārāyana',[19] 'whose nature is absolute bliss and goodness; who is fundamentally antagonistic to all evil; who is the cause of the origination, sustentation, and dissolution of the world; who differs in nature from all other beings . . .'[20] God is thus the creator of the world. But having created it he enters into it in a manner analogous to that in which the soul is in the body. This includes his entry into human souls as their inner self. 'The world inclusive of intelligent souls is the body of the highest self; and the latter the self of everything.'[21] Though however God is immanent in all things, he is also 'different from all beings sentient or non-sentient'.[22] To say therefore that the world is the body of Brahman is not to say that Brahman changes or is affected by imperfections or by evil. The world is non-different from Brahman in the sense that the effect, according to Rāmānuja, is non-different from its cause. But it is not identical with Brahman or God in himself. As for the human soul, this too is non-different from Brahman. It is even said to be a part of Brahman.[23] Though however the soul has Brahman as its inner self, it is not identical with him.[24] And if it lives a life pleasing to God, it will be permitted 'to attain to that supreme bliss which consists in the direct intuition of His own true nature',[25] after which there will be no return to *samsāra*, to the life of transmigration.

To critical minds Rāmānuja's philosophy is likely to appear as an attempt to have things both ways, to preserve the non-

---

[18]*The Brahma-sūtra*, p. 46. (See Note 1.)
[19]*The Sacred Books of the East*, vol. XLVIII, p. 256. 1, 2, 1. (See Note 3.)
[20]*Ibid.*, p. 770. IV, 4, 22.
[21]*Ibid.*, p. 227. 1, 4, 13.
[22]*Ibid.*, p. 256. 1, 2, introduction.
[23]*Ibid.*, p. 191. 1, 1, 4.
[24]*Ibid.*, p. 226. 1, 1, 13.
[25]*Ibid.*, p. 770. IV, 4, 22.

dualism of Śaṁkara and at the same time to allow for a theistic conception of the One and for devotion to a personal God. It is not simply a question of respect for Śaṁkara pushing his thought in one direction, while his adherence to the *bhakti* tradition pushes it in another direction. One main reason for the nature of Rāmānuja's philosophy is his conviction that our knowledge of the reality transcending the empirical world is derived simply from scriptural testimony. As we have noted, the Upanishads do not present any single uniform doctrine. On the one hand it is certainly asserted that Brahman is all, the sole reality. On the other hand attributes are predicated of Brahman which can be predicated only of a personal being, while talk about approaching God through divine grace or help clearly implies a distinction between the human soul and Brahman. Statements of the first kind lie at the basis of Śaṁkara's thought, while statements of the second kind provide Madhva with scriptural authority for the Dvaita philosophy. Rāmānuja's thought naturally tends to appear as a half-way house between the thought of Śaṁkara and that of Madhva. At the same time one can understand its appeal to those who believe that Brahman must be recognized as the sole reality but who wish to combine this view with religious devotion to a personal God.

As Madhva rarely identifies the authors of the views which he discusses, it is often difficult to know which particular philosopher or philosophers he has in mind. His general attitude however to the Advaitins can be summed up by saying that he regards them as faced with a choice. If they believe that the world is real and that Brahman is the sole reality, they must sacrifice the divine transcendence. If they believe that the world is not Brahman, and also that Brahman is the sole reality, they must deny the reality of the world. From the logical point of view they cannot have things both ways. And though Madhva abstains from criticizing Rāmānuja by name, it is pretty clear that he did not look on qualified non-dualism as a satisfactory position. Madhva did not of course deny that there was any sense in which Brahman (conceived as personal) was the sole reality. But he understood it as meaning simply that Brahman or God was the only independent reality, all other beings being ontologically dependent on God, as his creatures. In other words, he embraced a theistic interpretation of the sacred texts.

Some writers have suggested that Madhva was influenced by contact with Christians. As he appears to have been the only Indian philosopher of note to have expressed belief in an ever-lasting hell for the incurably wicked, this fact has been used to support the suggestion or hypothesis. Though however it is not impossible that Madhva had some contact with Christians, it is unsafe to argue from possibility to actuality. Stronger evidence than some points of similarity is required. In any case Madhva's philosophy can hardly be described in any other way than as theistic, God being frequently described as the Lord Vishnu.

Madhva's theism forms the theoretical basis for his emphasis on *bhakti*, which he defined in various ways, such as attachment to God preceded by knowledge of the divine greatness or as affection preceded by admiration. Commenting on the *Brahma-sūtra*, he quotes with approval the statement that 'devotion alone leads him (man) to the supreme'.[26] Devotion, he says, 'the intense love which, proceeding from a knowledge of His great-ness, becomes the tie between the Lord and the soul',[27] is the best of all means of coming close to God, 'and consequently it is spoken of as the only means'.[28] The light revealing God comes only through His grace, and devotion is the response.

What Madhva is saying in effect is that *bhakti* is the high road, indeed the only way, to union with God (which does not mean identity). Śaṁkara had indeed recognized it as a way to liberation. But, given his theory of non-dualism, he could hardly look on it as being on the same level as intuitive apprehension of identity with Brahman. For religious devotion was directed to the personal God, who was conceived as the appearance of the Absolute. Madhva however regards *bhakti* as the way of coming closer to God and of attaining salvation. Rāmānuja doubtless thought in much the same way. But it was Madhva, rather than Rāmānuja, who provided the theoretical basis or

[26]*The Vedānta-sūtras* (with Madhva's commentaries) translated by S. Rau, p. 228. (See Note 14.)
[27]*Ibid.*, p. 229. III, 3, 54.
[28]*Ibid.*

framework of thought, the metaphysics, for this emphasis on loving service of God.

From one point of view Madhva is doubtless justified in seeing in the Advaita philosophy a threat to religion. That is to say, if we conceive love and service of a personal God as essential features of religion, we are justified in seeing a tendency to undermine it in a philosophy for which the concept of a personal God is an appearance of a suprapersonal Absolute and which proclaims the identity of the human soul with this Absolute. To be sure, Śaṁkara had no wish to destroy religious devotion. Nor did he condemn it. On the contrary, he saw in it a path towards liberation. At the same time, an attitude of religious devotion to God presupposes recognition of a distinction between God and the human spirit. And if this distinction is said to be sublated at a higher level of knowledge, it follows that the religious attitude which is characteristic of the *bhakti* tradition is also sublated, or transcended and left behind. *Bhakti* may indeed be the right path for the majority of people. But if a man ascends to the higher level of knowledge of reality, he presumably sees an attitude which presupposes a distinction between *ātman* and Brahman as an expression not indeed of total but at any rate of partial ignorance. In this sense at any rate the Advaita philosophy can reasonably be said to be a potential threat to religion.

The matter can be expressed in this way. F. H. Bradley asserted that when the concept of God passes into that of the Absolute, God 'is lost and religion with him'.[29] Bradley was evidently thinking of religion in terms of the religious beliefs prevalent in the culture to which he belonged. And it is safe to say that many Jews, Christians and Muslims would agree with what he said. So presumably would Madhva.

What this amounts to is saying that if religion is defined in a certain way, it is reasonable to regard the Advaita philosophy as a potential threat to it. In view, however, of the fact that in ordinary language use of the word 'religion' is not confined to theistic religion, the position referred to clearly expresses a judgment of value. That is to say, loving service of a personal God

---

[29]*Appearance and Reality*, p. 447 (2nd edition, London, 1897).

is regarded as an essential feature of 'true' or 'genuine' religion, and it is to this 'true' religion that monism, or, more precisely, non-dualism, is seen as a threat. Obviously, anyone is free to make a judgment of value, to state what he or she judges to be true or genuine religion. But it is as well to recognize when a judgment-value is presupposed. It is at any rate arguable that the great emphasis which Madhva places on devotion to a personal God expresses such a judgment. He is indeed claiming that acceptance of the Advaita philosophy tends, as a matter of fact, to undermine the *bhakti* tradition. But his attitude obviously also expresses an evaluation of the *bhakti* tradition.

Let us now forget Madhva and ask whether the philosophy of Śaṁkara, considered in itself, can reasonably be described as a religion or religiously oriented philosophy. In asking this question I presuppose the broad sense of the word 'religion' which enables us to speak not only of Hinduism but also of Buddhism as a religion.

Given this sense of the word 'religion', it seems that the Advaita Vedānta must be recognized as a religious philosophy. It developed within Hinduism. It had as its own point of departure for reflection the sacred texts of the Hindus. It was geared, so to speak, to the realization of oneness with the ultimate reality, of which the deities of popular Hinduism were regarded as so many manifestations or as so many names. This process of seeing one eternal reality behind or as manifested in the gods and goddesses or of regarding the names of the deities as names of the One is discernible even in the Vedas. It is much more prominent in the Upanishads. It can be regarded as culminating in the Advaita doctrine. The Advaita Vedānta therefore can be looked on as one esoteric form of Hinduism. It is possible of course to have different attitudes to the Advaita system. Some may find it repugnant. But this is irrelevant. The point is that, whether attractive or unattractive, it represents a development of the Hindu religion, a development which is oriented to mystical experience and to final liberation through absorption in Brahman. It is not, in my opinion, a cogent objection, if it is said that the Advaita system is a philosophy and that philosophy should not be confused with religion. If the thought of Plotinus can properly be described as a religiously oriented philosophy, so can the philosophy of Śaṁkara. As has already been remarked, Śaṁkara's idea of truth cannot be justifiably represented as a purely pragmatist one. At the same time he clearly looked on his philosophy as an instrument for enlightening people about the goal of human life and the way to attain it.

The Advaita philosophy, it may be said, certainly proclaimed realization of oneness with the ultimate reality as an end to aim at; but is the ideal of oneness with ultimate reality necessarily a religious goal? If someone believed, with Thales – the early Greek philosopher who is reported to have maintained that water was the original element from which all things came – that water was the ultimate reality and so aspired to be reduced to water, would one call this a religious aspiration? Possibly one might, but it is not immediately evident that this would be an appropriate description. It will of course be objected that Śaṁkara conceived Brahman as spiritual reality, transcending all material elements and things. But he also identified the inner self with Brahman. To find Brahman therefore is to find oneself as the 'witness' or transcendental subject. Has this really anything to do with religion?

By emphasizing certain statements this line of thought can be made plausible. For example, if one understands a statement such as 'That thou art' absolutely literally, one can represent the Advaita philosophy as maintaining solipsism. But one can hardly follow this procedure without at the same time recognizing that one's interpretation is an account not so much of what Śaṁkara and other Advaita philosophers actually thought as of what one believes that they ought to have thought, given certain statements. Brahman cannot be identified with the world, as contrary epithets are applied to the world and to Brahman. For instance, the world is subject to change, whereas Brahman is not. Nor can Brahman be identified with the *prakṛti* of the Sāṁkhya philosophy. It is true that Śaṁkara conceives Brahman as not only the efficient but also the material cause of the world, in the sense that the world issues, in some mysterious fashion, from the One. But he argues explicitly against the Sāṁkhya system, maintaining that what is not intelligent cannot be the cause of the world. As for the self and its relation to

Brahman, it seems to me that Śaṁkara's theory is indeed ambiguous. On the one hand he represents Brahman as immanent in the human self, as present in the innermost core, so to speak, of the human being. On the other hand he identifies the real self, the self stripped of the 'adjuncts', the appearances, which constitute the empirical self, with the Absolute or One. His general attitude however seems to be expressed in the statement to which reference has already been made,[30] that the wave belongs to the ocean and not the ocean to the wave. Further, whether consistently or not, Śaṁkara describes Brahman as omniscient, as infinite joy or bliss, and as the intelligent cause of the world. As we have noted, the predication of such attributes to Brahman was one of the reasons given by Madhva for claiming that the human spirit could not be identified with Brahman. Madhva may well be right. My point however is that Śaṁkara conceives Brahman as possessing attributes which are customarily predicated of God. There is indeed in Śaṁkara's thought a movement from 'God' to God, to use Paul Tillich's phrase, a movement from Saguna-Brahman to Nirguna-Brahman, the unmanifested ultimate abyss of being. But this movement is common enough in mystically oriented systems of thought. And I do not think that its presence disqualifies a philosophy from being described as religious. After all, it is connected with a profoundly religious conviction, namely that the divine reality transcends human comprehension.

To some minds the philosophy of Śaṁkara seems to be little more than a piece of sublime nonsense. It can also appear as an example of an outmoded link between philosophy and a particular religion, in this case Hinduism. In regard to this second point one can reply that though western philosophy has in fact moved away from any link with a particular religion, there is no good reason why adherents of a given religion should not try to work out its metaphysical implications in a systematic manner. It may be said that this sort of thing should be described as theology rather than as philosophy. But use of the word 'theology' would be misleading in the present context, as the criteria of orthodoxy are extremely loose in Hinduism. As for

[30]p. 78.

nonsense, there is a sense in which the Advaita philosophy, on its own premises, belongs to the sphere of appearance and is, in part at least, an attempt to say what cannot be said. This can be admitted without embracing logical positivism. None the less, as an endeavour to interpret mystical experience the system seems to me to have an abiding interest. Some critics regard it as an expression of escapism and as socially harmful and undesirable. But this is an aspect of the matter which will be discussed in Chapter 10.

CHAPTER 5

ISLAM AND MYSTICISM

*Belief in the divine transcendence and mysticism – Al-Ghazāli
and philosophy – Suhrawardī and Ibn 'Arabī – Mullā Sadrā
and Sabzawārī – some general discussion*

I

Emphasis on the divine transcendence has been a prominent
feature of Islam. The prophet Mohammed's passionate faith in
Allah was obviously faith in a personal God, distinct from all
other beings. All other beings depended ontologically on God
as creator, while he was in no way dependent on them. No
creature could be said to be like Allah.[1] To be sure, belief in the
divine activity has also been a prominent feature of Islam. When
theological and philosophical reflection emerged within the
Muslim community, one of the first questions to be discussed
was whether belief in the universal causality of God, which
extended (as certain passages of the Koran seemed to imply)
even to the choices of the human will,[2] was compatible with
assertion of human freedom. Obviously, the Koranic pictures of
divine judgment and of rewards and punishments after death
suggested belief in the human being's power to obey or not to
obey the divine commands and prohibitions. The more liberal
theologians could therefore appeal to the Koran in support of
their recognition of human freedom. To the more conservative
theologians, however, this recognition expressed a dangerous
surrender to rationalism and was incompatible with belief in
God's universal causal activity. In spite of this difference for
neither party was there the slightest question of identifying God
with the world or of regarding the human soul as a mode of the
divine substance. For both of them the ultimate reality, Allah,
was transcendent, though he was of course also immanent in the
sense of being omni-present.

This emphasis on the divine transcendence helps to explain

[1]*Koran*, 42, 11.
[2]*Ibid.*, 16. 93 and 74. 31.

the fact that there have been and still are Muslim thinkers who have looked askance at mysticism. This attitude has doubtless been partly due to some unguarded and provocative utterances by mystics who claimed or seemed to be claiming their identity with God. To cite two familiar examples, when Abū Yazīd al-Bastāmi (d. 874) exclaimed 'glory be to me, how great is my worth' and Mansur al-Hallāj (c. 857–972) asserted 'I am the Truth', champions of the divine transcendence were scandalized. Abū-Yazīd, who seems to have been introduced to mysticism by an Indian convert to Islam, is said to have escaped penalties by feigning madness. But Al-Hallāj was put on trial and eventually executed. Some scholars maintain that the real reasons for his execution were of a political nature. Perhaps they are right, but the reasons given related to religious belief. In any case statements such as those made by Al-Hallāj have been regarded by a good many Muslims as symptomatic of a general tendency in mysticism. I remember talking with a highly educated Muslim from Pakistan, a philosopher who was then holding a high position in the educational world of his country, who clearly regarded mysticism as unorthodox and as incompatible with belief in the divine transcendence. For those who share this view faith in God and obedience to the Muslim law, the Sharī'ah, as expressing the divine will, is the safe way, whereas aspirations after oneness with God threaten due recognition of the radical distinction between God and creatures, the transcendent One and the Many.

It seems reasonable to suggest (though it is more or less conjecture on my part) that another ground for suspicion of or hostility to mysticism was provided by the marked tendency of some mystical writers to adopt what might be described today as an ecumenical attitude to faiths other than Islam. To take but one example, the famous Persian poet Rūmī (1207–1273) claimed that there were many roads leading to the one goal, namely union with God,[3] and in a poem he asserted that he was neither a Zoroastrian nor a Jew nor a Muslim, as these terms were ordinarily understood.[4] It is doubtless only to be expected

---

[3]*Discourses of Rūmī*, translated by A. J. Arberry, pp. 108–12 (London, 1961).
[4]Poem **XXXI** in *Selected Poems from the Dīvāni Shamsi Tabriz*, edited and translated by R. A. Nicholson, p. 125 (Cambridge, 1898, 1952, paperback 1977).

that mystical writers will tend to emphasize the inner relationship of the soul to God rather than religious labels and the
performance of legally prescribed observances. By making, however, statements such as those made by Rūmī Muslim mystics
could obviously give the impression of belittling the claims of
Islam to represent the final revelation of truth.

Though, however, mysticism has had and has its Muslim
critics, it is important to understand that mystical spirituality
has its roots in Islam itself. Mystical writers could appeal to
certain passages even of the Koran, where it is said, for example,
that love is due to Allah[5] and that God is nearer to man 'than
the vein of his neck'.[6] Indeed, the prophet himself might be
regarded as a mystic. Mystical spirituality in Islam is sometimes
said to have shown itself first at Basra, with, for instance, the
female mystic Rābi'ah al Adawijah (d. 901), and then at Baghdad, as with Al-Junayd (d. 910). At the same time it can be
argued that emphasis on the interior spiritual life, as contrasted
with a predominantly legalistic attitude, goes back to the very
beginning of Islam, and that it represents what has been described as esoteric Islam. In the spread of mystical spirituality
external influences doubtless had a part to play. Thus we cannot
exclude the possibility of Christian influence, and in Persia
Indian thought seems to have exercised some influence, though
its extent is difficult to determine. Not unnaturally, some Muslim writers have claimed that Indian thought was powerfully
influenced by Islamic beliefs, rather than the other way round.
For example, it has been maintained that the Nyāya-Vaiśesika
school in India 'took on a theistic turn as a result of Muslim
influence',[7] and that Rāmānuja may have taken from Islam the
ideas of submission to the will of God and of veneration for
one's spiritual guide.[8] Equally naturally, Hindu scholars are
inclined to emphasize the influence of Indian thought on philo-

---

[5]*Koran*, 2. 165.
[6]*Ibid.*, 50. 12.
[7]Quoted from a contribution by C. A. Quadir to M. M. Sharif's *A History
of Muslim Philosophy*, Vol. 2, p. 1402 (Wiesbaden, 1966).
[8]These suggestions seem to me to be conjectures, and unnecessary ones at
that. We can easily explain such facts as the development of a theistic element
in the Nyāya-Vaiśesika school and Rāmānuja's emphasis on the role of a
spiritual director or guide without postulating Muslim influence.

sophy in Persia. During the period of Moghul rule in India a number of Hindu writings, including the Upanishads and the Gītā were translated into Persian. The Moghul emperor Akbar (1542–1605), who pursued a policy of friendly toleration in regard to non-Islamic religions, arranged for the translation of Sanskrit texts into Persian. And Prince Dārā Shukūh, a translator and devout Muslim, believed that the Upanishads were the 'hidden books' referred to in the Koran.[9] Though, however, as Islam spread, Muslim thought became subject to external influences, it by no means follows that mystical spirituality as such was an alien importation. On the contrary, this spirituality characterized by love of God and the desire to realize the divine presence, was a native growth, acting as a complement to exoteric Islam, the profession of faith and observance of the law.

We are not, however, concerned here with mystical spirituality simply as such, for its own sake. We are concerned with its influence on or relation to philosophical thought in the Islamic world. In histories of European philosophy attention has naturally been paid to Islamic philosophy in so far as it was known by and exercised influence on Christian thinkers, its further development being generally neglected. This means in effect that attention is paid only to certain thinkers of the Middle Ages, such as Al-Fārābī, Avicenna and Averroes. This procedure is natural and understandable in the case of a history of western philosophy. At the same time it tends to give readers the impression that philosophy in Islam ceased with the death of Averroes in 1198, which is not in fact the case. We are concerned here primarily with aspects of Islamic thought of which little is generally said in histories of western philosophy.

II

When philosophical reflection began to arise within the Muslim community, the tools of thought, categories and models of argument, were naturally borrowed from the available storehouse, namely Greek philosophy. It was not, however, simply a question of tools. As a result of a process of translation of Greek

[9]*Koran*, 56. 77–80.

writings into Arabic,[10] Greek philosophical ideas, especially those of Aristotle and the Neoplatonists, came to exercise a marked influence on Islamic thought in the Middle Ages. Indeed, if we focused our attention simply on certain Muslim philosophers of the Middle Ages, we might easily receive the impression that philosophy in Islam was little more than an importation from the ancient world, an importation which was then adapted, with varying degrees of success, to the demands of Muslim orthodoxy. For example, in the first half of the tenth century Al-Fārābī not only made use of the Neoplatonist ideas of emanation and of a hierarchy of levels of being, identifying the Neoplatonist One with Allah, but also represented philosophy, in Aristotelian fashion, as the highest activity open to man. He did indeed find a place for the concept of prophetic revelation and for belief in the Koran as expressing revealed truth. But, for him, the different religions were so many expressions of truth in symbolic form, whereas the philosophical expression of truth was the same for all human beings. Again, Averroes (Ibn Rushd, c. 1126–98), the great commentator on the writings of Aristotle (whom he regarded as representing the culmination of human intellectual power), tried to harmonize philosophy with Muslim faith by means of a theory of different levels of understanding. Averroes did not defend a double-truth theory, in the sense of claiming that a proposition could be simultaneously true in philosophy and false in theology, or the other way around. What he maintained was that the Koran could be interpreted or understood at different levels. For instance, by its pictorial images of the after-life it catered to minds which could not grasp the truth either at the level of theology or, and still less, at the philosophical level. His theory bears comparison with Hegel's contention that art, religion and philosophy express the same truth but in different ways.

It is hardly surprising that to conservative theologians philosophers such as Al-Fārābī and Averroes seemed to be guilty

---

[10]At first the translations were made in Christian schools, often from Greek into Syrian and thence into Arabic, sometimes directly from the Greek into Arabic. In the ninth century a regular school of translators was established at Baghdad. Not only philosophical writings but also medical and scientific treatises were translated.

of sacrificing the purity of Muslim faith to rationalism and, in effect, of subordinating faith to philosophy. But critics could, of course, be philosophers themselves, intent not so much on rejecting philosophy as such as on combatting theories which they believed to be incompatible with the doctrines and spirit of Islam. Such was Al-Ghazāli (c. 1058–1111), a writer of Persian origin who taught for a time at Baghdad and who became a mystic. To be sure, in his *Incoherence of the Philosophers*, in which he singled out for attack Al-Fārābī and Avicenna (Ibn Sīnā, 980–1037), he wrote as though he was attacking philosophy as such. But in point of fact he himself employed philosophical arguments and metaphysical concepts. Averroes, who composed a rejoinder entitled *The Incoherence of the Incoherence*, was quick to notice this fact and virtually accused Al-Ghazāli of having been guilty of a lack of intellectual integrity, on the ground that he had attacked the Islamic Neoplatonists while being himself heavily indebted to Neoplatonism. As far as Al-Ghazāli's debt to Neoplatonism was concerned, Averroes was quite right. The relevant point in the present context, however, is that Al-Ghazāli tried to combine a metaphysics inspired by Neoplatonism with a doctrine of mystical spirituality which did not involve the claim that the human soul or spirit was identical with God. It is true that for him everything other than God was, in itself, not-being, and that creatures in general formed together God's 'face', the theophany. But there was nothing unorthodox in maintaining that finite things, apart from God, are nothing. It is a way of saying that they are utterly dependent on him for existence. 'Being is itself divided into that which has being in itself, and that which derives its being from not-itself. The being of this latter is borrowed, having no existence by itself. Nay, if it is regarded in and by itself, it is pure not-being.'[11]

As for the description of the world as the 'face' of God and the divine theophany, we read in the Koran that wherever one turns, 'there is the face of God'.[12] We also read that God is 'the

[11]*Al-Ghazāli's Mishkāt Al-Anwār ('The Niche for Lights')*, translated with an introduction by W. H. T. Gairdner, p. 58 (London, 1924; Asiatic Society Monographs, vol. XIV).
[12]*Koran*, 2. 115.

outwardly manifest and the inwardly hidden'.[13] In point of fact Al-Ghazāli, in expounding his claim that the human being could attain to an experimental, mystical knowledge of God, was careful to avoid the sort of provocative statements which had been made by Al-Hallāj. If a stage could be attained at which consciousness of self disappeared and there was simply the divine reality, this absorption in God was, for Al-Ghazāli, a psychological phenomenon, analogous to the absorption of the lover in the beloved, not an ontological identity. Thus he speaks of those who arrived at the idea of one reality 'experimentally and subjectively. From these last the plurality of things fell away in its entirety. . . . No capacity remained within them save to recall Allah . . . so there remained nothing with them save Allah. They became drunken with a drunkenness wherein the sway of their own intelligence disappeared. When drunkenness abated and they came under the sway of intelligence they knew that that had not been actual Identity, but only something resembling Identity.'[14]

One of Al-Ghazāli's main targets, Avicenna, had himself written a treatise (the *Ishārat*) in which he traced the stages of the soul's ascent to mystical union with God. But Al-Ghazāli did not of course criticize Avicenna on this score. What he objected to was, for example, Avicenna's account of the world as permeated by necessary causal relations. The objection was not that this account threatened belief in human freedom but that it was incompatible with belief in the universal divine causality. In Al-Ghazāli's judgment, this belief required an interpretation of the causal relation, from the empirical point of view, as factual succession. We see *B* succeeding *A*, but the real cause of the effect is God. What he wanted was obviously a philosophy in full accordance with the Koran, an interpretation of reality in which Muslim belief in the divine transcendence was preserved but which at the same time emphasized the complete dependence of the world on God not only in regard to its origin but also in regard to its existence at any moment. God was for him transcendent but also immanent, everywhere active. The world was the divine self-manifestation. Under the influence

[13]*Ibid.*, 57. 3.
[14]Gairdner, p. 60. (See Note 11.)

of Neoplatonism he represented God, the One, as absolute Light and the different levels of created being as corresponding to divine degrees of reflected luminosity. The human soul, attracted by the Light, can move upwards towards it, though it can never become the absolute Light, in the sense of being ontologically identical with it.

III

The metaphysics of light seem strange and bizarre to us, as the idea of light is associated in our minds with scientific theory, so that we naturally tend to look upon its use in metaphysics as a poetic metaphor which contributes nothing to knowledge of reality. This should not, however, prevent us from recognizing the important role which the concepts of light, illumination and darkness have played in religious and mystical thought. It is not simply a question of Neoplatonism and of philosophies influenced by Neoplatonism. The concepts are prominent in, for example, the Upanishads and in Buddhist writings, as well as in Christian and Muslim thought. Referring to India and to Tibetan Buddhism, Mircea Eliade remarks that 'experience of the Light signifies primarily a meeting with ultimate reality'.[15] Again, this meeting with the Light 'produces a break in the subject's existence, revealing to him – or making clearer than before – the world of the Spirit.'[16] For the matter of that, the metaphor of light still has a certain power. It can still be used quite naturally, even in a non-mystical context. For example, a recent work on the early development of Hegel's thought is entitled *Hegel's Development: Toward the Sunlight, 1770–1801*.[17]

The philosophy of light, represented by Al-Ghazāli, was to have a future in Persia, where Suhrawardī (1153–1191), a contemporary of Averroes, is generally credited with being the founder of the illuminationist tradition. Suhrawardī, who was eventually to fall victim at Aleppo to the intolerance of the doctors of the law and of Saladin, depicted the world as the theophany, the self-diffusion of absolute Light, and the way of

[15]*The Two and the One*, p. 43.
[16]*Ibid.*, p. 77.
[17]By H. S. Harris (Oxford, 1972).

sanctity as a progressive approximation to the model of the perfect or universal man, corresponding to the Platonic Idea or Form of human nature. The concept of the universal man was linked with that of the invisible Imam in Shi'ite Islam. An interesting feature of Suhrawardī's thought was his employment of Zoroastrian ideas. Thus he made use of Zoroastrian angelology to express an interpretation of the Neoplatonist theory of ideas.

In Zoroastrianism, which had existed in Persia for centuries before the Muslim conquest (A.D. 633–637), Ahura Mazda or Ormazd, the supreme deity and the author of all that is good (matter, considered in itself, was not regarded as evil), was conceived as Light and as the source of all reflected light. Though Zoroastrianism recognized a principle of evil, Ahriman, the sharp dualism between two ultimate principles, Ormazd and Ahriman, Light and Darkness, was characteristic of the later religion proclaimed by Mani, Manichaeism, rather than of the teaching of Zoroaster, for whom there was really only one God, Ahura Mazda. In any case we cannot exclude the possibility that the metaphysics of light in Islamic thought in Persia was strengthened or reinforced by the influence of native beliefs antedating the Muslim conquest. In fact, this seems highly probable. Some Islamic thinkers in Persia were quite prepared to make use of Zoroastrian ideas when they were judged compatible with Muslim faith.

In the course of time Suhrawardī's philosophy of light or illuminationism (*Ishrāq*) pretty well coalesced with the philosophy of Ibn 'Arabī (1165–1240). Born at Murcia in Spain, Abū Muhammad Ibn al-'Arabī was present at the funeral of Averroes in 1198, after which he went to the east. He died at Damascus. His thought can be said to centre round the idea of the divine self-manifestation or theophany. Referring to writers such as F. Schuon, R. C. Zaehner asserts that 'it is quite absurd to quote the late philosophic mystic, Ibn al-'Arabī, as an authentic exponent of the Muslim "tradition" since he has been rejected by the majority of the orthodox as being heretical'.[18] As Professor Zaehner presumably did not intend to make a tauto-

---

[18] *Mysticism, Sacred and Profane*, p. 31.

logical statement by including the rejection of Ibn 'Arabī as an essential condition of orthodoxy, we can understand him as meaning that Ibn 'Arabī claimed that the human soul, or at any rate the mystic's, was identical with God, which would certainly be unorthodox by Muslim standards. It is certainly true that Ibn 'Arabī asserted that the only existence is that of God, and that the self is one with God. And Zaehner was doubtless thinking of such statements. It is not however clear in what precise sense the statements in question should be understood. As for Schuon, he was indeed a westerner, but his books on Islam won high praise from the distinguished Iranian scholar, himself a Muslim, Dr. S. H. Nasr. In any case Ibn 'Arabī's thought is of considerable historical interest, even if most modern philosophers would understandably dismiss it as fanciful theosophy.

One of the first themes to be discussed, when theological reflection began to develop in Islam, was the relation between the divine attributes or names and the divine essence. This question arose directly out of the Koran, in which the unity of God is asserted while at the same time God is called by many names, in the sense that a variety of attributes, such as mercy, are predicated of him. Some theologians maintained that the divine essence should be regarded as lying, as it were, behind the attributes, though the latter were said to be not-different from God, that is to say, not separate entities. This line of thought found expression in the writings of Ibn 'Arabī, among others. For him, the divine essence, considered in itself, lies beyond human knowledge and description. It corresponds to the hidden or unmanifested God of the Koran.[19] It is as Lord, as creator and sustainer of the world and as endowed with attributes, that God is known, in the first stage, so to speak, of his self-manifestation.

This sort of idea immediately calls to mind the distinction in the Advaita Vedānta philosophy between the Absolute as devoid of qualities, Nirguna-Brahman, and the Absolute as endowed with qualities, Saguna-Brahman. Unless, however, one has some historical evidence other than similarity, it is rash to

[19]*Koran*, 57. 3.

conclude that Ibn 'Arabī derived his theory from India. As we have noted, the Koran provided a ground for it. Besides, the idea of a One beyond human understanding and description is not uncommon in the metaphysics of the past. It can be found in Neoplatonism, which formed much of the background of Islamic philosophy.

According to Ibn 'Arabī, God created the world in order to be known. Indeed, what he says seems to imply that the human being's knowledge of God can be regarded as God's knowledge of himself. But we have to consider what he really means. When the human being has knowledge of God, what he or she knows is an image of God, rather than the abyss of the divine being which lies beyond thought. In a poem Ibn 'Arabī speaks of man as giving God being by knowing him. This does not how- ever refer to God as he is in himself. It means that God is given being in man's mind through man's idea of him, this idea being at the same time God's manifestation of himself. God reveals himself in a variety of ways, and the conceptions of God in human minds are so many divine epiphanies. In other words, the different faiths can be regarded as so many theophanies.

When treating of the human soul's spiritual ascent Ibn 'Arabī emphasizes, as Suhrawardī had done, the idea of striving after approximation to the model of the perfect or universal man, the archetypal essence of human nature. Taken by itself, this idea suggests that of moral improvement, of an integration of the personality under the rule of reason, rather than that of mystical union with God. While however the concept of an integrated human being was indeed prominent in the writings of Muslim spiritual teachers, moral improvement was regarded as a pre- requisite for genuine mystical experience. Such experience could attain a form in which consciousness of self-identity is lost.

Ibn 'Arabī, as he himself admits, never provided a systematic exposition of his thought. He trusted, as he tells us, to the intelligent reader to understand his meaning. Not unnaturally, he was interpreted in more than one way. A fifteenth-century Muslim maintained that Ibn 'Arabī was a past master of the art of confusing people by referring to Muslim beliefs and then interpreting them in such a way as to seduce people into accept- ing erroneous doctrines. Evidently, this writer would endorse

Professor Zaehner's judgment above. Ibn 'Arabī's disciples however maintained that he could be properly understood only by people of his own intellectual and spiritual stature. Looking back from the point of view of a twentieth-century westerner, perhaps we can say that Ibn 'Arabī had a strong inclination, connected with mystical spirituality, to conceive God as the sole reality, but that with the help of a theory of the world as the divine self-manifestation or theophany he tried to reconcile this inclination with orthodox Islam, with belief, that is to say, in the divine transcendence. He employed Neoplatonist metaphysics, mediated by Avicenna, to state a theory of the hierarchy of being, in which the One in itself transcended human thought and knowledge. But his God-centred outlook can remind us of the Sufi writer who spoke of a man having made three successive pilgrimages to Mecca. On the first he saw the Ka'bah but not the Lord of the Ka'bah. On the second he saw the Ka'bah and the Lord of the Ka'bah. On the third he saw the Lord of the Ka'bah but not the Ka'bah. In any case, seeing God in everything, in the theophany, and seeing everything in God was certainly Ibn 'Arabī's spiritual ideal.

IV

The ideas of Suhrawardī and Ibn 'Arabī contributed to the development in Persia, under the Safawid dynasty, of that blend of philosophical, theosophical and mystically oriented thought which is known as the *Hikmat* or wisdom. Its best known representation is Sadr al-Din al-Shīrazī, commonly known as Mullā Sadrā (1572–1641). A devout adherent of Shi'ite Islam, he believed that the hidden or invisible Imam would one day manifest himself and convert the whole of mankind to the monotheism proposed by Abraham and confirmed by the prophet Mohammed. At the same time he was no enemy of philosophical thought as such. When he criticized the Sufis, the people whom he had in mind were those who not only threw overboard the exoteric doctrines and practices of Islam in the name of a wisdom which, in his opinion, they did not possess but who also despised intellectual effort. Despite this criticism, he can be said to have himself belonged to the movement of mystical spirituality, though he preferred to speak of 'gnosis', by which he meant an experiential knowledge issuing in practice or action and thus distinguishable from a purely theoretical knowledge which rarely, if at all, influenced conduct. Knowledge in this sense, however, he tried to integrate with both philosophical reflection and prophetic revelation.

Use of the Neoplatonist analogy of the diffusion of light in describing creation or the divine epiphany was a common feature of Islamic thought in Persia; and we find it with Mullā Sadrā. At the same time we can also see a shift from emphasis on the concept of light to emphasis on the idea of existence. The point of departure for reflection on this second theme was a theory advanced by Avicenna. Avicenna was himself a Persian by birth, and, of course, he wrote a treatise on mystical spirituality, in addition to his philosophical writings. Al-Ghazāli's criticism did not prevent Avicenna's thought exercising a powerful influence on subsequent Islamic philosophy.

Suhrawardī had interpreted Avicenna as holding that existence was an accident which accrued to an essence.[20] For example, before Tom Jones or Bill Smith came into existence, he was a possible essence, and at his coming to be this essence received existence. Mullā Sadrā attacked this thesis, arguing that a non-existent essence could not receive any accident at all. We can indeed perform an act of abstraction and talk about the existence of something, as though existence and essence were distinct. But it by no means follows that in concrete reality existence is, or can be, an accident which is received by an essence. For there is nothing to receive it. As Mullā Sadrā put it, 'existence, the act of being, is precisely the very existence *of* the substrate, not the existence of an accident *in* the substrate.'[21] Again, 'the existence of each non-necessary existent is its quality (essence) itself, with which it is united in a union which is *sui generis*.[22] In the abstract conceptual order essence is prior to existence. That is to say, we say of something that it exists. But

---

[20]Al-Fārābī had held much the same before Avicenna.

[21]Translated (by myself) from Henry Corbin's French translation of Mullā Sadrā's *Kitāb al-Mashāsir, Le Livre des pénétrations métaphysiques*, p. 133 (Bibliothèque Iranienne, Vol. 10, Tehran and Paris, 1964).

[22]*Ibid.*, p. 142.

in the concrete order existence and essence are really one. It is true that it does not pertain to the existence of anything in the world that it must exist. But the conclusion to be drawn is not that existence is an accident occurring to a non-existent essence but that nothing at all would exist, unless there were a reality which exists necessarily, the essence or nature of which it is to exist. This reality is absolute being or existence, Allah.

Mullā Sadrā's main point, that existence cannot be an accident accruing to an essence which is either non-existent or neither existent nor non-existent, seems to be sound. The matter would be expressed differently nowadays, but most people would agree that, given the essence-existence language, what he said was sensible. For how could existence be received by a non-existent substrate? A good many people, however, while prepared to agree with him on this point, would not be prepared to accept his proof of the existence of God. They might, for example, question the concept of a necessarily existing reality. It is obvious however that Mullā Sadrā was simply making use of what we might describe as a stock medieval argument for the existence of a transcendent One. Avicenna, for instance, had argued that there must be an absolutely necessary being to account for the existence of anything else, whether hypothetically necessary or not.[23] It would be too much of a digression if we were to pursue the theme further here.

The foregoing line of argument clearly implies a distinction between God and all other beings. God exists because he is what he is; he cannot not exist. All other beings depend on God for their existence. This distinction is in harmony with Muslim belief in the divine transcendence. It is also required by Mullā Sadrā's mystical spirituality, centering round the relationship of love. For even if in mystical union thought of self disappears, a distinction between lover and beloved is required, if the idea of love is to make any sense. At the same time it can hardly be

---

[23]The existence of y would be hypothetically necessary, if, given the existence of x, y must exist. Though Avicenna made a distinction between beings which, given God's existence, exist perpetually (the Intelligences of the spheres) and beings which come into existence and pass away (contingent beings), his view of the world was such that all beings other than God were, in a real sense, hypothetically necessary. It was this view of the world, permeated by necessary causal relations, that Al-Ghazāli attacked. (See pages 102–3.)

denied that Mullā Sadrā makes some statements which suggest a kind of acosmistic pantheism. He says, for example, that if 'it [Existence itself] is Reality in the true sense, all the rest are its states. It is the Light; that which emanates is the effusion of the Light. It is the origin and source; all other beings are its manifestations and theophanies.'[24] Mullā Sadrā also makes use of an analogy which had already been employed, that of ink and letters written in ink. The letters can be said to be nothing but ink, though at the same time they might be described as states of ink.

Such statements however should be interpreted in a sense which is consonant with Mullā Sadrā's Muslim faith. In terms of the light-metaphysics he clearly thinks of Light itself, absolute Light, as undiminished by the rays of varying intensity which proceed from it and would be nothing without it. To be sure, if one describes creatures as states of God, this suggests the monism of Spinoza. From one point of view Mullā Sadrā's mysticism impels him in this direction. From another point of view it does not, inasmuch as he conceives mystical experience as a union of love. He certainly does not intend to throw overboard Muslim belief in the divine transcendence; even if some of his assertions suggest that this is what he is doing.

Emphasis on the idea of existence was continued by Mullā Sadrā's successors, for example by Sabzawārī (1797–1878), who expounded what has been described as a scholasticized or more analytic version of Mullā Sadrā's thought.[25] Existence, according to Sabzawārī is from one point of view known by all, while from another point of view it is hidden. That is to say, we all have a pre-reflective awareness of the meaning of existence, in the sense that we all understand such statements as 'Tom exists' or 'Jane no longer exists'. We can all draw the appropriate conclusion from statements of this kind or respond by appropriate actions. At the same time we cannot conceptualize existence in itself, apart from essence. In this sense it

---

[24]*Le livre des pénétrations métaphysiques*, p. 181. (See Note 21.)
[25]On Sabzawārī see S. H. Nasr's essay in Sharif's *History of Muslim Philosophy*, Vol. 2 (see Note 7) and *The Fundamental Structure of Sabzawārī's Metaphysics* by T. Izutsu (McGill University, Institute of Islamic Studies, Tehran Branch, 1968).

eludes thought. Yet it is what unifies all that there is, and God is Absolute existence, the source of all existing things. This is of course substantially the same doctrine as that of Mullā Sadrā. But whereas Mullā Sadrā regarded recognition of the omnipresence of God, absolute existence or being, as a matter of spiritual illumination, a gnosis attainable only after due preparation and influencing conduct, Sabzawārī, while not denying that spiritual illumination had a role to play in any full realization of the truth, tried to provide philosophical arguments. In other words, a mystical orientation of thought is more obvious in the case of Mullā Sadrā than with Sabzawārī. At the same time it has been argued that in spite of his analytic approach Sabzawārī's metaphysics was in fact based on a mystical intuition of reality, so that he can be described as a 'philosopher-mystic'.[26]

V

The foregoing sections were not of course intended to be a potted history of Islamic philosophy as a whole. Well-known Islamic thinkers such as Al-Fārābī, Avicenna and Averroes have been referred to only briefly, and nothing at all has been said about one of the greatest intellectual luminaries of Islam, Ibn Khaldūn (1332–1406), the historian and philosopher of history. My intention was to show, by some admittedly brief accounts of some individual thinkers, not only that philosophical reflection in Islam did not cease with the death of Averroes but also, and especially, that a line of thought developed, from Al-Ghazāli onwards, which was associated with mystical spirituality. I now wish to suggest some general reflections about this line of thought.

In the first place the blend of philosophy, Muslim theology and spiritual doctrine which developed in Persia can be described as Sufism becoming reflectively aware of its presuppositions and implications. This statement may seem absurd, if we recall that the term *Sūfī* was first applied to Muslim ascetics

---

[26]*The Fundamental Structure of Sabzawārī's Metaphysics*, p. 102. (See Note 25.)

who were innocent of philosophy.[27] It seems even more absurd, of course, if our only idea of Sufis is that of whirling dervishes. It may seem untrue, if not absurd, even if we prescind from manifestations such as ecstatic dancing and consider the serious spiritual discipline characteristic of Sufism. In the Sufi movement great emphasis was laid on the need for the aspirant to closer union with God to put himself under the guidance and direction of an experienced teacher who could not indeed confer on his pupil mystical union with God but who could help the pupil to avoid self-deception, train him in the conquest of selfishness and desires apart from desire for union with God, and assist him in converting his intellectual assent to the existence of God into an awareness of the divine presence. Given this emphasis on personal experience and on love of God, it was natural that Sufi teachers should play down or belittle theoretical speculation. For it was a question of love, of seeing God everywhere and of living in the divine presence, not of philosophical or theological theorizing. Have I not myself admitted that Mullā Sadrā criticized Sufis for despising intellectual effort? And is it really credible that the adherents of the many Sufi orders were all given to philosophizing? This is not what Sufism was all about.

There is, however, no question of claiming that Sufism as such was a philosophical movement, nor that all Sufis were philosophers. Even when Sufi spirituality came to find literary expression, this could, and not infrequently did, take the form of poetry. At the same time Sufism certainly had its doctrinal presuppositions and implications. Desire for union with God, awareness of the divine omnipresence, detachment from all except God, had implications in regard to the nature of reality and the nature of the human being. It may appear to be a very extravagant statement when an eminent Islamic scholar asserts that 'Sufi doctrine consists of metaphysics, cosmology, psychology and an eschatology that is often linked with psychology and occasionally with metaphysics.'[28] But we are justified in claiming that Sufism gave itself, so to speak, a metaphysics and a cos-

---

[27]The origin of the term *Sūfi* is disputed. The common theory is that it was first applied to Muslim ascetics who wore garments of coarse wool (*sūf*).

[28]*Sufi Essays*, by S. H. Nasr, p. 45 (London and New York, 1972).

mology, not in the sense that all Sufis pursued or even valued philosophy, but in the sense that some thinkers, such as Al-Ghazālī, developed a religiously oriented interpretation of reality in the light of Sufi ideals.

The tools employed were largely taken from Greek philosophy, directly or indirectly, but the task to which the tools were put was inspired by that mystical spirituality which, in Islam, is commonly described as Sufism. Thus for Mullā Sadrā the vision or lively awareness of God in all things and all things in God required a spiritual illumination for which philosophical reflection could only prepare the way. The theoretical work presupposed Sufi spirituality, and it was intended to confirm and strengthen it, to have a practical result.

The Sufi vision of God in all things and all things in God naturally pushed the reflective mind in the direction of some kind of pantheism. We can see an example of it in Mullā Sadrā's conception of God as absolute existence and of all other beings as states of absolute existence. At the same time this direction of thought was counterbalanced not only by adherence to Muslim orthodoxy but also by the emphasis in Sufi mysticism on a relationship between the human soul and God, the relationship of love. This relationship was given expression in the erotic imagery of poets, and it also influenced the line of thought from Al-Ghazālī. The idea of the human being's loving response to an initiative on God's part, to the divine love, obviously militated against any ontological identification of the human soul with God.

Perhaps we can express the matter in this way. Muslim emphasis on the divine transcendence naturally provoked an emphasis on the complementary belief in the divine immanence. If however we leave out of account some unguarded ecstatic utterances, such as those made by Abū Yāzid al-Bastāmi and Al-Hallaj, emphasis on the divine immanence did not mean that the divine transcendence was denied or simply forgotten. After all, we have had occasion to refer to the doctrine of the divine abyss, the hidden essence of the Godhead, beyond human understanding. To combine the two beliefs, in God's transcendence and immanence, was one of the main tasks which faced the Sufi-inspired thinkers. Whether or not they fulfilled the task successfully is open to discussion. A Thomist would probably claim that the job could not be done without a clear theory of the analogy of being. However this may be, it seems clear to me that not only Al-Ghazālī but also Ibn 'Arabī and Mullā Sadrā had every intention of adhering to the Muslim faith. And Sufi-inspired speculation can quite reasonably be regarded as expressing the esoteric dimension of Islam, without which Islam would be much the poorer.

If one raises the question, as I have just done, whether thinkers such as Ibn 'Arabī and Mullā Sadrā were successful or unsuccessful in stating precisely the relation between God and the world, one may seem to presuppose that they intended to do this and tried to do it. It can then be objected that the presupposition is unjustified, and that one is judging Muslim thought from the point of view of a modern analytically minded philosopher. That is to say, one makes up one's mind what the Islamic thinkers, given their beliefs, ought to have been doing, and then one awards good or bad marks according to their fulfilment or non-fulfilment of a goal which was not, or may not have been, theirs.

There is clearly some truth in this line of objection. Mullā Sadrā, for example, thought that philosophical reflection could show that creation could not have taken the form of God's conferring an accident, existence, on non-existing substrates, essences. He certainly believed that philosophy had a role to play in the construction of a religious conception of reality. At the same time he thought that spiritual illumination was required to see the world as 'the face of Allah' in such a way that the vision effectively influenced one's life and conduct. In other words, though he disapproved of a religious attitude which involved rejection of all serious thought, he looked on philosophy as oriented towards something beyond itself, spiritual illumination. He was a spiritual teacher who presupposed the truth of Muslim belief and envisaged the personal appropriation of this truth in a realization of the divine omnipresence and activity, a realization inspiring conduct and action.

To depict Ibn 'Arabī or Mullā Sadrā as being simply a would-be analytic philosopher would indeed be unjust. But the fact remains that they did pursue philosophical thought and that they did try to clarify their view of reality. For example, Mullā Sadrā and other Pahlawi philosophers such as Sabzawārī tried to show how existence, being, could be both one and many. Existence as absolutely unconditioned was the One or Absolute, the divine essence in its hidden state, corresponding to absolute Light in itself. Analogously, however, to the way in which there can be gradations or varying intensities of light, which are none the less nothing but light, so there can be degrees of existence or being in the self-unfolding of absolute existence. Conditioned beings, beings determined as beings of this rather than that kind, stand, so to speak, at the opposite pole to absolutely pure and unconditioned being. But they are none the less existents, beings, and in this sense they can be described as states of existence.

This way of looking at reality obviously suggests a form of dynamic pantheism. At the same time the Sufi philosophers, as I have said, did not intend to throw overboard Muslim belief in the divine transcendence. Hence there are ambiguities in their accounts of reality. And there is no reason why one should not draw attention to the fact.

It may indeed seem that poetry is a better medium than abstract philosophy for exposing a religious vision of reality or for suggesting one. This was seen by Rūmī. He says, for example, that 'the philosopher kills himself with thinking. Let him run on; his back is turned to the treasure. Most of those destined for Paradise are simpletons, so that they escape from the mischief of philosophy.'[29] Is not poetry, with the concrete images which the Persian poets knew so well how to employ, a much better medium of expression for mystical visions than the conceptual, abstract thought of the philosopher which desiccates what it endeavours to express? If the philosopher appears to succeed on occasion, surely it is only when his thought takes on a poetic character and abandons attempts at precise statement in favour of suggestive pictorial analogies.

This contention cannot simply be dismissed. If a number of

[29]Quoted from *Rūmī, Poet and Mystic (1207–1273). Selections from His Writings*, translated from the Persian with Introduction and Notes by the late R. A. Nicholson, p. 93 (London, 1950). The passage comes from the *Mathnawī*, vi, 2347.

prominent mystics both in the East and in the West have written poetry, it was obviously because they found it a natural and appropriate medium of expression. But nobody supposes that poetry is simply a meaningless concentration of sounds. And if a mystical poet gives expression to a view or vision of reality which he or she believes to be true, and not simply an imaginative construction, it is difficult to see anything objectionable in examining its implications, inquiring into its coherence or lack of it, and asking whether or not its claim to be true is defensible by argument. Consider the following quotation from Rūmī: 'Simple were we and all one essence: we were knotless and pure as water. When that Light took shape, it became many, like shadows cast by a battlement, and all difference will vanish from amidst this multitude.'[30] If these statements were supposed to convey a truth about reality, that the One in some sense became Many, an attempt to answer the question 'in what sense?' seems to be permissible, even if in theoretical reflection the concrete images of the original tend to disappear. Again, Rūmī represented himself as searching for God among the Christians, in heathen temples, in a mountain cave, in the Ka'-bah, in philosophy, with Mohammed, and in the end as finding God where alone he could be found, namely in himself. Obviously, what he says, just as it stands, could stimulate a believer to seek for God immanent in the soul. Rūmī's way of expressing himself might often be far more effective than philosophical reflection. At the same time, if God is really believed to be present within the soul, it is legitimate to consider what is implied in regard to the soul's relationship to God. Is the human soul a modification of God? If not, what is the relationship?

It is not of course my intention to suggest that philosophy can take the place of poetry. My claim is simply, in the present context, that the kind of philosophical reflection which we find with thinkers such as Mullā Sadrā was a natural development within the Sufi movement. There was a place for poetic expression. But there was also a place for reflection on the presuppositions and implications both of mystical spirituality and of the vision of reality expressed in poetry.

---

[30]*Ibid.*, p. 135, *Mathnawī*, i, 672.

To turn to a rather different topic. It was stated above that the Sufi movement, in the general sense of Muslim mystical spirituality, represented the esoteric dimension of Islam. This statement, which has been made by others before me, seems to me to be clearly true. But it gives rise to the question whether Sufi-inspired philosophy was not so much a part or feature of Islam that it cannot have a wider, much less a universal significance. Consider the following assertion by Dr S. H. Nasr: 'Because Sufism is the esoteric and inner dimension of Islam, it cannot be practised apart from Islam'.[31] If Dr Nasr is right, does it follow that Sufi-inspired philosophy, the sort of philosophy which we have briefly considered, is also tied up with Islam and is a specifically Islamic phenomena? If this is the case, are we committed to rejecting Al-Fārābī's contention that philosophy speaks to the human mind as such, not simply to people belonging to a certain religion or nation or ethnic group?

To avoid possible misunderstanding on the part of anyone who is not acquainted with Dr Nasr's writings, it should be explained that he does not intend to imply, by the assertion just quoted, that union with God is possible only for Muslims. What he means is that Sufism is an historical phenomenon which presupposes a certain background or belief and tradition and involves a certain traditional discipline and training, and that it cannot, without distortion, be torn out of this background or matrix and presented as a neutral spiritual path or programme, divorced from all links with a particular religion. He is not suggesting that Christians, for example, or adherents of the *bhakti* movement in Hinduism cannot make progress on the way to closer union with God. He is objecting to what he describes as 'certain pseudo-Sufis'[32] who endeavour to make Sufism more accessible to non-Muslims by presenting it as a neutral faith for all, regardless of their religious affiliations. There are, as some Sufi writers claimed, different paths to God, but no one of them can be turned into a purely neutral faith without suffering distortion. A Christian, for instance, should follow the Christian path in which Christ plays an essential role. If a Christian

[31]*Sufi Essays*, p. 169. (See Note 28.)
[32]*Ibid.*, Note 11.

wishes to practise Sufism, he or she had better become a Muslim. A Christian can of course claim to be practising Sufism while remaining a Christian, but the person will not really be doing so. I think that this is substantially what Dr Nasr is saying.

It seems to me that the matter is rather more complex than Dr Nasr's statement, taken by itself, suggests. We might apply it, for example, to Zen Buddhism or to Yoga meditation and say that Zen and Yoga meditation are features of Buddhism and Hinduism respectively, and that neither can be presented, without serious distortion, as a neutral pursuit. But some people would doubtless argue that *Zazen* or transcendental meditation can perfectly well be regarded as therapeutic, psychologically beneficial practices which do not necessarily involve any religious presuppositions and can be pursued by anyone, irrespective of his or her religious affiliation or lack of it. However, Dr Nasr obviously has a point. Sufi spirituality certainly has religious presuppositions. So has Christian spirituality. And my question is whether, if we accept Dr Nasr's statement as substantially correct, we are thereby committed to regarding Sufi-inspired philosophy as a specifically Islamic phenomenon.

In one sense at any rate the kind of philosophy which developed in Persia is certainly a specifically Islamic phenomenon. This is obviously the case if we regard it as an expression of the esoteric dimension of Islam. It grew up within Islam, it presupposed Muslim beliefs, and it cannot really be understood except in terms of the historical context. Just as the Vedānta philosophy in India arose within Hinduism and has to be seen against this background, so did Persian gnosis arise within Islam and form part of its intellectual history. It does not follow that it received no influence from outside. But this influence was ingested, so to speak, by a Muslim organism.

It is possible, however, to admit this in regard to Sufi-inspired philosophy as a whole and at the same time to argue that Al-Fārābī was quite right in drawing attention to the universal character of philosophical truth. St Thomas Aquinas was a thirteenth-century Christian theologian, whose thought as a whole has to be seen in his historical context. But when he said, for example, that negative statements about a being presuppose some positive knowledge of that being, he was making a statement which was not true only in relation to his time, or true only in relation to his time, a truth only for medievals. Similarly, if Mullā Sadrā was right in maintaining that existence is not a real accident which accrues to a substrate devoid of existence, the truth of his thesis was not limited to his coreligionists. Al-Fārābī may have made far too sharp a distinction between religious faiths and philosophy, if by philosophy we mean philosophies, philosophical systems; but he was none the less making a point about truth which should not be ignored. To be sure, one might wish to restate Mullā Sadrā's thesis in other terms. But one would surely be restating what one believed to be, in some sense, a perennial truth, not a Muslim truth or a Sufi truth but simply a truth.

Having argued elsewhere[33] that there are propositions which can be described as perennially true, I am naturally favourably disposed to the foregoing line of thought. It hardly needs saying, however, that if we simply abstract individual propositions or arguments from Sufi-inspired philosophy and show, or try to show, that the propositions are true for all and the arguments cogent, this procedure, by itself, is very unlikely to satisfy anyone who believes that this philosophy possesses a universal significance and is looking for grounds to support this belief. The person may, for example, be unhappy with contemporary western philosophy and be hankering after a religiously oriented philosophy. If the person claims that Sufi-inspired philosophy possesses a universal significance, he or she is not necessarily claiming that this philosophy as it stands is the philosophy for all time. The person may be thinking of a specific tradition simply as an example of the kind of philosophy desired or as pointing the way to a line of philosophical thought in which serious attention is paid to religious experience in general, and to mystical experience in particular, in philosophical anthropology and in metaphysics. If it is objected that philosophy has progressed beyond a situation in which it was tied up with theological presuppositions and with confidence in the cognitive value of mysticism, the person may reply that he or she does

[33]*Philosophers and Philosophies*, pp. 22–23 (London and New York, 1976).

not regard the conception of philosophy prevalent in university departments as an exemplification of progress, not at any rate without important qualifications. As for presuppositions, the person may comment that it is not necessarily a question of presupposing the truth of a definite set of religious beliefs but rather of being aware of aspects of the human being and of the human being's encounter with reality to which Karl Jaspers, for example, drew attention but which are generally passed over by philosophers.

It is difficult to deal with this line of thought. If someone thinks that belief in God or in any transcendent reality is a superstition, perhaps a harmful one, the disappearance of which is desirable, and that striving after union with God is a vain, and perhaps a harmful pursuit, he or she will obviously regard Sufi-inspired philosophy as possessing no more than an historical interest and will disapprove of any demands for its resuscitation or for the development of anything analogous to it. If, however, someone shares the belief in God manifested by thinkers such as Al-Ghazāli, Mullā Sadrā, Sabzawārī and also Dr Nasr and is convinced that human life has a goal beyond this world, he or she will obviously be much more sympathetically disposed to the sort of philosophy which we have been considering. At the same time such sympathy is compatible with the conviction that Sufi-inspired philosophy as we find it in history belongs to the past, being historically conditioned, and that today any religiously oriented philosophical thought would have to take account of philosophy's self-criticism as it has developed in the West and of modern standards in philosophical thinking. There would have to be a great deal of reconstruction.

As for the actual development of Islamic philosophy in the modern world, at any rate a few philosophers belonging to Muslim nations have embraced systems or lines of thought which are clearly incompatible with Muslim belief. They obviously think that traditional Islamic philosophy is obsolete and no longer viable, and they need not therefore concern us here. More relevant is the sort of demand for the reconstruction of Islamic religious thought which was made by the Muslim poet and philosopher Mohammed Iqbāl, who was born in what is now Pakistan and died in 1938.[34] He urged that instead of relying on such worthies of the past as Avicenna, Muslim philosophers should look to western philosophy for instruments to be used in the task of reconstructing Islamic religious thought. Once an admirer of Ibn 'Arabī, Iqbāl came to the conclusion that Ibn 'Arabī's thought was too pantheistic, and he himself tried to contribute to the task of reconstruction in the light of western philosophy and scientific theory.

Some would doubtless claim that if anyone seriously tries to reconstruct the religious thought of Islam with the aid of modern western philosophy, he or she will end by dismantling the whole edifice of the traditional philosophy of Islam. For my own part, I do not think that the issue can be settled in an *a priori* manner. Islamic culture has had a splendid past, in such fields as poetry, architecture, art and philosophy. We can only wait to see what happens in the future and whether, in philosophy, some genuine continuity with the past is preserved or whether some non-Islamic system of thought will prevail. Given the fact that it is religion which unites the Muslim peoples, the first alternative is certainly a possibility. But I am no prophet. In his work on Sabzawārī's metaphysics Professor T. Izutsu asserts that eastern philosophers should 'reflect upon their own philosophical heritage deeply and analytically, bring out of the darkness of the past whatever is of contemporary relevance, and present their findings in a way suitable for the present-day intellectual situation'.[35] This is an admirable programme. The degree of success which its implementation might have cannot be foreseen. But this does not affect my main aim in this chapter, which has been to illustrate the close connection between philosophy and mystical spirituality in the line of Islamic thought which stretched from Al-Ghazālī in the eleventh century up to Mullā Sadrā in the first half of the seventeenth century and thinkers such as Sabzawārī in the nineteenth century.

[34]Among his publications is *The Reconstruction of Religious Thought in Islam* (London, 1951).
[35]*The Fundamental Structure of Sabzawārī's Metaphysics*, p. 151. (See Note 25.)

CHAPTER 6

WESTERN PHILOSOPHY AND
THE ONE

*Greek philosophy and Plotinus – philosophical thought in
medieval Christendom – Hegel and the Absolute – Bradley and
religion – science and metaphysics – Christian theology and the
philosophy of the One*

I

It has often been asserted, doubtless with truth, that Greek
religion was a matter of cult rather than of belief. True, we
normally and naturally think of worship and prayer as implying
belief. It is of course possible for the relevant ceremonies to be
performed and the appropriate words uttered without belief.
But unless we had reason to suppose the contrary, we would
normally assume that worship of or prayer to a deity implied
belief in the deity in question. The assertion however that Greek
religion was a matter of cult rather than of belief need not be
understood as denying this implication. It can be taken as meaning that emphasis was laid on cult as a social act rather than on
acceptance of any determinate set of beliefs. Greek religion did
not comprise a set of dogmas which all were expected to accept,
and there was no commonly recognized teaching authority in
the sphere of religious truth. The priests were performers of
religious rites and ceremonies rather than authoritative teachers.
As for the Roman empire, it did not really matter what one
believed, provided that one was prepared to perform certain
rites possessing social significance. For example, the significance
of the so-called emperor-worship was primarily social and political, even if devout Christians took seriously the implication in
regard to belief and acted accordingly.

Given the character of Greek religion, it was natural that
minds which were sceptical in regard to traditional myths and
not prepared to accept traditional ethical standards without
question should turn to philosophy, to reason that is to say, for

122

an interpretation of reality and for light on the ideal life for the human being. Up to a point an analogous situation can be found today. That is to say, there are obviously some people who have little faith in the teaching of any religious body and who are not prepared to accept without more ado the current ethical standards of a given society, and who therefore look to philosophy for solutions to their problems. One obvious major difference between the two situations is that a good many modern philosophers do not regard philosophy as capable of increasing our positive knowledge of reality or of solving substantive moral issues, whereas in ancient Greece there arose philosophers who were perfectly prepared to provide visions of reality and positive moral guidance. Some writers have regarded the pre-Socratics as being simply primitive scientists. But this is hardly an adequate description, as can be seen by considering the thought of Heraclitus, in so far as it can be pieced together from the fragments, not to speak of the Pythagoreans. In any case the intellectual ferment of the fifth-century enlightenment at Athens did much to stimulate the growth of the kind of philosophies which I have in mind, philosophies which, in the Hellenistic and Roman periods, ranged from the utterances of popular orators to developed and elaborate systems of thought.

Obviously, ancient philosophy had a variety of aspects, and it is possible to select for emphasis aspects or lines of thought which, considered by themselves, had little to do with religion. For example, it is possible to emphasize Stoic contributions to logical studies rather than the metaphysics of the Greek Stoics or the ethical teaching of the leading Stoics in the Roman empire. This procedure may indeed express a judgment of value about what is worthwhile in philosophy, but it cannot be condemned on this account. We are free to place the emphasis where we will. At the same time it is simply an historical fact that in the ancient world some philosophies presented what can be described as religious visions of reality and theories of the human being's moral vocation.

The most striking example of a religiously oriented philosophy, in which a theory of mysticism was associated with the metaphysics of the One and the Many, is probably the philosophy of Plotinus in the third century A.D. In it we find the idea of a One which is the transcendent source of the Many, transcendent in the sense that the One is represented as undiminished and unchanged by the process of emanation. And this idea is linked to a doctrine relating to the ascent or return of the human spirit to its ultimate source, a process culminating in mystical experience, in what Plotinus described as 'the flight of the alone to the Alone,'[1] an experience which, according to Porphyry,[2] Plotinus himself enjoyed on several occasions. One may indeed jib at calling philosophy 'religion'.[3] But the thought of Plotinus none the less provides what can perfectly well be described as a religious vision of reality, together with a religiously oriented account of the goal of human life and a positive evaluation of mystical experience as contact with the One. We may note too that whatever Plotinus himself may have thought about Christianity, some leading representatives of Neoplatonism, such as Porphyry, represented it as an intellectually superior rival to the Christian religion and as an intellectual or esoteric development of Greek religion.

To what extent the thought of Plotinus was actually influenced by mystical experience, it is difficult to say. The general framework of his system can doubtless be accounted for in terms of the development of the Platonic tradition and Hellenistic philosophy, without introducing 'the flight of the alone to the Alone'. It is also difficult to assess the influence, if any, of eastern philosophy on his thought. That there was some influence is not impossible. The East was not entirely a *terra incognita* for the Hellenistic world. For example, at the end of the fourth century B.C. Megasthenes was ambassador of Seleucus I Nicator at the court of King Chandragupta, and he wrote about India, even if he shed little light on Indian philosophy. Besides, if the report is true that Plotinus joined a military expedition led by the Emperor Gordian III in A.D. 243 with a view to learning about Persian and Indian thought (and I know of no good reason for doubting the truth of the report), he must obviously have known

---

[1] *Enneads*, 771b (vi, 9, 11).
[2] In his *Life of Plotinus*.
[3] In his valuable book *Philosophy of Religion: The Historic Approaches* (London, 1972) Dr M. J. Charlesworth devotes his first chapter to the theme of 'philosophy as religion'. I prefer the phrase 'religiously oriented philosophy'; but the author has of course his reasons for speaking as he does.

that there was such a thing as oriental philosophy. To be sure, as Plotinus left the expedition and returned to the West when Gordian was assassinated in Persia in 244, he can hardly have acquired much first-hand information. But presumably he had received some ideas, however vague, at Alexandria about eastern thought, ideas which aroused his interest and which he hoped to have an opportunity to expand and make more precise. At the same time we cannot argue safely from possibility to actuality. Moreover, though there are certainly some resemblances between the philosophy of Plotinus and the religiously oriented metaphysics of the One and the Many in India, we must remember that the Greek philosopher cannot possibly have been influenced by the thought of Saṁkara, who lived at a considerably later time. Again, we ought not to assert direct oriental influence, if the metaphysics of Plotinus can be accounted for in terms of the development of Greek philosophy in the Hellenistic world. Although, however, I have no intention of claiming that there was no such influence, it seems to me that all that we can say with a reasonable degree of confidence is that Plotinus was aware of the existence of oriental philosophy and that he wished to learn more about it. How much he actually knew about it, we cannot say.

However this may be, it is clear that for Plotinus philosophy was the path to religious truth, to a religiously oriented vision of reality. Plotinus could not appeal to sacred texts in the way in which the Vedānta philosophers appealed to the Upanishads. Mysticism could turn theoretical knowledge, knowledge about, into knowledge by acquaintance, experimental knowledge. But otherwise philosophy was the road to religious truth.

II

In medieval Christendom there was obviously a different situation, inasmuch as there was a factor which had not been present in ancient Greece, namely an authoritative teacher in the fields of religious and moral truth, the Church. In the closing decades of the Roman empire St Augustine had spoken of Christianity as being itself the true philosophy, the true saving wisdom that is to say, for which the search for God in Greek philosophy, especially in the Platonic tradition, had been a preparation, as far as the Gentiles were concerned. And if we were to use the word 'philosophy' in this sense, to cover the Christian faith itself, we could of course say that in medieval Christendom people looked to philosophy for a religious interpretation of reality and for moral teaching. To speak in this way, however, would be very misleading. For in the course of the Middle Ages a clear distinction came to be made between philosophy and Christian theology. The premises of philosophy were regarded as propositions the truth of which was known by the natural light of reason, whereas the premises of theology were truths revealed by God. It was to revealed truth, as mediated by the Church, that people looked for a vision of reality and for moral teaching, not to philosophy, even though philosophy included both metaphysics and ethics. It is true that in the thirteenth century there seem to have been some professors or lecturers in the faculty of arts at Paris who represented philosophy as being the highest activity open to man. But when taxed with unorthodoxy, they replied that they were simply explaining what Aristotle held and that they did not intend to commit themselves to his view.[4] In any case people in general obviously looked to the Church and to Christian theology for saving wisdom, not to philosophy in the sense in which philosophy was regarded as a distinct discipline.

If one asserted that in the Middle Ages philosophy was not religiously oriented in any sense, the assertion would be false. For one thing, philosophy, as a subject taught in universities, was studied before theology, which was then regarded as the highest of the sciences. Its study constituted a preparatory stage in the academic career. For another thing, most of the creative thinkers of medieval Christendom were primarily theologians and were naturally concerned to integrate philosophy with theology in a systematic manner. St Thomas Aquinas, for example, regarded philosophical thought as culminating in the knowledge of God obtainable by the human reason in its reflection upon the world, whereas Christian theology ('sacred doctrine' as he

---

[4]At this date it is impossible to estimate the sincerity of such replies. But the teachers in question could claim with truth that they were expected to keep their hands off theology.

called it) treated God's revelation of himself and of truths which could not be proved philosophically. Both metaphysics and theology however were concerned with knowledge *that*, knowledge *about* God, whereas mystical experience came as near as was possible in this life to knowledge by acquaintance. Finally, all three were transcended in the vision of God in Heaven. We can thus say that for St Thomas the metaphysics of the One and the Many had a religious orientation, inasmuch as it looked forward to higher levels of the knowledge of God.

Although, however, medieval philosophy can be said to have been religiously oriented in the sense described, the word 'philosophy', as then used, had a much wider connotation (as in the Greek world) than it has today. It covered a good many subjects, such as mathematics, which had no clear connection with religion. Besides, in the late Middle Ages there was a strong tendency to restrict the scope of what was considered to be provable in philosophy and to extend the range of what was known only by revelation. Thus in the Ockhamist movement in the fourteenth century philosophy tended to become a matter of logical studies, conceptual analysis and critical analysis of metaphysical arguments advanced by earlier thinkers. Philosophy in this sense was hardly a fertile soil for religiously oriented visions of reality. It was clearly not a source of saving wisdom. Whereas Greek philosophy ended with Neoplatonism, late medieval philosophy in the universities tended to resemble, in some respects at least, the analytic philosophy of the present century.

Given the general nature of philosophy in medieval Christendom, one would not expect to find any close connection between it and mysticism. It is not of course a question of there not having been any theories of stages in the spiritual life. We can find them, for example, with Richard of St Victor in the twelfth century and St Bonaventure in the thirteenth century. But such theories were regarded as belonging to mystical theology, not to philosophy as a discipline distinct from theology. When in the late Middle Ages John Gerson (1363–1429), chancellor of the University of Paris, insisted on the importance of ascetical and mystical doctrine, his aim was to contribute to the revitalizing of theology through emphasis on the Christian spiritual life. Theology, he believed, had become far too academic and arid, only too apt to forget that the Christian's primary need was to come closer to God. He was not suggesting that philosophers should abandon their appeals to propositions regarded as self-evidently true and to logical argument, and that they should appeal instead to mystical intuitions. Again, tradition has it that towards the end of his life St Thomas Aquinas enjoyed a mystical experience which led him to exclaim that what he had written appeared as straw. But presumably he meant that theoretical knowledge, knowledge about God, cut a poor figure in comparison with knowledge by acquaintance. He was not suggesting that the scholastic method employed in philosophy and theology should be thrown overboard and mystical hunches substituted instead.

The thought may well have occurred to the reader's mind that I seem to have forgotten all about thinkers such as Meister Eckhart (c. 1260–1327), the famous Dominican preacher and writer. Is it not the case, someone may ask, that his view of the relation between the One and the Many, God and creatures, was influenced by mystical experience or reflection on it? After all, his more provocative statements such as 'all creatures are a pure nothing'[5] and 'outside God there is nothing'[6] have provided ground for comparing him with eastern thinkers. Inasmuch as he is concerned with emphasizing God as the only reality rather than with magnifying the human self, his thought may indeed bear more resemblance, as some have argued, to the Sufi-inspired philosophy of Persia than to the Advaita Vedānta, to which it has been assimilated by others. But in any case his statements are clearly expressions of a mystical spirituality. There is no need to embark upon a discussion of the orthodoxy or otherwise of Eckhart's statements.[7] Whether orthodox or unorthodox, the provocative statements can be seen as an expression of shock tactics, as devices to stimulate people to change their vision of reality from conceiving God as an

---

[5] *Meister Eckhart. Die deutschen und lateinischen Werke* (Stuttgart, 1936f). *Die deutschen Werke*, pp. 69–70.

[6] *Ibid. Die lateinischen Werke*, 1, p. 41.

[7] When accused of unorthodoxy, Eckhart argued that his statements had been misinterpreted. For example, the statement that outside God there is nothing was perfectly orthodox if taken as meaning that nothing exists or can exist except in complete ontological dependence on God.

additional being 'out there' to seeing him at the centre of the soul and as communicating existence to all finite things. Eckhart was a preacher. And his statements were clearly expressions of a mystical vision and intended to facilitate in others a realization of God as the one true reality.

All this may well be true. The statements about the relation between the One and the Many which were made by writers such as Eckhart and Ruysbroeck (1293–1381) can reasonably be seen as reflecting not simply Neoplatonist metaphysics but also personal mystical experience. Ruysbroeck was undoubtedly a mystic. But the statements in question are hardly typical of medieval philosophy or theology. This is of course the reason why they drew the attention of critics of philosophical thought in the Middle Ages. It can obviously be argued that what has been described as 'speculative mysticism' constituted a healthy reaction to the academic and arid philosophical and theological studies pursued in universities. At the same time it was in a real sense peripheral to medieval philosophy as a whole.

To say this is not to deny that the metaphysics of the One and the Many was a prominent feature of medieval philosophy. Generally speaking, the thirteenth-century philosophers evidently believed that the existence of the Many could not be explained except by reference to one ultimate reality. And if we prescind from those fourteenth-century thinkers who were sceptical about the philosophical arguments of their predecessors and affirmed the existence of the one infinite God simply on faith, we can say that the metaphysics of the One and the Many, in some form or other, runs from John Scotus Erigena in the ninth century to Nicholas of Cusa in the first half of the fifteenth century, provided of course that we are prepared to consider Nicholas as a medieval thinker and do not assign him instead to the Renaissance. At the same time most medieval philosophers differed from the Vedānta thinkers and the Sufi philosophers by appealing simply to clearly stated argument and not to suprasensory perception or to spiritual illumination. Philosophy in the Middle Ages can indeed be regarded as contributing to the development of a general Christian world-view. It has to be seen against the background of a culture in which religious beliefs formed common presuppositions in a way which is not the case today. But this does not alter the fact that philosophical discussion was conducted through a process of argument and counter-argument, and not by appeals to mystical insight.

III

In medieval Christendom the One, God, was conceived as infinite. In the fourteenth century there was indeed a tendency, within the Ockhamist movement, to include infinity among the divine attributes which could be known only by faith. But this tendency does not affect the fact that God was believed to be infinite, whereas all creatures were finite.

If, however, the ultimate reality is conceived as infinite, the question arises whether there can be anything distinct from God, whether, that is to say, God must not be the only reality, containing all finite beings within himself. In other words, must not Eckhart be quite right in claiming that apart from God nothing exists? If God is infinite being, must not creatures be states of absolute being or existence, as Mullā Sadrā claimed?

Thomists answered such questions, as has already been remarked, in terms of the theory of the analogy of being. That is to say, in answer to the question whether recognition of finite beings as distinct from God would not commit one to defending the paradoxical assertion that there can be an addition to the infinite, the Thomists answered that the question did not really arise, inasmuch as finite things were not beings in the same universal sense in which God is being, so that the idea of adding creatures to God as two oranges might be added to one orange was nonsensical. Even John Duns Scotus, who maintained that we could not talk about God, much less prove his existence, unless there were some sense in which the concept of being is univocal, admitted that God and creatures are opposed to notbeing in different ways and that in the real order being is analogical. In other words, Scotus did not reject the concept of analogical predication, but he insisted that if any assignable meaning can be given to statements about God, analogical predication must rest on a basis of universal predication. If there were no such basis, all our statements about God would be meaningless. This basis having been established, we can then go on to argue that the infinite and the finite exist in different ways.

If however the theory of the analogy of being is rejected or forgotten, it is very difficult to see how a being which is said to be infinite must not be the sole reality. In other words, there is then a natural movement from the idea of a transcendent One to the concept of the Absolute. We can see this movement of the mind exemplified in the philosophy of Spinoza. There are of course other factors to be considered, such as the development of the philosophy of nature at the time of the Renaissance, with, for example, Giordano Bruno. But I do not wish to discuss Spinoza here, apart from noting that with him infinite substance became the sole reality, finite things being represented as its modes. Instead of Spinozism I prefer to discuss the philosophies of Hegel and F. H. Bradley and the relations between these philosophies and religion.

Inasmuch as Hegel lectured not only on the philosophy of religion but also on the philosophy of art and the philosophy of history, we might suppose that for him the field of philosophy was much wider than that of religion, religion being one of the first-order historical phenomena on which the philosopher re-flected. So it was in a sense. Otherwise he would not have been able to distinguish between, say, philosophy of religion and philosophy of art. At the same time Hegel explicitly asserts that religion and philosophy have the same subject-matter, namely 'God and nothing but God and the self-unfolding of God'.[8]

There is a good deal which could be said about this statement. I confine my attention to one point only, the relation between this statement and mysticism. To avoid misunderstanding, I do not claim that Hegel himself was a mystic. Richard Kroner described the philosopher as a 'Christian mystic'.[9] I cannot accept this description. But it does not follow that there is no connection at all between mysticism and Hegel's view of the relationship between philosophy and religion.

Hegel's philosophy can be approached in various ways, and

[8]*Werke*, xv, 37 (Hermann Glockner's edition, Stuttgart, 26 vols., 1927–39).
[9]On p. 8 of his preface to Hegel's *Early Theological Writings*, translated by T. M. Knox (Chicago, 1948).

emphasis can be laid on this or that theme or line of thought in accordance with one's estimate of what is most important, whether in terms of what Hegel himself is believed to have thought important or in terms of what one judges to be important today. One way of approaching it is to see it as an attempt to think the relation between infinite and finite in such a way that they are not left in sharp opposition to one another. To say that x is infinite is to say that it is not finite. The terms 'infinite' and 'finite' are thus opposed, and for ordinary logic, according to Hegel, they remain frozen in opposition. They are what Duns Scotus called 'disjunctive attributes' of being.[10] That is to say, every being is either infinite or finite, but it cannot be both. The mystics, however, such as Meister Eckhart, enjoyed an intuitive grasp of a relationship which transcended the sharp opposition between infinite and finite but which did not involve the reduction of the one to the other. Hegel quotes Eckhart to the effect that 'the eye with which God sees me is the eye with which I see him; my eye and his eye are one. . . . If God were not, I should not be; if I were not, he would not be either.'[11] Hegel remarks that the 'older theologians', such as Eckhart, had a better grasp of 'this depth', as he puts it, than their modern successors. And it is arguable that he tried to give philosophical expression to the intuitive grasp of this truth,[12] trying to avoid either reducing 'the One' to a mere label for the Many or reducing the Many to the One in a way which would involve acosmism. (When Hegel denies that he is a pantheist, he understands pantheism in an acosmistic sense.)

It is not, of course, claimed here that this is the only proper way of looking at Hegel's philosophy. One can perfectly well emphasize, for example, his attempt to overcome the dichotomy between thought and being, an attempt which is natural enough in the case of an idealist philosopher. I simply claim that it is one possible way of seeing Hegel's philosophy. And it is an approach which fits in with the general theme of this book. If

[10] In his ontology Scotus was influenced to a considerable extent by Avicenna.
[11] *Werke*, xv, 228. (See Note 8.)
[12] I have argued in this way in 'Hegel and the Rationalization of Mysticism' in *New Studies in Hegel's Philosophy*, edited by Warren E. Steinkraus, pp. 187–200 (New York, 1971).

anyone wished to argue that Hegel's references to people such as Eckhart and the later visionary Jakob Böhme (1575–1624) are simply a kind of sop for the devout and should not be taken seriously, it would be difficult to prove that the contention was wrong. For my own part, however, I think that Hegel seriously believed that mystics had enjoyed an intuitive grasp of the immanence of the One in the Many, a truth which he proposed to exhibit in systematic form with the aid of his dialectical logic.

In Hegel's thought the concept of God seems to me to undergo transformation into that of the universe considered as a totality, the universal which manifests itself in and exists and lives in and through its particulars. The One transcends the Many in the sense that it is not identifiable with any determinate set of finite things, those existing at the present moment for example. But though the One, through a process of abstraction, can be considered in itself, as distinct from the Many, it does not follow that it exists by itself. It exists in and through its self-manifestation in Nature and in human history. We may thus be put in mind of Taoism and of the distinction between the One as substance and the One as function. Hegel, however, was an idealist. He saw the One, Reality with a capital letter, as coming to know itself in and through the human mind. As he puts it, 'God knows himself in the human spirit.'[13] This of course is why he approves of Eckhart's statement that the eye with which God sees me is the eye with which I see God. Reality is the essence which develops itself. It develops itself by attaining self-consciousness, self-knowledge. Hence instead of Spinoza's description of the Absolute as substance we must substitute the definition of the Absolute as Spirit.

Within the sphere of religion itself the truth about the One finds progressively more adequate expression in the form suited to the religious consciousness. In Christianity, the 'absolute religion' according to Hegel, the immanence of the One is expressed in the doctrine of the indwelling Holy Spirit, uniting Christians in one community, one brotherhood, a union symbolized by participation in the Eucharist. From the philosophical point of view however the One is the universe considered

[13] *Werke*, xvi, 192.

as one reality which comes to know itself in and through the human mind. And participation in the life of the religious community tends to be transformed into participation in the life of the political community, the State. This does not imply that Hegel himself envisaged philosophy as taking the place of religion for humanity in general and the State as taking the place of the Church. It is more a case of Hegel seeing the interior union between human beings through the indwelling Spirit expressing itself in the objective sphere in political life.

The foregoing interpretation of Hegel has been expressed dogmatically, for the sake of brevity and clarity. At the same time this line of interpretation is not acceptable to everyone. For example, there have been and still are those who interpret Hegel in a more or less theistic sense. They interpret Hegel as holding, for instance, that God is self-conscious quite independently of the human mind. And they can indeed appeal to statements made by Hegel. After all, the philosopher not infrequently employed theological language. However I see Hegel as transforming the concept of God into that of the Absolute. The Absolute is defined as spirit, as self-thinking thought. But the essence so defined actualizes itself in and through a process, the development of man's religious and philosophical apprehension of reality presupposing the background of Nature, the condition of mental or spiritual life.

If this line of interpretation is accepted, we can see some resemblance at any rate between Hegel's philosophy and the Advaita Vedānta, inasmuch as the concept of God seems to be, for Hegel, the way in which the Absolute appears to the religious consciousness. In this case it corresponds to some extent to Śaṁkara's idea of Saguna-Brahman. At the same time Hegel's Absolute is very different from the Absolute, Nirguna-Brahman, in the Advaita philosophy. Brahman transcends all thought and is without qualities, as Nirguna-Brahman is for the mind a blank. For Hegel, the nature of the Absolute is knowable in speculative philosophy, which is really the Absolute's knowledge of itself. In his view, the conception of the ultimate reality as a blank was simply a phase or stage in the onward march, the dialectical advance, to positive knowledge of the Absolute.

These observations are relevant to the subject of the relation between Hegelianism and mysticism. Hegel had little use for appeals to mystical intuition as a substitute for a resolute and patient effort to achieve communicable understanding. In this sense he was a rationalist. At the same time his idea of identity-in-difference, of a One existing and living in and through the Many, can be seen as a means of conceptualizing a truth which he recognized as having been divined by a writer such as Eckhart. It may perhaps be arguable, as W. T. Stace argued,[14] that Hegel endeavours, unsuccessfully, to turn a mystical idea into a logical concept. But this is obviously not the situation as Hegel himself saw it. In any case the connection between his philosophy and mysticism is not that he was a mystic, nor that he believed that appeals to mystical experience could take the place of speculative thought (he believed nothing of the kind), but that he saw in mysticism the intuitive grasp of a truth which it was the business of philosophy to understand and exhibit in a systematic manner.

IV

There has been some discussion of the question whether Hegel's view of the relation between philosophy and religion committed him to the claim that for the philosopher religion was something to be left behind as an inferior expression of truth. On the one hand it can be argued that as art was also, for Hegel, an expression of truth and as he obviously did not think that the philosopher was debarred from enjoying aesthetic experience, even if he could not enjoy it at the same time that he was pursuing philosophical reflection, there is no good reason for supposing that he regarded the philosopher as debarred from religious experience, even if he could not enjoy religious experience and devote himself to philosophy at the same moment. On the other hand it can be argued, with Benedetto Croce, that if we interpret religion as a way of understanding the same truth which is presented in philosophy, the two cannot co-exist. If a person advances to the philosophical level, he or she must leave religion behind.

[14]In *Mysticism and Philosophy* (London, 1961).

For any thorough discussion of this matter, we would obviously have to distinguish between two questions. To what
conclusion was Hegel logically committed? And, what did Hegel
himself think about the matter? For the answers to these two
questions need not necessarily be the same. But I mention the
issue here simply to indicate that Hegel's position is not clear.[15]
At any rate it is not clear enough to prevent dispute.

If we want a clear statement (or what at first sight appears
to be such) about the fate of religion when the concept of God
is transformed into that of the Absolute, we can turn to F. H.
Bradley. 'Short of the Absolute God cannot rest, and, having
reached that goal, he is lost and religion with him.'[16] That is to
say, the concept of an infinite personal God logically demands
transformation into the concept of the suprapersonal all-inclusive Absolute or One. When this demand is satisfied, the basis
for religion disappears. One cannot sensibly worship or pray to
a suprapersonal Absolute.

A natural comment is that Bradley's statement is quite true,
provided that the term 'religion' is understood in the sense in
which he obviously understands it, whereas the statement is
false if we understand the term in a sense wide enough to
accommodate Buddhism and the Advaita Vedānta. That is to
say, Bradley understands religion in the way in which it is
commonly understood in a society in which the prevailing form
of religion has been Christianity. It is not indeed simply a
question of Christianity. It is a question of theistic religion in
general. Given this kind of religion, with its belief in a personal
God, its worship and its prayer, it is clear that its basis is
undermined by the substitution of the Absolute for God. If
however the term 'religion' is understood in a sense which is
much wider but which is still compatible with ordinary language
(inasmuch as Buddhism, for example, is commonly described as
a religion), we are not entitled to claim that acceptance of
Bradley's philosophy entails the discarding of religion. In other
words, what Bradley is really saying is that absolute idealism,

---

[15]For a discussion of Hegel on religion see, for example, Professor Emil
Fackenheim's *The Religious Dimension of Hegel's Thought* (Bloomington, Indiana,
1967).

[16]*Appearance and Reality*, p. 447 (2nd edition, London, 1897).

as he presents it, is incompatible with orthodox Judaism, Christianity and Islam. And this statement is true.

These comments on Bradley's statement are perfectly reasonable. It is, however, worth remarking that Bradley does not try to turn his philosophy into a religion to take the place of theism. In the non-dualist Vedānta philosophy the laying aside of the ego-consciousness and of individual personality is looked upon as a desirable goal. Absorption in Brahman, realization of the spirit's Oneness with the Absolute, is sought with an intensity or fervour which can be described as religious. I am not, however, aware that Bradley adopts anything which could reasonably be described as a religious attitude to the idea of the self being relegated to the sphere of appearance. He gives some reasons for inferring that the self is not really real, concludes that it must therefore be consigned to the sphere of appearance, and leaves it at that.

It is indeed true that Bradley evidently thinks that the value of religion is such that it will not, or should not, entirely disappear, especially if it is conceived, as he rather obscurely puts it, as 'the attempt to express the complete reality of goodness through every aspect of our being.'[17] But religion in this sense, he adds, is 'at once something more, and something higher than philosophy'.[18] Further, the religion which he has in mind seems to lie in the future, as a more or less remote possibility. He sees the need for 'a religious belief founded otherwise than on metaphysics, and a metaphysics able in some sense to justify that need'.[19] But he goes on to remark that the fulfilment of this need 'is a thing which I cannot myself expect to see . . . (though) I cannot regard it as impossible'.[20] It may be, therefore, that if he were told that his statement about the disappearance of religion referred only to Judaism, Christianity and Islam, and not to the Advaita Vedānta, he would reply that the Advaita Vedānta was not a religion but a metaphysical system which did indeed grow out of a religion but which relegated this religion to the

---

[17]*Ibid.*, p. 453.
[18]*Ibid.*
[19]*Essays on Truth and Reality*, pp. 446–7 (London, 1914).
[20]*Ibid.*

sphere of appearance, just as he, Bradley, relegated theistic religion to the sphere of appearance.

Someone might conceivably claim that Bradley grounds his philosophy on a mystical experience, on an experience in which 'the subject, the object and their relation are experienced as elements or aspects in a One which is there from the start.'[21] Though, however, he does sometimes give the impression of postulating an immediate pre-reflective awareness of the Absolute, he seems to be referring to pure feeling as the primitive and lowest level of knowledge, to the experience of a 'felt totality',[22] a state in which the subject-object distinction has not yet emerged and which can serve as an analogue to the concept of the Absolute. Elsewhere he speaks of an initial faith or of a presupposition which philosophy has to make if it is to reach its goal. In other words, the search for the One implies an initial faith or presupposition that there is a One to search for. A word such as 'presupposition' does not suggest a mystical experience. In any case I do not think that Bradley makes his meaning sufficiently clear to warrant the claim that he is postulating what would generally be described as a mystical experience. He appears to be saying simply that there is a primitive feeling of a totality as the lowest conceptual limit of awareness, and that realization of this fact should make us more ready to accept the idea of an Absolute which transcends the subject-object distinction. This primitive or basic feeling is presumably present in all as a state preceding the emergence of the subject-object distinction, and is not a relatively rare or exceptional mystical experience. However, if anyone wishes to describe this state of pure feeling as mystical experience, then he or she can go on to claim that Bradley bases his philosophy on mystical experience.

V

There is no great difficulty in finding some points of resemblance between the philosophies which we have considered and those of the East. It is not a question of derivation or borrowing but simply of similarity. For example, though Nāgārjuna and Brad-

[21]*Ibid.*, p. 200.
[22]*Ibid.*

ley were widely separated in space and time, there is a resemblance between the ways in which both thinkers tried to show how the concepts which we ordinarily employ in interpreting reality give rise to antinomies. Such similarities however form only one side of the picture. There are also dissimilarities, and among the most obvious is that of background or historical context. Both Hegel and Bradley lived in a culture which had been formed largely, though not of course exclusively, under the influence of the Judaeo-Christian religious tradition. For Hegel Christianity was 'the absolute religion', and Bradley's idea of the nature of religion was, as we have noted, strongly influenced by the religious tradition of the society in which he lived.

When seen against this background, the transformation of the concept of God into that of the Absolute is likely to appear as a half-way house on the way to abandonment of the idea of a spiritual One altogether. Hegel defined the Absolute as spirit or mind (*Geist*), and Bradley too insisted that the ultimate reality was spiritual. 'Outside of spirit there is not, and there cannot be, any reality, and, the more that anything is spiritual, so much the more is it veritably real.'[23] If, however, the Absolute is conceived as the universe, and not as a transcendent God, is there any good reason for claiming that it is spiritual? According to G. E. Moore, it is very difficult to discuss the question whether the universe is or is not spiritual, inasmuch as it is none too clear what is meant by describing it as spiritual.[24] If, it may be urged, the Absolute is conceived as identical with the universe, does not the phrase 'the Absolute' become superfluous? It is doubtless true that a universe transformed in the way envisaged by Bradley would not be the same thing as the world as we ordinarily conceive it. But Bradley was not able, nor did he claim to be able, to explain how appearances are transformed in an Absolute which is said to be identical with appearances. He was inclined to argue that the transformation could not be shown to be impossible, and that it must therefore be a reality. But this line of argument presupposes of course that there is an Absolute. And given the difficulty in explaining the relation

[23]*Appearance and Reality*, p. 552.
[24]See Moore's article 'The Refutation of Idealism' (*Mind*, vol. 12, 1903), reprinted in his *Philosophical Studies* (London, 1922, new edition 1960).

between appearance and reality in Bradley's philosophy, it is understandable if to a good many minds it seems both simple and more sensible to drop the idea of a metaphysical Absolute altogether and to maintain that if there is a One at all, it is simply the world in so far as science can show it to be a unity. We then have the contention, referred to in Chapter 1, that the task of synthesis has passed from metaphysical philosophy to science.

This is the conclusion which may seem to follow from the thesis advanced in a book, *The Tao of Physics*, to which reference was made in Chapter 2 of this volume.[25] For if eastern thinkers such as the Taoist sages are regarded as having had an intuitive apprehension of a unified cosmos in which all things are inter-related, and if modern physics is seen as confirming the antici-patory vision and as giving it body, so to speak, and articulate structure, it is natural to conclude that scientific theory has effectively taken the place of the anticipatory vision, not by denying it but by making it explicit and putting it on a firmer and wider foundation than it had before.

It is not my intention to imply that the author of the book in question, Frithof Capra, would endorse this interpretation of his thesis. He claims that eastern thought forms a philosophical framework in which modern science can be better accommo-dated than it can be in the framework provided by Western philosophy with its reluctance to consider anything which tran-scends conceptual thought and precise linguistic expression. This reluctance makes it difficult for western philosophy to accommodate a theoretical physics which is prepared to recog-nize the inadequacy of our ordinary conceptual apparatus and language to express new scientific theories. So it may well be that Capra looks on eastern thought as having a permanent value, and not as something which has been superseded by science.

At the same time the kind of eastern thought with which Mr Capra is concerned is that in which the One is said to be non-different from the phenomenal world. Given this conception of oriental thought (which is certainly exemplified in some philo-

---

[25]Pp. 66–7. (See Note 40 on p. 66.)

sophies), it would be hardly surprising if someone drew the conclusion that the metaphysics of the One has been superseded by modern science. For if the One is literally identical with the phenomenal world, is it not science which reveals the nature of the phenomenal world, and so of the One?

If ultimate reality is literally identified with the phenomenal world, the association which has often existed between the metaphysics of the One and religion tends to disappear. Bertrand Russell, while not believing that there was any being higher than man, refused to regard the world as a suitable object for religious devotion. And a good many people would doubtless agree with him. It may be objected that even Russell himself recognized that there could be something which might be described as 'cosmic emotion'. So there can. There have certainly been cases of what R. C. Zaehner called 'nature mysticism'. But this seems to me to involve, implicitly at any rate, the idea of an immanent One which is more than the world considered as a system of interrelated things. The One of Taoism, while not a reality existing quite independently of the world, is logically prior to the Many, as its source. Nor do I believe that Spinoza's infinite substance, considered as *Natura naturans*, is literally identical with the world as presented in physical science, though some people may be prepared to argue that it is. Anyway, my contention is simply that if the One is identified in a literal sense with the world of physical science, any association of the philosophy of the One with religion tends to disappear. If the association reappears, then the One tends to regain an element of transcendence.

Some years ago, while the 'death of God' movement enjoyed considerable notoriety, we were informed by some writers that what they called the religious *a priori*, the alleged orientation of the human spirit to a transcendent reality, was a concept which could no longer be seriously entertained. However this may be, the idea of such an orientation has found explicit expression in some recent philosophies, for example in that of Karl Jaspers. It is true that the philosophy of Jaspers has made little impact on philosophical circles in the West. Those analytical philosophers who are acquainted with his thought regard it as vague, ambiguous, subjectivist, lacking in precision of thought, clarity

of expression and solid argumentation. Philosophers who continue the tradition of systematic ontology are not attracted by
a thinker who rejected rationalist metaphysics and pursued what
they regard as a subjectivist line of thought. Christian theologians are apt to see in Jaspers' 'Comprehensive' a poor substitute for the God of the Bible, even though Jaspers frequently
called his One 'God', and also to look on his so-called 'philosophical faith' as a quasi-religious attitude, hovering uneasily
between agnosticism on the one hand and a definite religious
commitment on the other. At the same time Jaspers' thought is
a good illustration of a movement of the mind towards an
ultimate reality transcending the world as presented in science,
a movement, in his case, which does not precede but presupposes the development of modern science. Jaspers came to philosophy by way of jurisprudence, medicine and then psychology.
He was no enemy of science, and he paid serious attention to
reflection on science and the relation between it and philosophy.
Further, he took Kant seriously, Kant's criticism, that is to say,
of the idea of metaphysics as a science of supersensible reality,
parallel to physical science as directed to knowledge of the
material world. There is a sense in which Jaspers could have
endorsed Betrand Russell's statement that 'all *definite* knowledge
. . . belongs to science'.[26] At the same time Jaspers tried to show
how through genuine advertence to manifestations of finitude
and contingency, to what he described as limit-situations, the
human being could become aware of the ultimate ground of all
finite existence, not indeed as a visible, audible or tangible
object, but as a mysterious enveloping presence, so to speak.
'Becoming aware' is indeed a phrase which is open to objection.
For it inevitably suggests awareness of an object. The object of
which one becomes aware, for Jaspers, is not the One itself but
the phenomenal world as a 'cipher' or symbol for the ultimate
reality which transcends direct awareness and which the human
being remains free to affirm or deny. This is why he spoke of
'philosophical faith' – 'faith' in the sense that the existence of
the One cannot be proved in such a way as to compel the assent
of any mind which understands the truth, 'philosophical' in

---

[26]*A History of Western Philosophy*, p. 10 (London and New York, 1945).

order to distinguish the faith in question from assent to the doctrines of a particular religion. For Jaspers, all definite religions, like all metaphysical systems, were symbols of the divine reality.

Even though Jaspers' thought made relatively little impact on philosophical circles in the West, it did arouse a good deal of sympathetic interest in the East, in Japan for example. For one thing, his idea of the ultimate reality as transcending the distinction between subject and object resembled in some respects the Absolute of certain oriental philosophies. For another thing, his way of philosophizing was more acceptable in the context of, say, Buddhist thought than in that of western philosophy with its long-standing concern with precision, clarity and closely structured argumentation. Indeed, to some oriental readers his philosophy appeared as a stimulus to them to rethink their own traditions, thus acting as a bridge between West and East. It is mentioned here however more as illustrating a religious interest which cannot be described than as apologetics in the sense of an attempt to provide a rational support for the doctrines of a particular religion. His philosophy is reflection on experience, the human being's experience in transcending the sphere of science and of discursive thought in general towards an ultimate reality which, for Jaspers, traditional metaphysics tried, unsuccessfully, to pin down in adequate concepts.

If anyone wants a philosopher to tell them clearly what is what, to unveil the nature of reality for all to see, Jaspers is not the man for them. It is not so much a case of trying to say the unsayable as of trying to get people to see, by reflection on their own experience, that their experience is limited by the unsayable. Those who will not accept the idea of an unsayable unless it is said, and said clearly, must obviously abandon any hope of illumination from Jaspers. Then there are those who, while not rejecting the idea of the unsayable, think that it should at any rate be the possible object of confirmatory mystical experience. But they too will be disappointed, as Jaspers was unsympathetic to mysticism, regarding it as an attempt to turn the unobjectifiable into an object (of experience). His philosophy thus disappoints the expectations of very different classes of persons. At the same time it exemplifies a movement of the mind which I have elsewhere called 'the movement of transcendence'[27] and which, in my opinion, underlies the old metaphysical arguments for the existence of a One.

VI

Some philosophers might comment that metaphysics, at any rate what Professor W. H. Walsh described as 'transcendent metaphysics',[28] must be in a pretty bad way, if, to survive, it has to have recourse to the sort of subjectivism exemplified in the thought of Karl Jaspers. But a number of Christian theologians too have welcomed what they believe to be the downfall of metaphysics, especially of 'transcendent metaphysics', in the post-Kantian world. As a conclusion to this chapter I wish to make some brief remarks about their attitude.

Given the historical development of philosophical thought and the rise and fall of systems, it is understandable if Christian theologians are reluctant to see in metaphysics a natural ally. To take an extreme case, Hegel took the Christian religion under his wing, presenting it as kind of exoteric version of the truth of absolute idealism by interpreting the meaning of Christian beliefs in the light of his own philosophy. If, however, absolute idealism and the absolute religion, Christianity, express the same truth, though in different ways, it follows that if the truth-claims of Hegelianism are rejected and the system abandoned, Christianity shares in this fate. It is not surprising if theologians wish to avoid postulating such a link between the Christian religion and a particular philosophical system. For the matter of that, theologians may be reluctant to accept any support from metaphysics. If, for example, theologians look to metaphysics to prove the existence of God, and if each of the proofs successively offered is undermined by critical analysis, at any rate in common estimation, the theologian is left in a rather embarrassing situation. To make matters worse, metaphysicians have been apt to transform the concept of God into something else, such as Nature or a non-personal Absolute. If metaphysics could be got out of the way, people could then be faced with the

[27] *Religion and Philosophy*, ch. 9 (Dublin, London and New York, 1974).
[28] See Professor Walsh's *Metaphysics* (London, 1963).

clear option between believing and not believing in the God of the Bible.

The most drastic way of eliminating metaphysics is doubtless to argue that all metaphysical problems are pseudo-problems. In this case it is pointless to look for answers. Although however some theologians have shown satisfaction in logical positivism's attack on metaphysics, logical positivism has not escaped intact from the criticism levelled against it. Further, even if theologians can refer to St Paul's word about 'foolishness to the Greeks', to extend a welcoming hand to logical positivism is a somewhat risky procedure for any theologian who wishes to preserve the traditional Christian doctrines. Nor is it necessary. It seems to me that for the purposes of the theologians whom I have in mind, it is sufficient if the pretensions of metaphysics to provide us with knowledge of meta-empirical reality are rejected. For if these pretensions or claims are false, the metaphysician can hardly be a rival to the Christian theologian by providing, for example, that the ultimate reality is a non-personal Absolute.

As we have seen, however, there are metaphysical philosophers who are quite prepared to accept Kant's criticism of the idea of metaphysics as a science of supersensible reality, and who leave the way open for the response of faith to God's self-disclosure. Why should not the theologian be willing to extend approval to this kind of metaphysics? One can understand his not wishing to endorse the philosophy of Jaspers as it stands, in view of Jaspers' theory of philosophical faith as contrasted with faith in a particular revelation or what is believed to be such. But there are other philosophers, such as Maurice Blondel (1861–1949), who, though a university professor of philosophy, regarded his thought as Christian apologetics, though not indeed of the kind practised in the eighteenth century.

The theologian might, I suppose, reply that this kind of metaphysics, though much less obnoxious than what Kant described as dogmatic metaphysics, is none the less open to serious criticism, and that he does not wish to rely upon it. Further, some theologians might claim that it is a mistake to think that Christian faith presupposes an orientation of the human spirit to transcendent reality. In fallen man there is no such orientation. Not only faith itself but also the capacity for faith are a divine gift, the result of divine action. This is precisely why faith appears to the unbeliever as folly or nonsense. One might perhaps employ the neo-Wittgensteinian theory of autonomous language-games and say that the language of Christian faith can be understood only by those who participate in the relevant form of life. But to say this is not at all the same thing as to postulate in the human being as such an orientation to transcendent reality, an orientation which can be made the object of philosophical reflection.

Even if I were qualified to do so, I could not embark on theological discussion here about the nature of faith. But I can at any rate suggest the following line of thought. It can indeed be objected against philosophers such as Jaspers, Blondel and others that the orientation which they claim to see in the human spirit as such is simply an orientation experienced by religiously minded people like themselves. This, it may be said, is why such philosophers have not made more impact than they have. At the same time an orientation of the mind to a One (when the phrase 'the One' is not used simply as a label for the sum total of the Many) is discernible in other religions beside Christianity. Further, though we are certainly not entitled to assume without more ado, that mysticism is always uniform, of the same kind, mystical experience is a phenomenon which has occurred in both East and West. It is perfectly legitimate for the philosopher to reflect on religious phenomena in general, including mystical experience, and to try to assess their significance in the life of the human being living in a world of multiplicity. The philosopher may indeed confine himself to phenomenal analysis. But unless he regards Husserl's suspension of judgment in regard to existence as setting an absolute limit to thought, he is unlikely to avoid some sort of metaphysics, even if he disclaims any ability to develop a science of supersensible reality. Metaphysics of some sort or other is a natural development of human thought, and I do not think that it can ever be entirely eliminated. Christian theologians are of course entitled to pass judgment on metaphysics from their own point of view. And as the days are past when philosophy could be brought to heel by ecclesiastical authority (though in some places it is now brought to heel by the authority of the State), theologians who dislike or mistrust metaphysics are understandably pleased if it is subjected to destructive criticism by philosophers themselves. In spite of such criticism, however, the phenomena which give rise to metaphysics are still there. As metaphysics is part of philosophy, it naturally learns from philosophy's self-criticism and may restrict the scope of what it believes that it can achieve. But I doubt whether it will ever commit suicide and disappear.

CHAPTER 7

THE WORLD AND THE ONE

Introductory remarks – the world as the self-transforming One – a linguistic point – the process of understanding and the One – the One as transcendent

I

We can now turn to the question, why people should have thought in terms of the theories of the One which have been discussed in the previous chapters. Belief in the existence of a world of plurality is easily explicable in terms of sense-perception and self-consciousness. It is indeed possible for a sophisticated philosopher to argue that one has no knowledge that anything exists apart from one's own ideas. But, as Hume saw, nobody, not even the sceptic, acts on this assumption in ordinary life. To most people it would not even occur to ask for an explanation of belief in the existence of a pluralistic world. To be sure, G. E. Moore's way of proving the existence of physical objects external to the mind has seemed to some philosophers naive and unconvincing, a case of appealing to common sense when it is precisely the validity of the common sense belief which has been called in question. But the ordinary person would doubtless feel convinced that belief in a plurality of physical things was firmly grounded in sense-perception, and that Moore was simply drawing attention to this fact. Belief in a One, however, is a different matter. If someone expresses doubt about the existence of a One, we cannot dispel the doubt by pointing to the One as an object of sense-perception, in the way in which Moore could point first to one of his hands, then to the other. However the One is conceived, it is not a datum of sense-perception. This was obvious, for example, to the materialists in ancient India. Nor did the author of the *Lao Tzu* claim that the Tao was perceptible by the senses. On the contrary, he denied it. Nor would an Advaitin philosopher claim that Brahman is a possible object of sense-perception. And the same

148

applies to the theist in regard to God. In other words, the question 'what grounds are there for believing in the existence of a One?' is not a superfluous question.

If the One cannot be pointed out as an object of sense-perception, it seems to follow that if the existence of a One can be known at all, it must be known by inference, and that our programme should be that of examining and evaluating arguments for the existence of one ultimate reality. It is true that the early Taoist sages were more inclined to make assertions than to provide arguments for believing in the Tao. But a process of thought doubtless underlay such assertions, and if we wish to discuss it, we can reconstruct it in a tentative manner. It is also true that some philosophers of the One have appealed to suprasensory perception or mystical experience. But we can treat this appeal as an inference, as an argument from the occurrence of certain phenomena to a certain conclusion.

The objection can be raised that concentration on inference, or metaphysical argument, does not do justice to my expressed intention of discussing factors which have contributed to belief in a One. It may be natural for a philosopher to adopt this approach; but it is none the less a narrow approach, and also somewhat unrealistic. In the first place, many people believe in the existence of a One because they have been brought up to do so, not because they have inferred the existence of a One. In the second place, though inference has in fact been a conspicuous feature of metaphysics, it is arguable that argument is a surface phenomenon, a rationalization of some deep-seated need which requires a psychological explanation. In any realistic discussion of belief in the existence of an invisible One due weight should be given to such relevant factors. Exclusive attention to inference expresses an erroneous presupposition, namely that belief in a One is simply the result of inference or argumentation.

It is true that many people have believed in the existence of an invisible One because they were brought up to do so. For example, a person who has been brought up in a devout Muslim family is predisposed by his or her education to believe in Allah, even if such a belief can hardly persist as a living faith, a spring of action, unless it is personally appropriated and rests, in some sense, on religious experience. In any case belief in a One cannot be adequately and exclusively explained in terms of upbringing and education. If we tried to explain the doctrine of the *Lao Tzu* by claiming that the original author derived belief in the nameless One from his parents, and they from their parents and so on, people might think either that we were joking or that we had uncritically accepted the theories of the so-called Traditionalists,[1] who existed in France after the revolution. Obviously, this does not show that upbringing has no relevance when it is a question of explaining the prevalence of belief in an invisible One. It certainly is a relevant factor. But there is no need for the philosopher to dwell on it. He can simply accept it as an historical fact and focus his attention on the arguments offered by metaphysicians to justify the belief in question.

As for psychological explanation, some writers have indeed offered explanations of this kind. For example, Morris Lazerowitz represented the metaphysics of the One as expressing 'an important psychological rejection, caused by the unsatisfactoriness of life itself'.[2] That this way of accounting for the metaphysics of the One should have been proposed is perfectly understandable. Generally speaking at any rate, it presupposes a critical dismissal of metaphysical arguments, coupled however with the conviction that the long and complex metaphysical speculation of East and West cannot be adequately explained simply in terms of logical confusion but that it must have deep-seated roots of a psychological nature. Though, however, we are not entitled to claim that psychological factors are completely irrelevant when it is a question of explaining belief in an invisible One, it does not necessarily follow that philosophers should pursue amateur psychoanalysis. In point of fact the psychological explanations offered by philosophers are apt to take the form of generalizations, the questionability of which becomes apparent when we apply them to particular cases. Consider, for example, the explanation referred to above,

[1]The reference is to thinkers such as the Vicomte de Bonald (1754–1840). See, for example, the present writer's *A History of Philosophy, Vol. IX, Maine de Biran to Sartre*, ch. 1 (London, 1975).

[2]*Philosophy and Illusion*, by Morris Lazerowitz, p. 32 (London and New York, 1968).

namely that the metaphysics of the One is the expression of a rejection of life, this life, as unsatisfactory. Does this apply to Hegel's theory of the Absolute? I do not think so. Hegel is generally thought of, and not without reason, as having endeavoured to justify human life and history as they are. He did not reject the actual as unsatisfactory. He tried to show that it was eminently satisfactory. In any case it is reasonable to claim that the philosopher is well advised to leave psychoanalysis to others and focus his attention instead on the arguments which have actually been stated by metaphysicians and on the lines of thought which can reasonably be regarded as implied by their assertions or theories. It is not a question of denying any relevance at all to psychological factors. It is a question of the cobbler sticking to his last.

At the same time the idea of philosophy as consisting simply in the criticism of other people's arguments is a narrow one. It is also one which I do not accept. Further, if we confined our attention simply to explicit arguments advanced by metaphysicians of the One, we could not do justice to the lines of thought outlined in the earlier chapters of this book. So I shall allow myself a certain latitude in my discussion of factors relevant to belief in a One.

In this chapter I intend to discuss some aspects of the concept of the world of plurality as the appearance of the One. That is to say, I shall be concerned primarily with the world of plurality as object in an epistemological sense. The idea of the self as subject will be treated in the following chapter. As for the cognitive value, if any, of suprasensory perception or mystical experience, this theme will be reserved for Chapter 9. In other words, in the present chapter I shall be concerned primarily with the physical world in which we find ourselves.

II

Let us consider first the idea of the world of plurality as the appearance of a One which is conceived as the self-developing or self-transforming universe, the sort of idea which finds expression in Taoist philosophy. As we have noted, the early Taoist sages were more given to making assertions than to providing arguments. But reflection obviously lay behind their assertions. When Chuang Tzu asserted that terms such as 'great' and 'small', 'noble' and 'ignoble', 'up' and 'down' are relative terms and that in the universe nothing is great or small, noble or ignoble, up or down in an absolute sense, his assertion was clearly the product of reflection, of inference of some sort. Similarly, behind and supporting the Taoist conception of the unity of the universe we can reasonably discern a process of reflection, with its point of departure in ordinary experience. To take a simple example, it is obvious to anyone in an agricultural community that the ripening of crops depends on both sunshine and rain, that the animal kingdom depends on the vegetable kingdom, that human beings depend on all sorts of factors outside themselves, and that they in turn act on and modify their environment. No scientific research is required to become aware of such facts. And the facts can suggest to the reflective mind that all things are interconnected, that Heaven and Earth and Man, to use the ancient Chinese terms, form one complex interrelated whole.

Again, advertence to phenomena such as the regular succession of seasons can suggest the idea of a cosmic harmony, a balance of forces. In pre-Socratic philosophy Heraclitus conceived the world as exemplifying a strife or tension between opposites, a tension which could also be represented as a harmony. Similarly, in early Chinese cosmology the two basic forces, *yin* and *yang*, and the five elements were seen as gaining ascendancy in turn (water, for example, dominating in winter), the total result being a cosmic harmony. Allowance had to be made, of course, for phenomena which seemed to constitute interruptions in this harmony. And the Confucianists were inclined to explain such phenomena in terms of the moral failings of human beings, especially rulers.[3] It is perfectly understandable, however, that early thinkers should draw the conclusion that the universe forms an harmonious whole from phenomena which loomed large in the life of an agricultural community.

[3]Some more hard-headed Confucianists maintained that disasters such as floods and earthquakes had purely natural causes, and that the moral faults of human beings had nothing to do with the matter. As for the Taoists, they did not conceive the Tao as swayed by any moral considerations.

There is a further aspect of the interrelation of things to be considered. We are accustomed to regard a thing as changing in respect of quantity or quality while remaining the same entity. A young tree, for example, grows in size, but we think of it as remaining the same identifiable entity. In other cases, however, one kind of thing seems to be converted into another kind of thing. The tree may be consumed by fire, and the grass eaten by a cow does not remain grass. Such phenomena can suggest to the mind that the things which we see about us are all forms assumed by some original element which undergoes successive transformations. This is not indeed a necessary inference. For it is possible to adopt a theory of atoms such as that expounded by Democritus in ancient Greece or that defended by the Vaiśesika school in India. None the less, the idea that all things came out of some primary element is one which can understandably occur to the mind at a time when inquiries into the nature of the world are based simply on sense-experience and reflection on this experience. It is an idea which we find not only in pre-Socratic philosophy but also in India. Thus there are indications in the Upanishads of there having been speculation about water as the primary element. In the Chāndogya Upanishad[4] sound, breath and food are said to go back to water, while in the Katha Upanishad[5] the universal soul (*ātman*) is said to have been born from water.

Reflection however is likely to suggest that it is more satisfactory to derive things from an indeterminate matrix, capable of assuming determinate forms, than to derive them from an element of one particular determinate kind. Thus in Greek philosophy early attempts to find the ultimate matrix in this or that particular element were succeeded by Aristotle's theory of 'first matter', the purely indeterminate component of all material things, representing what is left, so to speak, if one thinks away all determinate forms. And in early Indian thought we can find indications of an analogous idea. For example, in the passage of the Chāndogya Upanishad to which reference has been made above, water is said to go back to the yonder world, the yonder world to this world, and this world to space. 'All things here

---

[4] 1, 8, 4–5; Hume, p. 185.
[5] 4, 6; Hume, p. 354.

arise out of space, they disappear back into space, for space
alone is greater than these. Space is the final good . . . this is
endless.'[6] This idea doubtless puts one in mind more of Plato's
concept of 'the Receptacle'[7] than of Aristotle's first matter; but
the notion of an indeterminate origin of all things is present.
And this notion is also exemplified in the doctrine of the nameless One in the *Lao Tzu*, the 'mother' of the myriad creatures[8]
and the 'uncarved block'.[9]

The ideas to which we have referred are doubtless of a primitive nature. At the same time they can be reasonably regarded
as the product of reasoning, of inference based on advertence to
phenomena. Taken together, they give us the conception of a
world which is unified in terms not only of the relations between
particular things but also of the derivation of all determinate
entities from an original matrix. To be sure, the indeterminate
matrix has not always been conceived as a dynamic principle.
For example, Aristotle's 'first matter' was conceived as pure
potentiality but not as itself originating activity. When however,
as in Taoism, the ultimate source of determinate entities is
regarded as being itself a dynamic, originating principle, we
have the idea of one self-transforming world. The process may
indeed be conceived as cyclical, as one of production and reabsorption. It was so conceived in Taoism. But this is not an
essential feature of the conception of the self-developing or
self-transforming One, even if it was a prominent feature of
ancient cosmological theories. These theories can therefore be
seen as looking forward to later cosmological speculation, to the
theory, for instance, of a self-diffusing creative energy, perhaps
originating in some 'big bang'. Obviously, we are not entitled
to look on modern cosmological speculation as having said the
final word. My point is that the development of cosmological
speculative theory exemplifies an intellectual process of unification, a unification of the Many in the conception of a cosmos,
a self-transforming One. The data for reflection may have been
at one time primarily the phenomena of ordinary sense-percep-

[6] 1, 8–9; Hume, pp. 185–6.
[7] *Timaeus*, 49f.
[8] *Lao Tzu*, 1, 1, 2.
[9] *Ibid.*, 1, 37, 81.

tion and at another time data revealed by scientific inquiry; but the same sort of basic intellectual process, the process of unification, has been at work.

There are indeed other factors which we can reasonably regard as contributing to the conception of the world as a unity, as a One. For example, there can be a feeling or experience on the part of the human being of unity with nature as a totality, of being a member of a greater whole, a feeling or experience to which we referred when treating of Taoism. Clearly, people who have lived all their lives in a great modern city and have rarely, if ever, been alone in nature, are unlikely to be acquainted with this feeling or experience. But that it exercised a powerful influence on a thinker such as Chuang Tzu can hardly be doubted. It finds expression in his statement (already quoted in the third chapter of this volume) that 'all things and I are one.'[10] There is nothing very odd in the occurrence of such a feeling or experience. We are beings in the world, in nature, and, as far as ordinary observation goes, we return to nature. This situation can form the basis, or provide an occasion for, a vivid awareness of nature as a kind of enveloping presence, an awareness which can both stimulate and reinforce a process of inference or reasoning culminating in the assertion of a self-transforming One.

Given this idea of the world, we can speak of particular things as phenomena or appearances of the One. That is to say, they can be conceived as the forms in which the One appears to a subject. To describe the Many as phenomena or appearances is not, in this context, to imply that they are illusory or unreal. For they are the real forms assumed by the One in its process of self-transformation. It is not a case of contrasting transient phenomena with an unchangeable invisible reality beyond them, Being as opposed to Becoming. For according to the conception of reality which we have in mind the ultimate reality is Becoming, the self-transforming universe, and the Many are the concrete shapes assumed by this process of becoming. The One is immanent in the Many and can therefore be said to appear in them, provided of course that there is a subject to whom it can appear. In fact it is possible to conceive the One, reality as

[10]*Chuang Tzu*, ch. 2.

a whole, as coming to know itself in and through the human mind. We then have the sort of conception of the world proposed by Schelling at one stage of his intellectual odyssey and also by Hegel, if, that is to say, we interpret the Absolute of Hegel as a name for the universe considered as a totality, as the One.

III

If the One is conceived simply as the self-transforming or evolving world, considered as one reality, anyone who is prepared to claim that the world can properly be regarded as one being or substance, can admit that there is a One. It is of course possible to question the propriety of conceiving the world as one being. A person might claim, for example, that to conceive the world in this way is to be misled by language, by our use of the phrase 'the world'. Or someone might maintain that though exhibition of the world as a unity constitutes a goal to which scientific theory aspires, their goal has not yet been reached and, for all we know, never will be. If, however, someone believes that there are sufficient grounds for conceiving the world as one reality, one being, he can obviously admit the existence of a One, provided that the One is conceived as synonymous with the world considered as one being.

This way of putting the matter, it may be objected, is too weak. If the One is conceived as the world considered as one all-inclusive reality and if a person admits that the world can be properly conceived in this way, that person must surely also admit the existence of the One. It is not a question of 'can admit' or of 'may admit' but of what the person is logically committed to saying.

It seems to me that a distinction should be made. It would be possible for the person to speak in this way: 'I recognize that what you call "the One" exists, namely the world. But I am hesitant about using the descriptive phrase "the One", for I think that it is potentially misleading. The phrase "the One" is commonly associated with the idea of an ultimate reality, whether conceived as personal or suprapersonal, which is not identifiable with the world of plurality as such. Even in the philosophy of F. H. Bradley the Many are conceived as transformed in the One, as no longer the Many of our experience. Further, the idea of the One has been commonly associated with some religious attitude, as, for example, in the Advaita Vedānta or in the Sufi-inspired thought of Persia or in the philosophy of Plotinus; and I do not think the physical world is a proper object of religious devotion, not at any rate if the world is conceived simply as the totality of interrelated physical things. In some philosophies the One has been equated with the self-developing universe, and this idea has been associated with mysticism of some kind. But I suspect that the association with mysticism can be maintained only if the universe is tacitly conceived as something more than the world of physical science. While, therefore, I am prepared to admit that what you call the One exists, provided that you are referring simply to the world as the object of scientific inquiry, I am reluctant to use the phrase "the One", because of its associations. I prefer simply to say that I admit that the Many are, or may be, so interrelated that they form one complex whole. You can say, if you like, that I recognize the existence of the One. In a sense this is true. At the same time I think that the statement is potentially misleading and should be avoided. Or one might say that I am prepared to admit the existence of a One, provided that the One is conceived simply as the world considered as the object of scientific inquiry. As far as I am concerned, this is the only One which exists. If anyone believes that there is a One which is not identifiable with the world of science, it is up to him or her to give reasons why I should share this belief.'

The retort might be made that the reluctance to use the phrase 'the One' which I have ascribed to an imagined person is superfluous. If someone recognizes the existence only of a plurality of things, distinct from one another, he obviously ought not to say that he believes in the existence of the One. If he did say this, his statement would be not so much misleading as false. If, however, he conceives the Many as so interrelated as to be members of one ultimate reality, the world or universe, there is no reason why he should not say that he believes in the existence of the One. It is true that the phrase 'the One' is potentially misleading in the sense that, taken by itself, it gives no indication of the nature of the One. But the person could always explain that he believes in the existence of 'a One', that the One the existence of which he recognizes is the world or cosmos, that this is the only One in which he believes, and that he therefore refers to it as 'the One'. This is a clear enough explanation of his position.

However this may be, we have considered some factors or grounds for believing in the existence of a One conceived as the self-developing world or universe. And we have noted that if the Many are described as appearances of the One as so conceived, this description does not imply that the members of the class of the Many are unreal or illusory. They may be transient, at any rate in comparison with the One itself; but this does not make them unreal, as long as they exist. As has already been re-marked, a dog is not unreal because it is born and dies. Let us consider, therefore, some lines of thought contributing to belief in a One which is not identifiable with the empirical world of plurality. It is true that by postponing consideration of the self as subject and of mystical experience to later chapters I have limited the area of discussion, so far as the present chapter is concerned. That is to say, I shall have to confine my attention as much as possible to the physical world. But some metaphy-sicians have in fact approached the idea of the one ultimate reality in this way. To see this one has only to recall, for ex-ample, the Five Ways of St Thomas Aquinas, which take as their point of departure various features of the world about us.

IV

Reference to the Five Ways of St Thomas Aquinas should not be understood as implying that I intend to recount and discuss these particular arguments, or indeed any particular arguments for the existence of a transcendent One which have been offered by past philosophers. What I wish to do is to outline a movement of the mind which seems to me to underlie at any rate a number of such arguments. Sometimes, of course, arguments for the existence of God have been clearly apologetic in nature; that is to say, they have been intended to support a pre-existing reli-gious belief. We can find arguments of this kind in Jewish, Christian and Muslim thought. If, however, we prescind from this aspect of the matter or extend our field of reflection to include the metaphysics of the One as a whole, including, for example, the philosophies of Plotinus and Bradley, it is reasonable to see in the arguments the expression of a basic movement of the mind towards a One, the Absolute, a movement which implies what Bradley regarded as an initial faith that there is a One to seek for. To put the matter in another way, it seems to me that the metaphysician of the One is not going to be satisfied with anything less than one final explanation of the existence of the Many, and that this presupposes that there is a One to be found. It may be said that if the metaphysician makes any presupposition at all it is not that there is a One but that being is intelligible. My point is, however, that for the metaphysician the existence of the Many is intelligible or shown to be intelligible when it is related to one ultimate source or origin. Different metaphysicians have taken different particular points of departure and have developed different explicit arguments; but in these arguments we may detect a common basic movement of the mind towards a One. And it is about this movement of the mind that I wish to make some remarks. Obviously, what I say will be of a tentative, exploratory nature. But there does appear to be a movement of the mind which survives, so to speak, criticism of particular arguments and reasserts itself in other ways. It is a case of trying to discern a basic movement in the thought itself rather than of trying to delve into psychological factors other than thought.

Partly, I suppose, in opposition to any claim that the existence of things external to the mind is subject to genuine doubt and stands in need of proof, some writers have insisted that from the start we find ourselves in a world. That is to say, when we become conscious of ourselves, we become conscious of ourselves as present in a world, not as self-enclosed entities outside of which there may or may not be other realities. Through self-awareness we distantiate ourselves from other persons and things, but as within a common environment, within what Joseph Conrad calls 'the visible and tangible world of which we are a self-conscious part'.[11]

---

[11]In the prefatory note to his story *The Shadow Line*.

It is obviously true that we do not find ourselves without any world, existing apart from any environment. But it is also true that our concept of the world is not something which is there ready-made from the beginning. It is progressively developed. And getting to know the world, to form an articulate idea of it, involves a process of mental discrimination, not simply in the sense of distinguishing oneself from one's environment but also in the sense of distinguishing between the variety of objects and persons in the environment. The world takes shape for us largely through a process of distinction, of identifying distinct objects and persons in what we might describe as a general field. Obviously, the content of what we think of as the world in which we are is far from being equally luminous to us. Our world extends from the sphere of what is distinctly known through the sphere of what is known only in a global way to the obscure sphere of the unknown, though knowable in principle. The limits of these spheres are of course subject to change. Our knowledge of the world can be extended in a variety of ways, not only through personal experience, personal acquaintance with people and things and institutions but also of course through history and the sciences. And this extension of knowledge involves a process of discrimination, of making the Many stand out, as it were, from a vague background. What we come to know is a pluralistic world.

This process of discrimination is required for life. In other words, it certainly has a pragmatic or vital function. We could not live if we made no discrimination between things. For example, success in keeping ourselves alive depends on our ability to discern what will sustain life and what will not. Though, however, the discriminating intelligence is a biologically useful instrument, it does not follow that all the distinctions which we make are purely subjective, that they are all imposed on what is itself without distinction. To be sure, we can make what the scholastics called purely mental distinctions. But the claim that all distinctions are of this kind is implausible. Two animals, for example, function as distinct organisms, and it would not be plausible if one claimed that the distinction lacked what the scholastics called a foundation in fact. Your dog is not my dog, no more than you are I. Our world is a world of real plurality, not one of a merely imagined or projected plurality. Things are not indeed isolated entities, unrelated to one another. But the terms of the relations are distinguishable.

It may seem that I am intent on defending the point of view of naive realism, and that I assume that things are just what they appear to be on the level of ordinary experience. The validity of this assumption, it may be objected, is refuted by modern science, which presents us with a very different world, a world in which the apparent substantiality of what we ordinarily take to be distinct things dissolves before the eyes of the mind. It is indeed true that science does not simply do away with our ordinary view of the world. This ordinary view has an obvious pragmatic value, and we cannot do without it. Not even an Einstein can dispense with the common sense conception of the world. For a great part of his life man acts, and must act, on the assumption that this conception conforms with reality or at any rate as though it conformed with reality. As a philosopher might put it, we require two languages, the language based on ordinary experience and the language of science. They should not be confused. One should not try to use both at the same time. But neither represents the absolute and final truth. Which we adopt and use depends on our interests and purposes. Each has pragmatic value. We can also say that each has cognitive value. But the cognitive value is closely linked to the pragmatic value, to human needs, interests, purposes.

Obviously, it is not my intention to deny that science presents us with a rather different view of the world from that of pre-scientific experience. Nor have I any intention of denying that there is room for different points of view, different language-games. A sunset may mean one thing to the artist, Turner for instance, something else to the farmer, and something else again to the atomic physicist. It might conceivably have these three meanings successively for the same individual. The point, however – one which has already been made – is that modern science does not refute the conviction that there is a pluralistic world. I would not myself care to say that a table is a whirling mass of sub-atomic particles and not a solid object. For in many contexts the table can perfectly well be described as a solid object, in comparison with water or air for example. In any case, if we do say that the table is not a solid object but a mass of moving sub-atomic particles, we are not thereby denying plurality. If the world of ordinary experience is a pluralistic world, so is the world of science. Science exemplifies the analytic, discriminatory movement of the mind, which pertains to an understanding of reality.

As I have laid, and continue to lay, emphasis on the mind's movement of unification, it is essential that I should not lose sight of the complementary analytic, discriminatory function of the mind. Let me take an example from ordinary life. If one is invited to a party and enters a room full of fellow guests whom one does not know, it would be absurd to claim that one sets about trying to unify them, to perform a work of unification. On the contrary, one tries to discriminate. If one's host or hosts fail to make any introductions, one has to try to make the acquaintance of individuals as individuals. One's interest is what can be described as discriminatory. In science too analysis, discrimination, is a conspicuous feature of the process of understanding. Also of course in philosophy. If, for example, we are considering religious language, we want to obtain a clear view of the different functions of terms in such language. We do not seek to confuse them, to conflate them, but rather to analyze, to discriminate. People have sometimes poked fun at the medieval philosophers for their subtle distinctions. But, basically, they were simply pursuing a proper concern of the philosopher.

Emphasis on analysis, however, should not blind us to the complementary role of synthesis, to the role of unification in the process of understanding. Conceptual mastery over a plurality involves unification. This can be seen by reflection on ordinary language with its abundance of class-names. The process is also exemplified in science, in its attempt to coordinate phenomena under what we call 'laws' and in the way in which more particular laws and theories are subsumed under more general laws and theories. Indeed, the process of unification is especially conspicuous in science, inasmuch as the scientist is concerned with the universal rather than with the particular, with, say, atomic structure as such rather than with individual atoms, with the characteristics of a kind or type of living thing rather than with the particular members of the class as such. Unification is also a conspicuous feature of metaphysics. It can be seen in the attempt to identify the most general characteristics of things as beings. And it can obviously be seen in the metaphysics of the One. This movement of unification is part of the process of understanding, of obtaining conceptual mastery over a plurality. In the metaphysics of the One it is a question of understanding, of making intelligible the existence of the Many.

This line of thought is, of course, open to serious objections. For example, it is possible to argue that instead of speaking of the philosopher as trying to identify the most general characteristics of things as beings I ought to speak of him as trying to exhibit the basic and most general concepts by means of which we conceive things, concepts which find concrete exemplification in language. In other words, I have no adequate justification for assuming that the categories in terms of which we conceive the world are categories of things. They may be simply categories of our thought, categories which we impose on the world about us, not arbitrarily or capriciously but because of their instrumentalist or pragmatic value. Nietzsche may well have been right when he proposed a view of this sort. The categories may help us to deal with our environment, to act successfully in the interchange between human beings and their environment. But it by no means follows that they are 'the categories' of things, objective categories, as Aristotle supposed and presumably Whitehead too. Again, it is all very well to say that in the metaphysics of the One it is a question of understanding or making intelligible the existence of the Many. It first has to be shown that the existence of the Many requires explanation. If we consider any individual thing, such as a cow, its existence is generally susceptible of a perfectly adequate empirical explanation. When no such explanation seems to be forthcoming, we do not abandon the search for one. And even if we are prepared to accept the claim that there is no empirical explanation, is recourse to the One of any real help? Obviously, the metaphysician can say that he is concerned not with giving empirical explanations of the existence of particular things but with explaining the existence of the Many as such, the whole class. But how do we know that there is an explanation? If the existence of every member of the Many can in principle be explained without reference to a One, we have all that we require. The class of the Many is not an additional thing, the existence of which requires an additional explanation over and above the explanations which can be given of the members of the class. The metaphysician of the One seems to presuppose the existence of a One, that there must be a One. And this presupposition is gratuitous, at any rate from the philosophical point of view.

In regard to the first line of objection, it seems to me that any claim that the categories by which we think of the world are purely subjective is exaggerated. If the claim were true, I do not see that we would have any means of ascertaining that it was true. For, *ex hypothesi*, we could not compare our conception of the world with the world in itself. This point apart, we have indeed to allow for the formation of our categories by a process of trial and error over the centuries or, rather, over the millenia. At least this is what we have to do, if we are not prepared to accept a Kantian view of the matter. We also have to allow for the possibility of seeing things in different ways. At the same time in the process of trial and error, in the course of experience, certain categories or concepts are found to be required for life, in the dialectic between man and his environment and between human beings. This statement may indeed appear to lend support to the view that our categories have a purely pragmatic value. But this is not necessarily the case. For what proves to be required for life, to be indispensable in the development of society and of knowledge, may well be required because it corresponds with the actual state of affairs. Indeed, this is more probable than the opposite. That the concept of a person, for example, is a purely subjective imposition is not a view which I am prepared to accept. Again, that there is no such thing as an objective relation, in the sense that no thing is objectively related to any other thing, is a view which it is difficult to endorse. To be sure, Chuang Tzu was perfectly justified in pointing out the relative character of terms such as 'far' and 'near'. In a story by a Russian writer an old lady living in a remote hamlet or village in the country likes to relate how once she embarked on an expedition to a village about, say, fifteen miles away and marvelled at the greatness of God's world. For her this village was far off. To others, in different circumstances, with more experience or knowledge, it would be very near, in comparison, for instance, with Paris or New York, about which the old lady knew nothing. But that I am my father's son and not he mine seems to be objectively true, and not a situation which can be changed simply by altering the meanings of words. I am not trying to canonize one particular list of categories, Aristotle's for example. But I am not prepared to accept the contention that a categorical scheme is necessarily nothing but a subjective imposition, lacking any objective foundation.

As for the second objection, in a sense it makes my point for me. That is to say, the objection is that the metaphysician of the One presupposes that there must be a One; and I have already stated that in my opinion the metaphysician does make a presupposition. But what I had in mind was not an arbitrary or gratuitous presupposition. Suppose that someone claims that the belief that the world is intelligible is a presupposition or an assumption, an assumption involved in the attempt to understand the world. I am not altogether happy about this claim, as it seems to me that we first understand this or that, and that if there is a presupposition, it has a foundation in our actual knowledge. However, let us take it that the attempt to understand the world involves the assumption, at least as a working hypothesis, that the world is intelligible. This assumption is progressively confirmed by increase in scientific knowledge, which involves, besides analysis, a movement of unification in terms of laws and scientific theory. It is indeed possible to arrest the movement at this level and go no further. If, however, the mind does proceed further, onto the metaphysical level that is to say, the movement of unification then takes the form of a movement towards the One as the source of the Many. If we prescind from the interests of religious apologetics, I doubt whether anyone would proceed to this level of metaphysical reflection, unless he experienced the sort of wonder at the existence of the Many which even Wittgenstein admitted to having experienced and which finds expression in the statement by Martin Heidegger that the fundamental question of metaphysics is 'Why is there something rather than nothing?'[12] Given, how-

[12]*Was ist Metaphysik*, p. 38 (Frankfurt a.M., 1949). The question, as it stands, is ambiguous. The significance of 'why?' is not clear.

ever, this stimulative impulse, the process of understanding, of making intelligible the existence of the Many, involves the movement of the mind towards the One. On the existential level the process of unification, of synthesis, culminates in the idea of the One as a reality, as the real source of the Many. To set out on this path is to give expression to what Bradley described as an assumption or initial faith, but this is inseparable from the movement of unification, the process of understanding in the relevant context. It is for this reason that the metaphysician will not be satisfied with anything short of the One. It may be said that further questions can be asked about the source of the One, and that there is no good reason for stopping at this point. But where else would we expect a process of unification or synthesis to stop except at the One?

This is a pretty flimsy basis, someone may say, for belief in the One. It seems to be equivalent to an admission that the metaphysics of the One provides no solid knowledge. It may well be true that a process of synthesis or unification, in the relevant context, culminates in the idea of a One of some kind. But the statement that this is the case amounts to a tautology. What is being said is in effect that if one embarks on the metaphysics of the One and persists in it, one will end by asserting the existence of the One. Though this is doubtless correct, it in no way proves that there is a One.

It seems to me, however, that something more than this is being said, which is that the process of understanding involves synthesis or unification, as well as analysis, and that this process of understanding, when pursued on the metaphysical level, leads to the idea of the One. Nobody can be compelled to embark on metaphysics. But if one does embark on it and persists, one will arrive at a certain point. This is, I think, the movement of the mind which lies at the basis of proofs of the existence of a One conceived in a determinate manner, a One of this or that kind. To be sure, what I have been saying may seem to be excessively intellectualist, in the sense that emphasis has been placed simply on the process of understanding. As however has already been noted, treatment of phenomena such as mystical experience has been postponed to a later chapter. We are concerned here simply with a movement of thought discernible in those arguments which take as their point of departure the world about us, the world of plurality. Further, we are concerned not with discussing particular proofs but with discerning a general line of thought which is exemplified in them. Reflection on the proofs suggests that there is a presupposition. My contention is that the presupposition belongs to the nature of understanding, that though the movement of the mind in obtaining conceptual mastery over the Many can be arrested, it is none the less a movement towards the One.

V

Even if what I have been saying is allowed to be basically true, why should not the One be conceived as the world itself, the world considered as one reality? Provided that we allow for the role of analysis in understanding, there is nothing unreasonable in claiming that understanding a plurality, obtaining conceptual mastery over it, involves a process of unification. But if it is a question of the Many in general, the natural movement of unification surely terminates in the idea of the world or cosmos. We do not need to go any further. We can find our One in what Joseph Conrad called 'the visible and tangible world of which we are a self-conscious part'. The idea of a transcendent One is not required.

It seems to me true that the world is, so to speak, the first candidate for the status of the One. We do indeed tend to unify the Many in the global concept of 'the world'. Further, I doubt whether our tendency to conceive the world as a unity can be ascribed simply and solely to the influence of language, to our being bewitched by use of the term 'the world'. We have the term or phrase because we need it, because we need to have a way of referring to the totality of interrelated phenomena.

At the same time when we reflect on the concept of the world, it tends to break up into a multiplicity. Consider for a moment, the concept of the nation. We naturally tend to think of the nation as a one, as a real whole, to which we belong. But is the nation something apart from individuals, past, present and future? It is true that any adequate account of a nation-state would involve mention of certain relations, the relevant relations

between the individuals which compose the nation. But is it in
actual fact anything more than individuals related in certain
ways? I recognize of course that there is a strong tendency to
think that there is. If we talk about sacrificing oneself for the
nation, we tend to conceive the nation as an entity greater than
the sum of the individuals which compose it. And it seems to be
true that we mean by the nation something more than the
individuals which compose it here and now. Thus we can talk
about making sacrifices for the future of the nation. We tend to
conceive it as an entity having a past, a present, and a future.
But when we reflect on the matter in a hard-headed way, can
we really find any unity beyond the members of the nation, past,
present and future, considered as related in various ways? Analogously, though there is a strong tendency to conceive the world
as a One which is more than the sum of its interrelated members,
there can be a counterbalancing tendency to analyze the concept
of the world into that of its members as related in a variety of
ways. If the first tendency found expression in the Taoist conception of the One as the mother of heaven and earth and the
myriad creatures, the second tendency found expression in Kuo
Hsiang's interpretation of the One as a collective name for the
Many.

The matter can be put in this way. In the previous section of
this chapter reference was made to the discriminatory or analytic
activity of the mind, through which an articulate picture of the
pluralistic world is built up. We then went on to consider the
synthesizing activity of the mind, the movement of unification.
If the first activity gains the upper hand, so to speak, triumphing
over the second and asserting plurality at the expense of unity,
the concept of the One, if it is admitted at all, will be regarded
as a collective idea of the Many. In this case there is no ground
for describing the Many as appearances of the One. If the
second activity gains the upper hand completely and the One
is conceived as being alone 'really real', the Many will be regarded as 'mere appearances' of the One, as being illusory or,
at best, semi-real. Their existence can hardly be denied altogether. They certainly appear to a subject. But from a higher
point of view they will be regarded as analogous to dream-
images. If however neither side wins a complete victory but the

tension between the two tendencies is resolved in a synthesis, the mind postulates a One which is non-identifiable with the pluralistic world of our experience. In this case the Many will be regarded as appearances of the One only in the sense in which the effect manifests the cause. We are probably unwilling to say, as some philosophers used to say, that any effect is like its cause. For though this statement may be true in regard to generation within a living species there are obviously cases in which it is highly implausible. A Ford car does not resemble the people who made it. And if I roll a cigarette, it is not a photograph of myself. So in this context the use of the word 'appearance' may well seem inappropriate. However, effects do manifest something in their causes, even if it is only productive power. And the Psalmist speaks of the heaven as showing forth or manifesting the glory of God.

What I have in mind therefore is a dialectic between the analytic and synthesizing activities of the human mind. If we conceive the mind, in its effort to obtain conceptual mastery over the Many, as seeking to unify them in the concept of the One, the first move is naturally to identify the One with the world considered as a totality, as one reality, the Many being its (real) appearances, provided that there is a subject to whom they can appear. The analytic mind however does not find the One and tends to reduce the world to the interrelated Many. If the mind does not stop there and abandon the concept of the One or interpret it as a collective name for the Many, it is driven, in its movement of unification, to locate the One beyond the world, not in a spatial sense but in the sense that the One is conceived as non-identifiable with the collection of the Many, with the class.

Though I think that some such line of thought underlies some of the arguments for the existence of a transcendent One, arguments, that is to say, which take as their point of departure the visible and tangible world about us, I must confess that there are aspects of it which seem to me problematic. I mention two of them. In the first place I am not altogether happy with a reductive analysis of the concept of the world. On the one hand it seems to be defensible. The *Lao Tzu* represents the Many as proceeding from a One which 'stands alone and does not change.'[13] Where in the world is such a reality to be found? If there is such a reality, must it not be conceived as transcending the pluralistic world? On the other hand, is not the world in some sense a unity, a One? At any rate is it not arguable that science progressively tends to show that it is? In the second place, it can be objected against the concept of a transcendent One, distinct from the Many, that the One then becomes a being among others, a member of the class of the Many and so not deserving the title of 'the One'. As far as I can see, the only way of coping with this sort of difficulty is by means of a theory of the analogy of being. Though however a theory of this kind seems to me to be an indispensable instrument for the theistic metaphysician, it is hardly a magic wand, one wave of which is sufficient to eliminate all problems.

However this may be, at the close of Plato's *Parmenides* agreement is expressed that if the One is not, then nothing is.[14] This, I am inclined to think, is a conviction which tends to govern the thought of the metaphysician of the One. In a sense this is what he presupposes, not necessarily in the sense that he explicitly presupposes it, but in the sense that, as Bradley saw, the One is what he is looking for. I have associated this presupposition or initial faith with the nature of understanding, in so far, that is to say, as understanding a plurality, obtaining conceptual mastery over it, involves a movement of synthesis, of unification. In other words, I have tried to justify the presupposition by appealing to the mind's reflection on its own activity, on the dynamism of its own movement.

In this chapter we have confined our attention to one particular line of thought. It can of course be objected that even if this line of thought is exemplified in some of the arguments which have been advanced in support of belief in a One which is non-identifiable with the visible and tangible world in which we are situated, there are other factors which have influenced philosophers of the One and which I have not mentioned. This is quite true. Little, for example, has been said about the self, the concept of which plays a prominent role in some versions of the metaphysics of the One, notably so in the Vedānta philo-

[13]*Lao Tzu*, 1, 25, 56.
[14]*Parmenides*, 165–166.

sophy, whether in the Advaita Vedānta or in other Vedānta schools or sub-schools. But in the next chapter I intend to discuss this theme. The self can of course be considered part of the world which we have been considering, a self-conscious part, as Conrad put it. The thought however of the self as subject has sometimes occupied a prominent position in the metaphysics of the One, and it calls for explicit treatment.

CHAPTER 8

THE SELF AND THE ONE

The self as in the world – the self as subject and as agent – the pure subject and the One – the unity underlying subject and object – the metaphysics of the One as revealing a capacity in the human being – the self and monism

I

In the last chapter Joseph Conrad's reference to 'the visible and tangible world of which we are a self-conscious part' was quoted. Conrad was not of course a professional philosopher, and it would be both pedantic and unfair to take his words literally and object, for example, that not everything in the human being is visible and tangible. In regard however to the statement that human beings constitute part of the world, a self-conscious part, this would seem to most people to be obviously true. We are inside the world, not outside it.

We cannot indeed think and speak about the world without objectifying it, without making it an object of thought and something about which we speak. In doing so, it might be argued, we distantiate ourselves from the world, as subjects, hold it over against ourselves and thus place ourselves outside it. I and the world are correlative, and the former cannot be part of the latter.

It seems to me that if this line of argument were accepted, we would be committed to some odd claims. It would appear to follow, for example, that if I can think and speak about the nation, the nation of which I am a member, I cannot in fact be a member of the nation in question but must stand outside it. If this conclusion is absurd, why should it not also be absurd to claim that because we can think and speak of the world we are therefore outside the world and not part of it? If I can think of the nation as including myself as a member, why cannot I think of the world as including me within itself? In point of fact we do think in this way. We think of the world as from within the world; we think of the world as including us, not as excluding us. We can of course abstract from the presence of human beings in the world and consider, for example, simply the system or systems of heavenly bodies. For the matter of that, I can abstract from my membership of a particular nation and think and speak globally about the other members. I can find fault with the nation for this or that reason, while exempting myself, justly or unjustly, from the condemnation. But the mere fact that I can objectify the nation, turning it into an object of thought and speech, does not show that I do not belong to it. Nor does the fact that we can objectify the world by thinking and speaking of it show that we are not in the world.

The conception of ourselves as in the world, as conscious members or parts of the world, can form the basis for the sort of philosophy which we find in one phase of Schelling's thought. If, that is to say, we assume an evolutionary view of the world, we can see the world as becoming conscious of itself in and through the mind of man. Obviously, I do not mean to imply that we think of the world as a totality as thinking and speaking. What I mean is that we can see human beings as immanent products of the evolving world, and that inasmuch as human beings are members of the world, we can conceive the human being's knowledge of the world as being in a sense the world's knowledge of itself, as the world attaining self-consciousness in and through its own production.

If this point of view seems to anyone to smack of superfluous mystification, he or she can leave it alone. I am concerned not so much with recommending it as with making the point that the idea of human beings being in and part of the world can be used in support of the conception of the world as the ultimate reality which comes to know itself in and through the mind of man. As I have already indicated, I think that this sort of view can be found not only in the objective idealism of Schelling but also in the philosophy of Hegel, unless indeed more weight is given to his use of theological language than I am inclined to give it. It is also a conception of the world which can perhaps be regarded as being, in some respects at least, an up-dated or modern version of Taoist philosophy.

II

The foregoing summary account of the human being's relationship to the world is open to challenge, not indeed on the ground that it is completely false but on the ground that it is only partially true and that an important relevant factor has been passed over in silence. It is of course true that we think of ourselves as being in the world, and this idea is justified up to a point. When I think of myself, objectify myself, what I objectify, myself as object, is indeed in the world. At the same time it is I, as subject, who objectify the world and myself as in the world, and where in the world is this subject to be found? Is it not arguable that while the empirical self, the self as object of self-consciousness and of thought, is in the world, the self as subject, the self as objectifying but not as objectified, is not in the world? In a well known passage of his *Tractatus*, Wittgenstein asks, 'where in the world is a metaphysical subject to be noted?'[1], and his answer is that 'the subject does not belong to the world but it is a limit of the world'.[2] If, he says, one were to write a book entitled *What I Found in the World* and listed the objects which one had found, the pure subject could not be mentioned. For it is not found in the world. It is the subject of the finding. And this subject is unobjectifiable. This is a fact which the German philosopher J. G. Fichte illustrated by inviting his students first to think the wall and then to think him who thought the wall. Obviously, however far back we go in the endeavour to turn the self into an object, there is always an I-subject which eludes objectification. This is what Indian Vedic philosophers called 'the witness'; and it is not in the world but, as Wittgenstein puts it, the limit of the world, correlative to the world, my world, but not a member of it. To be sure, if we assume that nothing exists which is not in the world, we have to say that the pure subject does not exist, that there is no pure subject. But this does not effectively eliminate the subject. For it is presupposed even by the statement that there is no subject to be found.

It is important to understand that acceptance of this view

[1] *Tractatus Logico-Philosophicus*, 5, 633.
[2] *Ibid.*, 5, 632.

does not necessarily imply that there is no sense in which it is true to say that the self, the human being, is in the world. The Buddhist thinkers found no permanent abiding self, no *ātman*, and analyzed the self into successive states (momentary states according to one Buddhist theory) which were causally linked. The states were regarded as psychical, not physical (the Buddhists were not materialists), but the self, as so conceived, was none the less in the phenomenal world. David Hume later defended a similar phenomenalistic analysis of the self, though the antecedents and context of his thought were obviously different from that of Buddhism. This phenomenalistic view was adopted by the associationist philosophers such as Alexander Bain; and Bain's theory provoked F. H. Bradley's remark, 'Mr Bain collects that the mind is a collection. Has he ever asked himself who collects Mr Bain?'[3] In asking this question Bradley was not simply joking. He was making a serious point and reminding his readers that Bain had forgotten the subject. But Bradley was not denying that there is any sense at all in which we can talk about successive mental states. And the succession of states certainly belongs to the world. In other words, the empirical self, the self of the Buddhists, of Hume and of Bain, belongs to the world. But the I-subject, which objectifies the empirical self, does not belong to the world.

Much the same can be said in regard to Śaṁkara, the famous Advaita philosopher. Śaṁkara did not accept the Buddhist phenomenalistic analysis of the self as consisting of nothing but a succession of momentary, psychical states. But he did not deny that there is a succession of states. And he regarded them as belonging to the phenomenal world. The empirical self, the self as objectifiable, belonged to the phenomenal world, but the self as pure subject, *ātman*, did not. It was thus a question not of denying that there is any sense in which the self is a member of the phenomenal world but of asserting that there is more to the self than as objectifiable, and that this something more, the subject, transcends the phenomenal world.

What I wish to do is to reflect on the relevance, if any, of this theory of the I-subject to the metaphysics of the One. But I

[3]*Ethical Studies*, p. 39, note 1 (London, 1927).

want first to make some comments about the theory considered in itself. In particular, there is a distinction which should be borne in mind when considering the ways in which metaphysicians have used the theory.

On the one hand, a purely phenomenalistic analysis of the self in terms of a succession of states which can be seen, as Hume put it, by looking into the mind, by introspection, seems to me unacceptable. If the validity of this analysis is assumed, it becomes very difficult, as Kant saw, to account for the unity of consciousness, the synthesis of a plurality of states as 'my' states. Bradley's question to Alexander Bain cannot be simply dismissed as irrelevant or beside the mark or foolish. Further, though the idea of distinct mental states, cut off from one another by a hatchet, is open to the sort of criticism which Henri Bergson levelled against the associationist psychologists, experience shows that in some sense I can be aware of mental states, of myself as successively affected by different attitudes for example; and it is obvious that it is I who objectify myself in this way. In other words, I do not think that the idea of the I-subject, as contrasted with the me-object, can be simply eliminated, even if ingenious attempts have been made to do so. Gilbert Ryle tried to dispose of the line of thought expressed by Fichte by making some amusing remarks about a reviewer whose review of a book is reviewed by another reviewer, and so on indefinitely.[4] This seems to me to be a different sort of case. Another person can objectify me, turning me into an object of thought. This person can be objectified by a third person. And so on indefinitely. But in self-consciousness there is a distinction between subject and object such that the subject, as subject, is, so to speak, a terminal point. It is the structure of self-consciousness which is in question. And the phenomenologists, such as Edmund Husserl, seem to me quite justified in emphasizing the subject-object relation, as far as the phenomenology of consciousness is concerned.

On the other hand, when Kant refused to turn the idea of the pure subject into a 'constitutive' idea, he was drawing attention to an important point. The fact that in self-consciousness the

[4]*The Concept of Mind*, p. 196 (London, 1949).

self functions as subject does not prove that there is in the human being a distinct entity, hidden away inside, which can be identified as the real self, the self as object being relegated to the sphere of mere appearance. To be sure, the self as object is appearance in the sense that it is the self as appearing to a subject. But to say this is to say that the self appears to itself. In other words, the distinction between I-subject and the me-object lies within the self, in so far as the self is self-conscious or aware of itself. The distinction arises in self-consciousness. In point of fact I am inclined to talk about the person rather than about the self, and to claim that the I-subject is a function of the human person in consciousness, the human person being the one living, sensing, feeling, imagining, desiring, thinking and willing organic being. When the person is conscious, he or she functions as subject. As for the object, it is the self in self-consciousness; otherwise it is something other than the self, another person or a thing for example.

It is probably a determination to find a permanent self which lies behind the hypostatization of the I-subject as a distinct entity, hidden away inside and identifiable with the real or inner self. This is understandable. For if we postulate a succession of distinct momentary mental states, as in the Buddhist theory of momentariness, the self seems to dissolve into a multiplicity of entities, and it is then natural to turn to something like the Hindu theory of *ātman* as a needed complement.[5] At the same time the identification of the I-subject with the real self is hardly satisfactory. Is the I-subject to be conceived as an entity which is not always functioning as subject but only sometimes? Or is it to be conceived as being always subject? In the first case we have indeed a permanent entity, but it is not always the I-subject, and it is something very different from what we ordinarily have in mind when we talk about 'myself', 'himself', 'herself', 'ourselves'. In the second case we seem to be committed to the claim that the self is always conscious, even when it appears not to be, as in so-called dreamless sleep. Whether there is or is not such a thing as dreamless sleep is not a question

[5]Historically, the *ātman* theory preceded the Buddhist phenomenalistic analysis of the self. But the latter was in turn criticized by adherents of the former.

which the philosopher as such is properly qualified to answer. But let us suppose that there is dreamless sleep. If we maintain that the real self is a permanent entity which is always functioning as subject, we must claim that there is consciousness even in dreamless sleep. Śaṁkara, if I understand him correctly, maintained that this is the case, on the ground that we can remember having enjoyed dreamless sleep, and that we could not have this recollection if we had been totally devoid of consciousness. But this does not seem to me a convincing argument. For one might very well claim that it is a question not of our remembering the experience of dreamless sleep but of our not remembering any dreams, which is a different matter.

What we are confronted with in the first instance is obviously the human being, the human person. The human being is an agent. And it would not occur to us to conceive the human being as acting anywhere else than in this world. If we think of man, as Marx did, primarily as standing in a dialectical relationship to nature, his physical environment, we conceive him as a being in the phenomenal or empirical world. The human being's actions however can be seen as the fruit of thoughts, intentions, desires, which start, as it were, within and then express themselves outwardly, overt action being the prolongation, as Josiah Royce put it, of an idea. It is therefore understandable if we look for the essential self within, through introspection. If we find there only successive states, we may conclude that the self is nothing but this series of transient states. Reflection suggests however that this is an unsatisfactory analysis of the self. As has already been remarked, it is then difficult to account for the unity of consciousness, to which Kant drew attention. The idea may then occur to us that introspection, looking into the mind, is impossible without the I-subject. For it is I who look into my own mind. We may therefore be tempted to identify the real self, the permanent self, for which we are looking with the I-subject or transcendental ego. But this theory too is unsatisfactory in a number of ways. If the phenomenalistic analysis of the self seems to dissolve the self into a multiplicity of distinct states, so that unity is lost, identification of the real self with the I-subject also seems to imply a bifurcation of the self. Most of what we ordinarily think of as the self will be conceived as the empirical self, belonging to the phenomenal world, while the real self, as pure subject, will be conceived as the limit of my world, as being in some sense outside the world. The self is then reduced to what Bradley, in spite of his criticism of Bain, described as a miserable metaphysical point, a 'poor atom'.[6] Further, it is difficult to avoid solipsism. I do not mean to imply that even the resolute adherent of the theory which identifies the real self with the I-subject or transcendental ego is likely to defend solipsism seriously. This is most unlikely. What I mean is that it is difficult for the adherent of this theory to explain how he can succeed in avoiding solipsism. For example, you are all objects for me as subject, just as I am an object for each of you as subject. That is to say, you all belong to 'my world', and I, as subject, am the solitary being which stands outside this world.

Both theories therefore are unsatisfactory. At the same time both make points which should be borne in mind. It may therefore seem that what we require is a synthesis, not indeed in the sense of a conflation but in the sense of a theory which would do justice to the truth in the rival positions while avoiding the one-sidedness and errors of each. In any such attempt at synthesis however it should be remembered that the human being is not simply a spectator, a subject in an epistemological sense, but also an agent. In the agent we can see both continuity and change exemplified, continuity throughout change. If we seek for a permanent self in the sense of a changeless entity concealed under changing transient states, we shall probably end up with the idea of what Bradley called a metaphysical point. If we pay more attention to the human being as agent, as acting in the world, we may find it easier to harmonize the ideas of continuity and change. For example, a plurality of distinct actions can often be seen as unified by relatively stable purposes and ideals, which bear witness to a continuity in the human person.

It is not my intention to claim that I can produce the required synthesis. I do not suppose that a definitive and universally accepted synthesis can be achieved in any case. At any rate the

---

[6]*Appearance and Reality*, p. 81. It should be remembered that Bradley tried to show that the concept of the self is 'contradictory', presenting us with 'a riddle without an answer' (p. 80). No theory was considered satisfactory.

history of philosophy does not suggest that this is likely. My aim
has been to make some critical comments about a theory of the
self which has seemed to some philosophers to be relevant to
the metaphysics of the One, to lend it support. We can now go
on to inquire to what extent, if any, it has relevance. In other
words, I intend to assume, for the sake of argument, that the
real self can be identified with the I-subject, with what a number
of Indian thinkers called 'the witness' and discuss the relevance
of this theory to the metaphysics of the One, in spite of the fact
that the theory seems to me unacceptable.

III

The Sāmkhya philosophers evidently did not think that the
conception of the self as 'the witness' had anything to do with
the theory of the One. In the Sāmkhya system a distinction was
made between *purusa*, the self as subject, as witness, and *prakrti*,
the primordial matter or material element which evolves into
nature as we know it. All physical elements of the human person,
including intelligence (*buddhi*) were regarded as evolutes of *prakrti*. It was only the pure subject, *purusa*, which transcended
nature and was eternal. This does not mean however that for
the Sāmkhya philosophers there was only one pure subject. On
the contrary, they postulated a plurality of subjects, corresponding to the plurality of human organisms, a view which they
supported by reasons of a common sense nature, such as the
diversity of ideas and actions.[7] Liberation took the form of the
freeing of the witness, the pure subject, from all elements belonging to *prakrti*. The pure subject then entered into a state of what
might be described as splendid isolation. There was no merging
with any One. In other words, in the Sāmkhya philosophy we
find an example of the theory of the pure subject as the real self
being included in a pluralistic system.

This theory of a plurality of pure subjects is open to the
objection that there is no way of distinguishing between disem-

---

[7]See, for example, the selections from the *Sāmkhya-Kārikā* as given in *A
Source Book in Indian Philosophy*, pp. 426–445, especially section 18 on p. 432.
There is a translation of Is'vara Krishna's *Sāmkhya-Kārikā* by S. S. Sury-
anarayana Sustri (Madras, 1935).

bodied pure subjects. When Aristotle was presenting his theory of a plurality of pure intelligence, the movers of the various spheres, it evidently occurred to him that to postulate a plurality of purely spiritual beings was open to serious criticism if, as he believed, matter was the principle of individuation within a species. For in this case how could one distinguish one pure intelligence from another?[8] A similar question could be asked of the Sāmkhya philosophers, inasmuch as all distinguishing elements were assigned to the sphere of *prakrti*, from which the *purusas* were said to be freed at final liberation. The Sāmkhya thinkers tried to reply to this line of objection. But their Advaitin critics remained unconvinced. It is all very well, for example, to suggest that the *purusas* retain some sort of relation to their bodies and other evolutes of *prakrti* with which they were in association. In the West St Thomas Aquinas defended this sort of view in regard to disembodied souls. But then he thought in terms of the human person, composed of soul and body, so that the disembodied soul was for him not, strictly speaking, a person and retained an orientation to its body. If we identify the real self with the I-subject, the witness, it seems to follow that final liberation involves the end of any relationship to the evolutes of *prakrti*. And in this case there seems to be a real difficulty in seeing how one *purusa* can be distinguished from another.

Even if, however, we assume that there is no way of distinguishing pure subjects, at any rate after final liberation, and that there is only one subject, it does not necessarily follow that this one subject is the One, in the sense of the ultimate reality on which all else depends ontologically or of which all else is appearance. As we have seen, the Sāmkhya philosophers believed in a plurality of *purusas*. But even if they had found themselves driven to admit that there was only one, they would not have been thereby compelled to deny the reality of *prakrti* and the world of nature or to regard nature as a mere appearance of the one subject. To be sure, their critics, the Advaitins, maintained that plurality belonged to the sphere of appearance, and that there was really only one *ātman*, which was not different

[8] *Metaphysics*, 1074a 33–8. It was for this reason that St Thomas Aquinas maintained that each angel was the sole member of its species, and that there could not be a multiplicity of angels (pure spirits) belonging to one species.

from Brahman, the one ultimate reality. But Śaṁkara did not arrive at the conclusion that *ātman*, the inner self, was one with Brahman, the ultimate reality, simply because of the difficulty in distinguishing between one *ātman* and another. He appealed, as we have already noted, to the passages of the Upanishads in which it is said that Brahman is the sole reality and that the inner self is one with Brahman, this doctrine being regarded as confirmable by suprasensory perception or mystical experience. In other words, the doctrine of Brahman, the Absolute, was derived from the sacred texts and was not a conclusion from the difficulty of distinguishing between pure subjects. In fact the conclusion would not necessarily follow from the premise that there was only one subject or witness. To put the matter in another way, we cannot make the transition from the Sāmkhya system to that of the Advaitins simply by postulating only one *purusa* or pure subject instead of a plurality, though this would indeed remove one obstacle to making the transition.

For the sake of clarity it may be desirable to sum up what has been said in this section. Having assumed a theory of the self which I do not myself accept, I raised the question of the theory's relevance to the metaphysics of the One. My conclusions are two. First, if we understand by the metaphysics of the One the thesis that there is an ultimate reality on which all else depends ontologically or of which all else is the appearance, the theory of the self in question does not imply the metaphysics of the One. Witness the Sāmkhya philosophy. Secondly, if we accept the view that there cannot be a plurality of pure subjects but only one, this view is indeed relevant to the Advaitin form of the metaphysics of the One, in the limited sense that it removes one obstacle to acceptance of the philosophy of non-difference. For we obviously cannot claim simultaneously that there is only one reality, namely Brahman, and that there is a plurality of distinct real selves. The trouble is of course that the thesis that all selves are one self is difficult to swallow.

IV

Let us now consider subject and object together, as correlative. Some philosophers have argued that there must be an underlying unity which is presupposed by and grounds the subject-object relation. Consider, for example, the Scottish philosopher Edward Caird. He first maintains that subject and object are distinct but inseparable. He then goes on to argue that 'we are forced to seek the secret of their being in a higher principle, of whose unity they in their action and reaction are the manifestation, which they presuppose as their beginning and to which they point as their end'.[9] A somewhat similar idea can be found in the philosophy of F. H. Bradley. Thus he tells us that 'the subject, the object, and their relation, are experienced as elements or aspects of a One which is there from the start'.[10] The subject-object relation, according to Bradley, presupposes and emerges out of a 'felt totality',[11] which is 'a being and knowing in one'.[12] These last words remind us that one of the main elements in the idealist movement of the nineteenth century was to close the gap between thought and things in themselves which is present in the critical philosophy of Kant. The idealists wished to bring together, and ultimately to identify, thought and being. It seems to me that thought is itself a form of being. In any case the post-Kantian idealists tried to unite what Kant had divided, knowing and thought, represented by the subject, and being, represented by the object, or, as Schelling put it, the ideal order and the real order. If we take it that Spinoza had brought the two orders together and that Kant had separated them, we can see the nineteenth-century idealists as trying to reunite them. Their tendency was to relate the subjective and the objective to a common source, the One or Absolute. Schelling, for example, found the common origin of subject and object in an Absolute which was described as the 'indifference' (identity or non-difference) of subject and object.[13]

It is doubtless true that in some rather vague way a good many people have believed (some of them might say 'felt') that there must be a unity underlying the subject-object relationship. Anyone who thinks in this way is likely to feel sympathy with

[9]*The Evolution of Religion*, vol. 1, p. 67 (Glasgow, 1893).
[10]*Essays on Truth and Reality*, p. 200.
[11]*Ibid.*
[12]*Ibid.*, p. 159.
[13]This refers to Schelling's so-called system of identity, not to the speculative theism of his later years.

Caird's point of view. But the general belief or conviction that there must be a One of some sort can be occasioned by a variety of factors. Here we are concerned simply with the relevance of the subject-object distinction to belief in an underlying unity or One. And I wish to attempt to disentangle approaches to the matter which may become confused and which should be distinguished. This way of tackling the matter may seem aridly theoretical and even tiresome, but it is none the less profitable.

In the first place let us consider Edward Caird's assertion that subject and object are distinct but inseparable. If the terms 'subject' and 'object' are understood in the technical senses given them in epistemology, the statement is true. For 'object' means object-for-a-subject, object in a cognitive relationship, while 'subject' signifies a subject as standing in a cognitive relation to an object. Given these meanings, subject and object are clearly distinct, inasmuch as 'subject' refers to the knower whereas 'object' refers to the known. They need not be separate entities. In self-consciousness I as knowing am not a separate entity from myself as known. But there must be a distinction. There is also a sense in which it is true to say that subject and object are inseparable. If 'object' means object-for-a-subject, there can be no object without a subject. And if 'subject' is taken to refer to an actual knower or thinker, there can be no subject without an object. For to know nothing is not to know, and to think about nothing is not to think.

In other words, the terms 'subject' and 'object' are, or can be understood as, correlative terms, distinct but inseparable as Edward Caird puts it. So are 'husband' and 'wife' correlative terms. There can be no husband without a wife, though there can be a widower without a living wife, and there can be no 'wife' without a husband, though there can be a widow without a living husband. But can we argue from the fact that 'husband' and 'wife' are correlative terms to the conclusion that there is an underlying unity out of which husband and wife emerge? If not, why should we be able to argue to an analogous conclusion from the fact that 'subject' and 'object' are correlative terms?

It may be said that I have been caricaturing Caird's position. He may have stated a truth about language, about the use of terms; but when he argued that there must be an underlying unity, he was evidently thinking not about the words 'subject' and 'object' but about the realities signified by the words. He was maintaining that the existence of the subject-object relation presupposes an underlying unity. His thesis may be true or false, but it should not be caricatured. To refer to another philosopher, when Schelling maintained that the subject-object relationship presupposes an underlying unity, he was thinking of the emergence of a relationship which introduces a rift, as it were, in reality, with the subject on the one hand and the object on the other. His idea was that this rift emerges out of an original unity in which the subject-object distinction was not present. Schelling was not talking simply about words.

This is no doubt true. Schelling was not talking *merely* about words. But let us consider the subject-object relationship as a real phenomenon, as that to which words refer, as that about which we talk. According to Edward Caird's own admission, 'strictly speaking, there is but one object and one subject for each of us'.[14] What he means is this. For me as subject all of which I am conscious, all that I conceive, all that of which I think, is object. You are object for me, just as I am an object for you. For me as subject all else constitutes my world. And 'my world' coincides with 'the world'. For if I try to think of a world which extends beyond my world, it becomes part of my world by the very fact of being thought.

In this case I cannot even conceive a unity underlying the subject-object distinction. For by the fact that I try to conceive it, it becomes an object for me as subject. There is thus a sense in which an approach to the metaphysics of the One by way of the subject-object distinction debars me from even conceiving a One. I am imprisoned in the subject-object relationship, with myself as subject, and I cannot get out of it. In other words, the subject-object relationship can be understood in such a way as to imply solipsism, in the sense that I am the only subject, all else being object for me as subject.

This line of thought is relevant to the proof of the existence of God given by the Scottish philosopher J. F. Ferrier. Ferrier maintained that every object is essentially object-for-a-subject.

---

[14]*The Evolution of Religion*, vol. 1, p. 65.

Nothing can exist except as subject or as object-for-a-subject. Ferrier saw that in the first instance everything is yoked, as he put it, to me as subject. For I have to start with my conception of the world. And if everything is essentially object-for-a-subject, the world is object for me as subject; it is yoked to me. What Ferrier wanted to prove of course was that nothing exists except as object for an infinite and eternal subject, God or the Absolute. And he argued that I can unyoke the world from myself as subject and yoke it onto God. Indeed, I must do, since I cannot seriously suppose that nothing existed before my birth. It is questionable however whether this appeal to common sense will work, once the initial yoking of the world to myself as subject has been postulated. If I try to think the world apart from myself as subject, what I think is object for myself as subject. God too, as thought by me, becomes object for myself as subject. Once I have divided up reality into myself as subject and every-thing else as object for myself as subject, there is no escape. It is true that Ferrier had no intention of defending solipsism. But this is not the point at issue. The question is whether he laid down premises from which solipsism logically followed, whether he wanted it to or not. And it is somewhat difficult to see how an affirmative answer to the question can be avoided.

Needless to say, common sense rejects solipsism. And this is not, I think, a case of childish naivety or of unenlightened prejudice. Solipsism is incompatible with experience. We ob-viously experience others as active agents in a common world, in, for example, cooperation for the attainment of shared ends or goals. And we can remark in passing that Jean-Paul Sartre has given some vivid examples of ways in which one can ex-perience oneself as object for another as subject. It is when one abstracts from the concrete human person and allows oneself to be hypnotized by the subject-object relationship when the sub-ject is oneself and all else is object for oneself as subject that solipsism shows its head. To be sure, there is a sense in which each one of us can talk meaningfully about 'my world'. We have to allow for a plurality of perspectives. Further, though we naturally think of these perspectives as so many perspectives of a common world, problems can be raised in regard to the har-monization of the ideas of a common world and of a plurality of perspectives, problems which it is difficult to solve on the theoretical level. Common sense is not sufficient to solve such theoretical problems. But this does not alter the fact that if I adopt a point of view which implies solipsism, I cannot postulate any One, in the sense of a unity underlying subject and object as their common sense. For, as was noted above, any unity which I conceive must be, by the fact of my conceiving it, object for me as subject.

It is not of course my intention to claim that all philosophers who have laid emphasis on the subject-object relationship or who have approached philosophy in this way have entangled themselves in solipsism. This would be false. Schelling, for example, may have started by reflecting on the subject-object relationship, but we very soon find him trying to form a unified picture of reality in which human beings are seen as persons, as expressing or objectifying themselves in social institutions, in ethical systems, in their art and religion, and as creating a moral order within the framework of the common natural order. Schelling was no solipsist. Nor of course was Edward Caird. What I was doing was to show how the following out of a particular line of thought effectively bars one, logically speaking, from postulating any unity transcending or underlying the subject-object distinction. When philosophers have widened the meanings of 'subject' and 'object' in the sort of way in which Schelling did, we are faced with a different situation.

Now let us assume that there is a common world in which human beings exist and act. It is within this world that the subject-object relationship arises whenever anybody is aware of something, conceives something or thinks about something. The emergence of the distinction between subject and object is contingent upon the existence of beings who are capable of exercizing the function of subjects, distantiating themselves, from the epistemological point of view, from the object of awareness. Is it not natural to claim that the underlying unity is simply the common world, within which and out of which the distinction emerges? It is true that we can think about the world, thus objectifying it. But it does not follow that the common world is actually an object, in the epistemological sense, from the start. It *becomes* an object in this sense, when one of the beings in the world *becomes* a subject. And this process of becoming presupposes a world which *can* take the form of subjects and objects. Is not this world the underlying unity? At any rate are we not entitled to claim that this is the case, unless a good reason can be produced for thinking otherwise?

This point of view, it may be said, is naive, an expression of uncritical common sense. What we call the world is the world as human, as conceived, the world in relation to a subject. If we try to think the world as not related to a subject, it is highly questionable whether this can be done. For by the very fact that it is thought or conceived, the world is object for a subject. But let us assume that we can conceive the world as not being object for a subject, that we can cancel out, so to speak, the subject-object distinction. We are then left with a mysterious blank, with what Schelling described as the vanishing-point of all differences. Must not the underlying unity be conceived in the way in which Schelling claimed that it must be conceived? We come in the end to the nameless Tao or One of the *Lao Tzu*, the Nothingness or Not-being of the Neo-Taoist 'dark learning', the Emptiness of Mādhyamika Buddhism, the Absolute of Schelling's system of identity. The alternative is to admit that we cannot get beyond the subject-object relationship and to abandon the search for an underlying unity.

A counter-attack can be conducted on these lines. Consider the claim that we cannot get outside the subject-object relationship. What does this really mean? Surely it is equivalent to saying that we cannot think of anything without thinking of it. This is obviously true. But it by no means follows that we cannot think of the world as existing before any subjects were around. Further, we can have reasonably definite ideas of what it was like. And we can think of the subject-object relationship as emerging in this world with the emergence of centres of consciousness. There is no need to bring in such metaphysical ideas as the nameless Tao, Not-being, Emptiness or the Absolute as the vanishing-point of all differences. Given the concept of an evolving world we can see potential subjects emerging within it. When a potential subject actualizes its potentiality of becoming aware of something, conceiving something, thinking of something, the subject-object relation arises. This involves, as Schelling and others noted, a distantiation, a distinction; but it is a distinction within the world. It may be the case that there is an ultimate reality other than the world, transcending it. But as far as the subject-object distinction is concerned, what it immediately presupposes is the world.

We have been considering some theoretical puzzles which can arise out of reflection on the subject-object relation. To the plain man such puzzles are likely to seem artificial or unreal, devoid of practical importance, the sort of games which philosophers like to play but which can be profitably disregarded by the rest of mankind. Though this is understandable, the reply can be made that if philosophers raise such puzzles, other philosophers have to discuss them, even if the solution of the puzzles lies in their dissolution. For this should lead to a clearer view of the situation. In particular, one has to try to see how the puzzles arise. And I should like to make a tentative suggestion, which may be relevant to this aspect of the matter.

The strictly epistemological relation between subject and object is only one of the ways in which the human being functions as subject. Human beings desire objects, and they can desire the realization of ideal ends. In such desires the human being functions as subject in relation to an object, whether the object is an actually existing thing, such as a loaf of bread, or an ideal object, such as social reform. Further, subject-object relationships of this kind make no sense except in the context of a world. Again, the human being can function as subject in interpersonal relationship, such as love, and hatred too for the matter of that. A human being can of course love another human being without being loved in return; but in mutual love both function as subjects in the relationship. Again, these interpersonal relationships are really not intelligible except in the context of a world. If however I focus my attention simply on the subject-object distinction in a strictly epistemological or cognitive sense, and if I bear in mind the phenomenon of self-consciousness, I am likely to make a distinction between the pure subject and its object. The side of the object includes all that I conceive or think about, myself, other people, things. Understanding of this fact gives rise to the problem of solipsism. It does so at least if I find myself unable to distinguish successfully between the world as representation and the world in itself. If, however, I recall that I can function as subject in other kinds of relationship, such as those referred to above, solipsism tends to lose any plausibility which it may possess when I concentrate my attention exclusively on the subject-object relation in a strictly epistemological sense.

In brief, I am inclined to suggest that the relevant puzzles which seem artificial or unreal to the plain man arise when the real self is reduced to the pure subject of transcendental ego, and that they tend to disappear when we avoid this reduction and think in terms of the human person instead, the living, sensing, desiring, remembering, thinking and willing totality. I have said this before, but it is a point worth repeating. I suspect that it is a point which the plain man tends to grasp instinctively, even if he could not state it.

V

There is indeed an obvious sense in which the subject-object distinction is relevant to the metaphysics of the One. That is to say, the distinction is a condition for the raising of the question of the One. Without this distinction it would not be possible to pursue metaphysics at all. Even if we cannot deduce the existence of a One transcending the empirical world simply from the occurrence of the subject-object relationship, we could not discuss the question except within the framework of the distinction between subject and object. Unless the human being could get his or her head above the stream, so to speak, and objectify the world in which we find ourselves, it would not be possible to ask whether the world is itself the ultimate reality or whether we must seek the ultimate reality beyond it. It can be pointed out however that it is not a question simply of the metaphysics of the One, nor simply of metaphysics in general, nor of philosophy only for the matter of that. We cannot think about anything at all, whether it is the One or going to the theatre, or one's next meal, without objectifying, constituting something an object of thought over against oneself as subject. The subject-object distinction is a condition of all human thought. Indeed, it can be claimed that what I have been saying is equivalent to asserting that we cannot think about anything without thinking about it, that is to say distantiating oneself from it as subject from object. This is true, but it is true in regard to all discursive thought, not simply in regard to the metaphysics of the One. Unless human beings could pursue what we call thought, they could not pursue metaphysical speculation. This is doubtless true, but there is no need to make a song and dance about it. Elsewhere I have said that man's ability to raise metaphysical questions or problems is due to his capacity to stand back from or out of the world, a capacity which 'is rooted in his nature, as an "ecstatic" being',[15] and that, paradoxically, he transcends 'the physical cosmos as a being in the world'.[16] Such statements are true in a sense. For we cannot consider problems about the world without objectifying it and so setting ourselves, as subjects, over against the world, though at the same time we are in the world, involved in it, regarding it from inside. But this situation is not peculiar to metaphysics. Metaphysics is one form of discursive thought. And all discursive thought, metaphysical or otherwise, involves the subject-object distinction. If we employ such a pompous term as 'ecstatic' to describe man because he can think about the world, we can also describe him as 'ecstatic' because he can objectify himself in self-consciousness. The subject-object relation occurs in both cases. Indeed, it occurs in all cases of knowing something, thinking about something.

That thinking about something, whatever the something is, involves objectification, and thus the subject-object distinction, is doubtless true. And I dare say that I did not pay sufficient attention to this fact, when I was writing at an earlier date about the self and metaphysics. At the same time the movement of the human spirit towards a One which transcends the Many seems to me to express an orientation which I would not hesitate to describe as religious and which is hardly revealed when I am thinking about a glass of lemonade as something which would contribute to quenching my thirst. What I am suggesting is that the metaphysics of the One, when it is not a purely academic

---

[15]*Religion and Philosophy*, p. 119 (Dublin, 1974).
[16]*Ibid.*

exercise,[17] tells me something about the human being. The human being is in the world and lives and acts in the world. But the human being can also reach out, as it were, towards what transcends the visible world and try to grasp it conceptually, objectifying it in a variety of ways, as the Tao, as Emptiness, as Brahman, as God. I am not concerned at present with these conceptualizations. I am concerned with the movement itself, which seems to me to reveal the human being as open to the transcendent. The possibility of the metaphysics of the One rests, in my opinion, on this openness of the human being.

Other writers have drawn attention to the connection between the sort of metaphysics which I have in mind and religion. For example, in his book on metaphysics Professor W. H. Walsh asserts that if we reflect on the background and the interests of what he describes as transcendent metaphysicians, 'we can see that the practice of religion tends to play a very large part in their lives',[18] and that this religious practice demands the basic conviction of the metaphysicians in question, namely that 'the familiar world is not the only world'.[19] The same sort of thing is implied by Gilbert Ryle's suggestion, in regard to the eclipse of metaphysical speculation, that the theological fire has died down, and that as a consequence the kettle of theological philosophy cannot continue to be on the boil.[20] Perhaps we can express this point of view by saying that the language of the metaphysics of the One is an expression of the religious form of life, and that use of this language declines in proportion as people cease to participate in the corresponding form of life.

In other words, a *de facto* connection between religion and the metaphysics of the One can be admitted even by those who do not adhere to the religious beliefs in question or participate in 'religious practice' which implies such beliefs. In this case the connection would obviously not be regarded as in any way proving the truth of such beliefs. The fact that some human beings have hankered, so to speak, after a reality transcending

[17] If, for example, I occupied myself simply with trying to improve or defend arguments offered by a past philosopher of the One, I might be described as pursuing the metaphysics of the One as a purely academic exercise.

[18] *Metaphysics*, p. 184 (London, 1963).

[19] *Ibid.*

[20] *The Nature of Metaphysics*, edited by D. F. Pears, p. 160 (London, 1957).

the familiar world does nothing to show that there is a reality of this kind, though it may of course show something about these human beings. Bertrand Russell, for example, insisted that human desires and emotive attitudes are no sure guide to the nature of reality. The fact that a person stranded in the desert desires water does not prove that there is water to be had.

To some people this line of thought seems to be obviously correct. It is undeniable that if I am stranded in the desert and desire water, this does nothing to show that there is water at hand to quench my thirst. But does not the fact of my thirst show something about the world? If, for instance, the world were such that hunger and thirst could not in principle be satisfied, there would presumably be no living organisms needing food and drink. If such organisms had arisen, they would very soon have perished. It is arguable that the fact of my thirst reveals something not only about me but also about the world in which I exist. And one might argue in an analogous way that the movement of the human spirit reveals something about reality; that the movement might be interpreted in terms of final causality, in terms of attraction.

It may be said that there are very great differences between the two cases. For one thing, all human beings need food and drink. Without them they would perish. What I have called the movement towards the One is not, however, universally experienced, and there can be times when few people experience it. For another thing, we are acquainted by experience with the relation between hunger and thirst on the one hand and the objects which can satisfy these needs on the other. But we are not acquainted by experience with any transcendent One. And the movement towards it may well be a movement towards a phantom.

There are of course differences. But they are what one would expect. From one point of view the human being is a 'worldly' being, involved in the empirical world, acting in it, seeking ends or goals in it. In virtue of this aspect of his nature man is naturally inclined to think of the metaphysics of the One as so much airy nonsense. At the same time the problems which find expression in the metaphysics of the One reassert themselves, and by doing so they reveal another aspect of the human being.

It is possible to write off the recurrence of these problems as due to logical confusion, psychological causes or what not. But it is also possible to see in it a manifestation of final causality.

These brief and disjointed remarks are not intended as a proof of the existence of the One. They are intended to indicate simply that the idea of the metaphysics of the One as being one expression of an openness in the human being to a transcendent reality is not quite so silly as references to travellers stranded in the desert may suggest. As for the succession of metaphysical systems, we shall return to this theme in the final chapter of this book.

VI

By way of conclusion I should like to suggest another way in which reflection on the self can be relevant to the metaphysics of the One, though I shall have to make my point very briefly and without discussion of the issues raised.

In the process of evolution Herbert Spencer saw a movement from a relative homogeneity to an increasing heterogeneity, from the relatively undifferentiated to increasing differentiation. Perhaps we can say that he saw a movement towards increasing individuality, an idea which formed the basis for his social philosophy. Obviously, unless we are prepared to recognize the existence of universal entities, a notion which Aristotle submitted to trenchant criticism, we have to say that anything which exists is individual. At the same time we can certainly see in the process of evolution the emergence of a consciousness of individuality. Thus the human being is a self for itself. It is a centre of consciousness and can be aware of itself as a centre of consciousness. This is why the sort of puzzles connected with 'I and my world', puzzles to which reference has been made above, can arise. I have argued that the human being cannot be reduced to the pure subject or transcendental ego, and I have no intention of abandoning this view. None the less, the human being is a centre of consciousness and a self for itself, aware of its individuality in a way in which we have no good reason for supposing that a stone can be aware of itself.

This feature of the human being militates against monism, if we mean by monism the thesis that there is only one reality, transcending all distinctions and relations. If we assume that the empirical world manifests a creative energy, and if we are prepared to see, with Schelling, human persons, individual selves, as creating a moral order within the framework of the natural order, in any theory of the ultimate reality, the One, we must find room for this consciousness of individuality and not embrace a theory which obliterates it or dismisses it as mere appearance. There is also of course the social consciousness to consider. But I confine my attention to one point, the consciousness of individuality, the appropriation, so to speak, by the self of its own being. And though theism is not without its difficulties, it seems to me that reflection on the self favours a theistic interpretation of reality rather than the sort of theory which we find in the Advaita Vedānta.

CHAPTER 9

MYSTICISM AND KNOWLEDGE

The theme of the chapter – experience and interpretation – ineff-ability and argument – reflection on mysticism as an element in the construction of a world-view – concluding remarks

I

There can be various different approaches to the study of or reflection on mysticism, psychological, physiological, theological, literary. In this chapter I am concerned simply with the claims, made by or on behalf of mystics, to have had contact with or to have experienced suprasensory perception of an ultimate reality which transcends the empirical world in the minimal sense of not being identifiable with the Many, so that the phrase 'the One' would be nothing more than a collective name for the Many. In other words, I am concerned with the question whether there is any way of assessing the truth or falsity of such claims. The approach is a limited one, and the subject-matter is limited. I shall pay no attention to physiological phenomena, such as levitation or ecstatic dancing, and I shall not aim either at edification or at developing a mystical theology. I am concerned simply with the cognitive value, if any, of mysticism, in the sense just mentioned.

It sometimes happens that we are told something which turns out to be untrue or to be based on a misinterpretation of what actually occurred. And I do not suppose that anyone is likely to claim that we should accept without question the assertion of a particular mystic that he or she has had intuitive experience of a transcendent reality. It has, however, been argued that, although mystical writers have given rather different interpretations of their experiences, there has been a significant measure of basic agreement between reports of mystics belonging to different cultures and different periods, and that when this agreement is present, it is only reasonable to accept what the mystics say. After all, the mystic is, by definition, the person who has had certain experiences, while the non-mystic is, also by definition, the person who has not enjoyed these experiences. In other words, the mystics speak from the vantage-point of knowledge which non-mystics do not possess. Unless therefore there is good reason for thinking it probable that mystical writers are lying or suffering from delusions, it is much more reasonable to accept their testimony than not to accept it. As the non-mystic has never enjoyed mystical experience, he is in no position to assess the truth or falsity of the mystic's claims. To be sure, a given philosopher might reject the mystic's claims in an *a priori* manner, on the grounds, for example, that to exist is to be a possible object of sense-perception, and that there cannot be a reality which is not a possible object of sense-perception. But if the mystic's claim was true, this thesis would be false. And if the philosopher refuses to consider the possibility that his own theory is false, he is simply giving expression to dogmatism and prejudice. He should be prepared to admit the possibility that other people know what he does not.

The situation is not however as simple as this. Unless we have reason to suppose that the mystic is lying or deluded, we can take it that he[1] knows that he has experienced certain psychological states of mind. If however we are prepared to recognize a distinction between experience and interpretation, there is the possibility that the mystic misinterpreted his experience in all good faith, in terms of his pre-existing beliefs. A measure of agreement among mystical writers would not necessarily show that this possibility could be discounted. For the measure of agreement in interpretation might be due to a measure of agreement in pre-existing beliefs. Whether or not we are entitled to make a distinction between experience and interpretation is a question about which something more will be said later. But, given this distinction, the mystic might well be mistaken in his interpretation of a psychological state which he had really experienced. In this case of course his claim to have encountered

---

[1]Strictly speaking, I should add 'or she'. Not all mystics have been male. But to express this fact verbally on all occasions would be extremely cumbersome. And I can only apologize to anyone who is irritated by what may appear to be male chauvinism.

a transcendent reality could not simply be taken at its face value.

There is of course a sense in which the mystic is in a better position than the non-mystic. For, as we have noted, the former has had experiences which the latter has not. Moreover, the mystic may obviously feel certain of the truth of his interpretation of his experience or experiences. I do not deny this. But is it inconceivable that in reflection subsequent to the relevant experience a mystic should ask himself whether he really encountered a transcendent reality? To dispel such doubt he might conceivably address to himself the same sort of arguments that he would use, if he had the requisite intellectual ability and training, in discussion with a sceptical non-mystic. In other words, when it is a question of assessing the validity of claims to knowledge of a transcendent reality, the difference between the mystic and the non-mystic is not perhaps as great as it may appear to be at first sight.

In any case we are not talking here simply and solely about the way or ways in which a non-mystic might assess claims to have experiential knowledge of a transcendent reality. We are talking in a more general manner, though I admit of course that the questioner of the claims is much more likely to be the non-mystic. It should be added however that 'non-mystic' does not necessarily mean a person without religious beliefs. For it is possible, for example, to believe in God and at the same time believe that the divine transcendence is incompatible with claims to have seen God or to have experienced him directly. In the fourth chapter attention was drawn to the existence of this sort of attitude among some Muslims. It can be found in Christianity too. Emphasis therefore on the need for assessing the truth or falsity of claims made by mystics is not necessarily an expression of lack of religious belief.

II

Is there however any way of deciding whether a mystic's claim to have experienced or encountered a transcendent reality is true or false? It may seem that there is no such way. Suppose that someone claims to have seen the Queen of England shopping in a Woolworth's store in Oxford Street, London. We can think of ways in which the claim might be checked, quite apart from the inherent improbability (though not of course impossibility) of the situation in question. For example, if we had good ground for believing that at the time when the Queen was allegedly shopping in Woolworth's she was actually opening a new hospital or bridge in Scotland, we would conclude that the person who claimed to have seen the monarch in Woolworth's was either mistaken or romancing. But how could we check a claim to have encountered a transcendent reality or to have had experience of oneness with the ultimate reality, whether it is conceived as Brahman or as God? There does not seem to be any available empirical test. A philosopher might indeed exclude the claim on *a priori* grounds, on the ground that it could not possibly be true. But the theory to which he appealed would have to be shown to be necessarily true. For if it were not necessarily true, it would be refuted by the mystic's claim, if it were valid. It may seem therefore that the only way of assessing the truth or falsity of the mystic's claim is by appealing to some theory which is necessarily true and which excludes the possibility of the mystic's claim being valid. But is there such a theory? If so, what is it?

Someone might protest that there is in fact a way to check a mystic's claim to have had experiential knowledge of the One, namely to repeat the experience, to enjoy it oneself. This may sound a fantastic suggestion. If a friend says that there is a wolf in the garden, it is an easy matter to check his statement empirically. Given certain conditions, such as clear eyesight and the presence of light, anyone can do so. But mystical experiences are relatively rare and there may be psychological predispositions which are not to be found in all and sundry. Further, the theologian may say that the mystical experience of the divine presence is a gift of God and cannot be enjoyed at will. In principle however it is possible for mystical experience to be repeated. After all, one of the arguments in favour of the mystic's claim, an argument mentioned above, is that there is a measure of agreement among mystics belonging to different cultures and periods. This argument clearly implies that mystical experiences of a similar nature are in principle repeatable. To be sure, it may not be an easy matter to actualize this possibility. But if, for example, one goes through the preparatory discipline enjoined by, say, a Sufi teacher, and if one then has the kind of mystical experience referred to by Sufi mystics, this is a good reason for accepting the mystic's claim. What better reason could there be? Even if there are different kinds of mysticism, in principle each kind can be explored empirically.

This line of argument may sound impressive at first hearing, but it is open to serious objection. Suppose that a group of people is travelling in a desert and stops to rest. One member of the group gets up and looks around him. He reports to his companions that he has seen an oasis in the distance. The others get up, look in the direction indicated, and confirm the first man's report. Unless they are all lying, they have all had similar experiences. Perhaps, when they proceed on their journey, they actually find the oasis which they thought that they saw. But it may turn out that there is no oasis where they hoped to find one. In this case it would be rational to say that their interpretation of their experiences was mistaken. The fact that several people had the same sort of experience makes no difference to this disappointing situation. Analogously, it can be argued, a number of people may have what are commonly described as mystical experiences. And it may be that they interpret these experiences in a recognizably similar manner. But it does not follow that their interpretation is correct. It is true of course that in the case of the travellers in the desert the similarity of their interpretations can be explained without its being necessary to postulate that there actually was an oasis in the area where they thought there was one. But it may also be possible to explain the similarity in the mystics' experiences without its being necessary to suppose that they actually enjoyed suprasensory perception of or contact with a transcendent reality. If, for example, the feeling of being acted upon by a mysterious reality was involved, this might be explained in terms of psychological causes. And even if there is no adequate explanation of this nature at hand, we surely ought to suspend judgment rather than jump to the conclusion that the mystics' interpretation of their experiences must be accepted.

In discussions of mysticism this distinction between experience and interpretation has often been made. It may however be challenged, on the ground that there is no such thing as raw, uninterpreted experience, on which an interpretation is then imposed. To experience, it has been argued, is to experience something *as* something, as *x* or *y*. Suppose that Chuang Tzu claims to experience unity with nature. If he is not lying, this is what he experienced, namely unity with nature. To say that his interpretation is mistaken is really to say that he did not have the experience. We cannot distinguish between the interpretation and the uninterpreted experience, for there is no such thing as uninterpreted experience. Similarly, if a Sufi mystic claims to have experienced the empirical world as 'the face of God', this *is* his experience, namely of the world as 'the face of God'. Either he had the experience or he did not. The Sufi mystic's experience is doubtless different from that ascribed above to Chuang Tzu. But this is irrelevant in the present context. The point is that we are not entitled to admit that a person had a certain experience and at the same time reject his or her interpretation of it. What Chuang Tzu experienced was unity with nature. If the interpretation is wrong, he did not have the experience. Similarly, what the Sufi experienced was the empirical world as 'the face of God'. If the interpretation is wrong, the Sufi did not have the experience. For all experiencing is experiencing *as*.

There seems to be something wrong here. If there is, what is it? Presumably, any experience must be of a certain kind. Suppose that I said that I had had an experience, and that you then asked me 'what sort of experience?' If I replied 'an experience of no sort, of no kind', you might well conclude either that I was joking or that I had not had an experience at all. In other words, it seems that there must be some truth in the argument presented in the last paragraph. At the same time it is difficult not to believe that there is some justification for making a distinction between experience and interpretation. Is it possible to reconcile the two beliefs?

Let us consider a situation taken from ordinary life. I am walking along a street, and I have the experience of hearing a sudden, loud, sharp noise, which I interpret as the sound of a pistol shot. I certainly had an auditory, not a visual experience.

I heard a loud noise as a loud noise. I did not see a bright colour as a bright colour. And unless my knowledge of the English language is deficient, I can hardly be mistaken in claiming that I heard a loud noise, or that I had an auditory experience as of hearing a loud noise. But I may very well be mistaken in claiming that the noise was the sound of a pistol shot. It may have been the noise caused by the sudden bursting of a tyre. In other words, I know that I had an auditory experience of a certain kind. It is not the job of someone else to tell me that I had a visual experience of a bright light and not an auditory experience of a loud noise, not at any rate unless the person has good reason for thinking that my knowledge of the English language is so weak that I am given to describing visual experiences as though they were auditory experiences. But my causal interpretation of my experience may very well be mistaken. Hence we have to make room for some distinction between experience and interpretation.

Now let us apply this line of thought to mystical experience. Suppose that a Christian or Muslim mystic has an experience as of being acted upon, and suppose that he describes the experience as one of being acted upon by God, of being caught up, so to speak, into God. Unless we have reason to believe either that the mystic is lying or that he is unintentionally using the wrong words, we must, I think, take it that he has had the experience as of being acted upon rather than as of acting. But must we therefore accept his statement that he was acted upon by God? If we believe in God, we may indeed be predisposed to give a more favourable hearing to his claim than if we did not believe in God. But we are certainly not obliged to accept the claim simply because it has been made. After all, we might allow that someone had a feeling or experience as of being acted upon by an external power and yet regard the claim that the person was actually acted upon by an external reality, whether divine or otherwise, as the expression of a mistaken inference. If it is urged that the mystic does not infer but experiences directly, the reply can be made that the mystic's account of his experience, whether made to himself or to others, is conceived subsequently to the experience, in reflection on it, and that his claim to have been acted upon by a transcendent reality is the expression of an inference, probably made in the light of his pre-existing beliefs.

It seems to me therefore that it is possible to admit that any experience must be of a certain kind, that experiencing is experiencing *as*, and at the same time to allow for a distinction between experience and interpretation. But let us turn to another aspect of our theme.

III

We are discussing mysticism from what is obviously a narrow point of view, namely as evidence for the existence of a reality, a One, which is transcendent at any rate in the sense that it is irreducible to the Many. It may be said that mystics themselves have rarely been concerned with offering their experiences as proof of the existence of a transcendent reality. Those who have left writings behind them have been concerned with encouraging others to follow in the path of spirituality and contemplative prayer rather than with proving the existence of a One. The idea of arguing to the existence of God from religious experience in general and mysticism in particular is a relatively modern phenomenon and should not be ascribed to the classical mystical writers. It would be absurd to assert that St John of the Cross, for example, the sixteenth-century Spanish mystic, wrote his works to prove the existence of God. He was addressing religious believers, not agnostics or atheists.

This is quite true. But we are not at present discussing the reasons why mystical writers composed their works. We are discussing a line of argument which, as has been noted above, is a relatively modern phenomenon. It has sometimes been said that adoption of this line of argument was due to the widespread criticism of the older or traditional arguments. That is to say, people who wanted to argue in support of the existence of God had to find a new argument. However, although criticism of the older arguments was doubtless one of the factors which contributed to the development of an argument from religious experience, it was not the only factor. The conviction that living faith rests on religious experience and is sustained by it was another. It was felt that if the aim of trying to prove the existence of God

is to facilitate genuine personal belief, the line of thought employed should keep as close as possible to actual religious life
and attitudes and not treat God as though he were an astronomical hypothesis. As for mysticism, growing knowledge of
non-western cultures and of the role played by mysticism in
oriental religion contributed to turning the mind to reflection on
this area.

However this may be, we are concerned here with argumentation from the occurrence of mystical experience to the existence of a transcendent reality, a One. And we are concerned
with the argument as argument, from a philosophical point of
view. As I have remarked, this is a restricted or narrow approach
to discussion of mysticism. But it is the one which we have
selected.

In the previous section we defended the view that a distinction
can and should be made between experience and interpretation.
The question arises however whether, if we have not ourselves
enjoyed mystical experience, we can know what it is. This seems
to be a question of some importance. For if an argument is to
be based on mystical experience, we ought surely to know what
it is. But can we? If we have not enjoyed mystical experience
ourselves, we have to rely on the testimony of mystics. But we
find some of them saying that the higher or deeper mystical
experiences are ineffable, that they cannot be described. In this
case how can we know what they are, unless we have enjoyed
them ourselves? And even if we have, how could we explain
what we are talking about to anyone who has not had the
experience in question? A line of argument based on experiences
which cannot be described might perhaps carry some weight
with religious believers who are prepared for the occurrence of
such experiences. But an apologetic argument is presumably
addressed to doubters or unbelievers rather than to believers.
And an agnostic or atheist is not likely to be favourably impressed by an argument in which appeal is made to ineffable
experiences, transcending description.

One way of coping with this problem is to call in question
the alleged ineffability of mystical experience on the ground that
writers such as St John of the Cross have not only written at
some length about their experiences but have also succeeded in

conveying an idea of their nature.[2] This line of thought cannot be simply dismissed. It would be a gross exaggeration to say that the writings of mystics such as St John of the Cross and St Teresa of Avila are completely unintelligible. But neither can the idea of ineffability be simply dismissed. There are doubtless a fair number of people who would not describe themselves as mystics but who at some time in their lives have experienced a feeling of unity with nature and who are confident that they have a good idea of the sort of experience or feeling of which nature mystics have written. There are also some states referred to by Christian mystics of which a good many people at any rate can form a sufficiently clear idea to distinguish between what is being referred to and something different. When however we turn to the writings of religious mystics who refer to what a mystic such as St John of the Cross regarded as the highest mystical states, we find them saying that they cannot be expressed. According to St John of the Cross, for example, a person who has not experienced the state of transforming union with God can no more understand what it is than one would be able to know what an animal was like which had been discovered by an explorer on some remote island and which bore no resemblance to any animal with which one was acquainted.[3] I must admit that this illustration has its defects. It seems to me doubtful whether there could be an animal which bore no resemblance at all to other animals. For if the creature were describable as an animal, it would have to bear some resemblance, however minimal, to other animals. None the less, we can hardly exclude the possibility of there being experiences or states which our language cannot describe in such a way as to enable us to know what they are without our having experienced them. Further, I doubt whether the fact that St John of the Cross tried to say something about such experiences is incompatible with what he says about indescribability. One of his main purposes in writing was to make people who were seriously devoted to contemplative prayer aware that if they came to find themselves in unfamiliar territory, they need not conclude that they had gone astray and

[2]See, for example, *The Transcendence of the Cave*, by J. N. Findlay, p. 202 (London, 1967).
[3]*Ascent of Mount Carmel*, Bk. 2, ch. 3, section 2.

seek to retrace their steps. He tried therefore, by the help of analogies and images, to say sufficient about higher mystical states to enable people to recognize them if and when they experienced them. It does not follow that he thought that he could make them understand the nature of the states before they experienced them. The view has indeed been defended that mystical writers 'are using language in a non-communicative fashion'[4], with the aim of stimulating people to enjoy *their* experiences. Although there is some truth in this contention, it seems to me an exaggeration, if it is claimed that mystical writers did not intend to communicate anything to anyone!

Besides, we have to remember that St John of the Cross was not talking about knowledge *that*, knowledge which is in principle communicable, but about knowledge by acquaintance. The feeling or experience of unity with nature is not knowledge *that*, factual knowledge. But as a good many people have experienced this sort of feeling, they know the sort of thing to which reference is being made. If however reference is made to states which, *ex hypothesi*, very few people have experienced, very few people will have any clear idea of what is being referred to. And the language which has meaning for those few who have experienced the states in question may give a very misleading impression to those who have not. Even if 'ineffability' is considered too strong a word, it may well be applicable in regard to a great many people.

If this is the case, it inevitably affects the utility and efficacy of any public property argument, so to speak, which appeals to mystical experience as evidence for the existence of God. If there is a state of transforming union with God, this would presumably provide a better ground for asserting the existence of God than a state or experience which can be accounted for simply in terms of pre-existing religious belief. On the assumption however that the state of transforming union can be understood only by the very few people who have experienced it and who, one supposes, stand in no need of a proof of God's existence, the majority of people are unlikely to be convinced by any argument which appeals to it.

[4]*Western Approaches to Eastern Philosophy*, by Troy Wilson Organ (Athens, Ohio, 1975).

What is not always noted by those who discuss the value of mystical experience as evidence for the existence of a transcendent reality is the bearing of the idea of ineffability or indescribability on the contention that a purely naturalistic account of mysticism is possible, and that to postulate a transcendent reality of any kind is to adopt a superfluous hypothesis. It has been maintained, by J. H. Leuba for example,[5] that we cannot find any factor in mystical experience which cannot be explained in physiological or psychological terms. It has also been maintained that even if a completely satisfactory naturalistic explanation is not available here and now, we cannot exclude the possibility that one will be forthcoming in the future, and that the critical mind should therefore suspend judgment and not have recourse to a supernatural explanation, unless perhaps as a purely temporary hypothesis, pending further investigation. A presupposition seems to be that mystical experience in itself has no intrinsic connection with religion, if we conceive religion as involving belief in a divine reality. To put the matter in another way, the distinction between experience and interpretation, to which we have already referred above, is presupposed, any connection between mystical experience and religion being assigned to the sphere of interpretation. This point of view, however, seems to demand that we should know what mystical experience is, including the states which religious mystics have conceived as states of close union with God or of oneness with the Absolute but which they have also regarded as indescribable by discursive thought. For we can hardly claim to be able to give a naturalistic account of something with which we are not acquainted or of which we have at best only a very hazy idea.

My point can be illustrated by referring to the claim that mystical experience is producible by drugs, in the sense that there is no detectable difference between drug-induced states and mystical experiences which have occurred without the use of drugs.[6] This thesis obviously assumes that we can compare

[5]In *The Psychology of Religious Mysticism* (London, 1925; revised edition, 1929; reprint, London and Boston, 1972).
[6]Thus in *Exploring Mysticism* (Berkeley, Los Angeles and London, 1975, p. 190) Dr Frits Staal expresses his 'suspicion' that mystical experience, taken by itself, has no connection with religion, if religion is understood as involving belief in God or the gods.

the former with the latter. Up to a point this may be possible. There is no doubt that after taking certain drugs some people have temporarily seen the world as transformed, as startling or wonderful, with heightened colours and so on. Again, under the influence of drugs some people have felt or experienced oneness with others or with nature. There are similarities between descriptions of certain drug-induced states and descriptions of experiences enjoyed by nature mystics. Further, it appears that some drugs may bring about phenomena similar to physical phenomena which have occurred in the case of religious mystics who have not taken drugs, though it must be added that the mystics themselves have tended to discount such phenomena as passing by-products of religious experience. We can also detect some similarities between descriptions by religious mystics of what might be called preliminary stages of contemplation and descriptions (such as they are) of states of mind experienced in the attempt to penetrate beneath the discriminating mind, an attempt which need not, in itself, have anything to do with religion, at any rate with religion as involving belief in a transcendent reality. At the same time, if there are mystical experiences which elude description and of which only those who have enjoyed them can possess any real knowledge, the outsider is not in a good position to compare them with drug-induced states. In other words, he is not in a position to experiment or to adopt a purely empirical approach to the matter. It is all very well for someone such as Aldous Huxley to claim that under the influence of mescalin he had experiences similar to the highest mystical states. How can he know that this is the case? If we assume, for example, that St John of the Cross's allusions to the state of what he calls 'transforming union' are sufficient to give us some idea of the state in question, there does not in fact seem to be much resemblance between this state and the experiences enjoyed by Huxley under the influence of drugs. And if we take seriously St John of the Cross's assertion that the state transcends description, Huxley obviously does not know that there is any resemblance between it and his own drug-induced experiences.

If I have not made any reference to conduct, to possible differences between, on the one hand, the effect on life and conduct of the experiences which religious mystics have regarded as the highest experiences and, on the other, experiences produced by the taking of certain drugs, this is mainly because I doubt whether discussion of this topic would contribute to further clarification of the point which I have been trying to make. Reference to conduct in the present context is apt to give the impression that one thinks that a person's conduct proves the truth of his or her beliefs; and I do not wish to spend time in dispelling this impression. In any case discussion of conduct would involve discussion of complex issues which may be of theoretical interest but which we can pass over here. I have confined my attention to a point relating to knowledge, to the cognitive value of mysticism.

In treating this matter I have argued that in any discussion between a religious apologist and an agnostic or atheist about the value of mysticism as evidence for the existence of a transcendent reality both sides are likely to encounter difficulty in explaining precisely what they are talking about. It is probably those mystical states which a writer such as St John of the Cross regarded as the highest or most profound which would provide the best support for an argument to the existence of a transcendent reality, if we could make clear the nature of the states in question. If however they are not describable, we cannot do so. This makes a difficulty for the religious apologist. At the same time it also makes a difficulty for the person who wishes to argue that a purely naturalistic explanation can be given, or could in principle be given, of all those states which are commonly described as mystical. I conclude therefore that the discussion between the religious apologist and the agnostic or atheist is bound to be inconclusive. That is to say, it is bound to be inconclusive, if we once assume that they are engaged in discussing the cognitive value of experiences which transcend linguistic expression and of which, probably, not even the religious apologist would claim to have personal knowledge. In a sense both are in the dark. They are certainly labouring under a severe handicap.

There are two objections which occur to me. In the first place it might be objected that I have contradicted myself. On the one hand I have accepted the claim that all experiencing is experiencing of something *as*, in which case all experiences should be describable. On the other hand I have accepted the idea that some mystical experiences are indescribable. But these two positions are incompatible. In the second place, even if some experiences are in fact indescribable, this does not seem to be peculiar to mysticism. For example, can we convey to a person blind from birth what the visual experience of colour is like? A person blind from birth has not got knowledge by acquaintance of this experience. Nor can we convey it.

The second objection tends to cancel out the first. A visual experience of colour is presumably an experience of something, even if it is only a patch, as coloured. It is an example of experiencing *as*. And if we cannot describe it to a person blind from birth in such a way that he or she will know what the experience really is in itself, it follows that the thesis that all experiencing is experiencing *as* does not entail the conclusion that all experiences must be describable. As for the second objection in itself, it is perhaps sufficient to point out that, whereas most people are not blind from birth, few would claim to have enjoyed mystical experiences of the kind which St John of the Cross, for example, declared to be indescribable. In any case it is really not a question of nothing at all being sayable about such experiences. Here Professor Findlay in *The Transcendance of the Cave*, certainly has a point. The conviction of a mystic such as St John of the Cross is obviously that there can be certain kinds of experience which our language is not capable of describing so that those who have not enjoyed the experiences will know what they are like. Someone may wish to insist that this is true of all experiences, not simply of certain mystical experiences. The fact of the matter is, however, that in the case of many kinds of experience we know perfectly well the sort of thing to which reference is being made, for the simple reason that we recognize it from our own experience. St John of the Cross assumes, and it is a reasonable assumption, that most people are not in a position to recognize in terms of their own experience the nature of what he regards as the highest mystical states. I do not think that his contention can be refuted simply by appealing to the statement that all experiencing is experiencing *as*. And to claim that what cannot be adequately described is unreal borders on dogmatism.

IV

To some people the foregoing discussion is likely to seem not only tiresome but also, in some sense, irrelevant. The sceptic of course may find himself in substantial agreement with a good deal of what I have said. So indeed may the religious believer who thinks that mystics have made claims which are incompatible with the divine transcendence. But there are people who are genuinely impressed by mystical experience as evidence for the existence of a divine reality and who may well believe that discussion of the distinction between experience and interpretation and about the question how seriously we should take assertions that some mystical experiences at any rate are indescribable somehow misses the point, skating round it, as it were, but never really coming to grips with it. Such people may indeed be prepared to admit that a mystical writer is naturally inclined to interpret his or her experiences in the light of pre-existing beliefs, Hindu or Christian beliefs for example, and that for this reason one can hardly argue simply from the occurrence of mystical experience to the truth of a particular religious creed. They may also be prepared to admit the possibility of there being experiences which are commonly described as mystical but which have little, if anything, to do with religion as ordinarily understood. At the same time they may be convinced that in the history of religion, both western and eastern, there are phenomena which appear to have a basic family resemblance and which can reasonably be regarded as cases of intuitive perception of or contact with a reality other than the physical world about us and the individual self, considered as such. If someone rejects this view of the matter on the ground, for example, that Kant showed that there is no such thing as intellectual intention, this is an example of dogmatism. For if we can reasonably claim that there are cases of intellectual or suprasensory intuition, Kant was wrong, or at any rate his thesis cannot justifiably be taken as an assured premise. Further reflection and argumentation is indeed required, if we wish to argue in favour of theism against monism or in favour of monism or in favour of monism against theism. But in regard to the existence of a reality which is transcendent in the sense that it cannot be identified with the physical world about us or with the individual self, mystical experience in East and West provides evidence which it is more reasonable to accept as evidence than not to do so. This aspect of the matter is simply by-passed, if we focus our attention simply on logical questions, such as the question whether experiencing is necessarily experiencing *as* and, if so, whether we can still make a distinction between experience and interpretation. Nobody really doubts that mystical writers of the past have interpreted their experiences in the light of pre-existing beliefs. But mystical experience can none the less be reasonably regarded as presenting cumulative evidence that there is more to reality than the visible and tangible.

It may be said that those who think in this way are likely to be people who are already religious believers and who are predisposed to look on mystical experience as providing experiential evidence in support of their beliefs. If, for example, a person believes in the existence of a personal God who calls human beings to close union with himself, he or she is naturally predisposed to seeing cases of such union where it is reasonable to do so. It would be an odd situation if the divine call were entirely ineffectual. Again, if a person believes, with Śaṁkara, that there is only one true reality, Brahman, that person is predisposed to see in mystical states, in which consciousness of self is lost in what seems to be consciousness of a meta-phenomenal reality, confirmatory evidence of the truth of the Upanishadic doctrine of the One. Again, if a person believes, with the Sufi thinkers, that God is in all things and all things in God, he or she is predisposed to see confirmation of this belief in cases of mystics who have claimed to have a vivid awareness of the divine presence. The confirmatory evidence can of course react on the pre-existing belief, reinforcing or strengthening it. But the belief predisposes a person to see certain phenomena as evidence which supports the belief. It is indeed a case of predisposition, not of predetermination. As we have noted, a Muslim may dismiss the claims of mystics as incompatible with belief in the divine transcendence. But it is none the less true that those who are genuinely impressed by mysticism as evidence for the existence of a transcendent reality are likely to be found among religious believers.

There is of course a good deal of truth in this point of view. After all, if one believes in the existence of a personal God with whom human beings can communicate, it is natural to expect to find examples of such communication, ranging from ordinary prayer and praise to a closer spiritual communion. And if a person believes on the authority of sacred texts that the innermost self is one with Brahman, he or she is predisposed to favourable consideration of claims to have experienced this oneness. At the same time I do not think that the class of those who are genuinely impressed by mysticism as evidence for the existence of a transcendent reality can be simply equated with the class of those who are already firm religious believers. Consider the type of agnostic who would like to believe in God and who does not stand, as it were, entirely outside religion, in the sense of having, as some would put it, no religious sense, but who regards the world as ambiguous, as pointing in some aspects beyond itself but of being of such a nature in other respects that belief in a transcendent source, at any rate if conceived as a personal and good God, is unwarranted. It is not inconceivable that such a person should be led by reflection on mystical experience to incline to, or even to come down on, the side of belief.

Such a person, it seems to me, would probably be considering mysticism not simply as an isolated set of phenomena but rather as one factor among others which should be taken into account in forming an overall view of reality. In other words, he or she would be reflecting on mysticism as an element in a cumulative argument, as one of a number of converging lines of thought. It is possible to feel sceptical about any argument to the existence of a transcendent reality which is based simply and solely on what we are able to understand in accounts of mystical experience and yet to believe that in developing a general view of reality one can see in mysticism a significant factor.

What I have in mind can be illustrated by reference to Henri Bergson. This reference should not be understood as equivalent to an unqualified endorsement of his style of philosophy, which tends to be impressionistic, vague and imaginative, lacking in precise conceptual analysis and in proper attention to the logical structure of his arguments.[7] At the same time I think that after his initial popularity and fame he has been unduly depreciated. In any case, in the course of his philosophizing he gradually builds up a general world-view, approaching it through reflection on different aspects of the world and of human life. It was not a question of deliberately constructing a system but rather of a number of lines of thought converging towards a rather loose synthesis. Thus in *Creative Evolution* he considers biological phenomena in the context of the theory of evolution and proposes the idea of the *élan vital*, the creative cosmic impulse or energy as responsible for the movement of evolution with the emergence of novelty, of life out of the apparently lifeless and of mind out of the level of organic life. Bergson does indeed speak of the *élan vital* as 'God', presumably because he regards the creative activity in question as one of the divine activities. But the concept of the *élan vital*, as presented in *Creative Evolution*, is obviously far from being all that the Jew or Christian or Muslim understands by the term 'God'. The concept represents for him the furthest extent to which he feels entitled to go on the basis of the data which he has been considering. Later, however, in the *Two Sources of Morality and Religion*, Bergson turns his attention to the moral and religious life of the human being. He is not blind to aspects of the religious history of mankind which seem to us, looking back, bizarre or repugnant. On the contrary, he draws attention to the presence of such features. At the same time he sees in mysticism, especially in Christian mysticism (and, we might add, in Sufi mysticism) a source of active love and a key to the nature of the ultimate reality. The *élan vital* then appears as a creative source, not simply of the levels of organic life but also of active love and as a possible object of love. In other words, the *élan vital* of *Creative Evolution* now appears as personal, as much closer to the concept of God as we find it in theistic religion. Reflection on mysticism is used not so much to prove the existence of a creative power as to indicate the nature of this power. In Bergson's words, 'God is

[7] I have presented a critical discussion of some aspects of his theory of morality in *Philosophers and Philosophies*, ch. XI (London and New York, 1976).

love, and he is object of love: this is the whole contribution of mysticism'.[8]

The emphasis which Bergson lays on Christian mysticism, as represented, for example, by St Teresa of Avila, may give the impression that he was writing under the influence of Christian presuppositions. Though however in the course of time he came very close to Christianity,[9] he did not start with Christian beliefs. He would have claimed, I suppose, that it was his own reflections which led him progressively nearer to the Christian religion, reflection on mysticism being one of the influential factors. In other words, he claimed that his approach was empirical. It may be said that in this case he should have paid more attention and given more weight to oriental mysticism. It must be remembered however that he had already written about freedom, and one of the chief features of Christian mysticism which attracted him was that, in his judgment, it left room for the idea of human creative activity in cooperation with God or as a kind of prolongation of the divine activity. It can reasonably be suggested that it was a question of presupposing certain judgments of value rather than of presupposing religious beliefs about the nature of reality. In the formation of Bergson's own beliefs, his general view of reality, various lines of thought interacted on one another. Thus reflection on mysticism interacted with his conception of the *élan vital*. The result of the converging lines of thought was a general picture of reality.

There are of course other philosophers who might have been mentioned to illustrate the point that a general picture of reality can have persuasive force, provided that it seems to people to 'click', to correspond with and enrich their own experience, to widen their existing outlook without contradicting convictions which they are not prepared to abandon or revise. One of the great attractions to some minds of the philosophy of Hegel is doubtless its comprehensiveness, the way in which it brings together in an overall view of reality reflection on a wide variety

[8]*The Two Sources of Morality and Religion*, translated by R. A. Audra and C. Brereton, with the assistance of W. Horsfall-Carter, p. 216 (London and New York, 1935). The French original appeared at Paris in 1932.

[9]At the end of his life Bergson said that he would have become a Catholic, had it not been for his reluctance to seem to be deserting the Jewish community in their hour of need, during the Nazi persecution of the Jews that is to say.

of themes, such as nature, human history, social and political life, art, religion and the development of philosophical thought. To be sure, it may appear repugnant or fantastic to some minds, but it can also tend to persuade by the cumulative power of interacting lines of thought. Marxism too can exercise a powerful attraction, as seeming to make sense of human history. With Bergson however we find a conspicuous emphasis on religious mysticism; and for this reason his thought is much more suitable for illustrative purposes in the present context of discussion than is the philosophy of Hegel, not to speak of the thought of Karl Marx. Besides, whereas with Hegel we may have the feeling that data are being accommodated to or fitted into a preconceived scheme which purports to rest on a logical deduction, Bergson's approach is, or claims to be, more purely empirical.

What all this amounts to, it may be said, is the claim that a general view of reality can exercise a persuasive force on the minds of those who are predisposed to accept it. This is doubtless a true psychological statement. We can add that sometimes a general view of reality can come as a kind of revelation, producing a change in a person's previous ideas. Some people seem to have been influenced in this sort of way by the writings of Teilhard de Chardin. But they were probably dissatisfied, if only vaguely and perhaps without realizing it themselves, with their existing outlook or ideas and were thus predisposed to react favourably to what presented itself to them with the force of novelty and seemed both enlightening and enriching. In other words, the relevant general view of reality appeared to them as what they had been looking for but had been unable hitherto to find. All this can be admitted. Nobody is likely to quarrel seriously with the contention that from the psychological point of view general views of reality can seem persuasive and exercise an influence. From the point of view of cognitive value, however, in regard to truth, argument and proof are of great importance. And it is in this respect that general views of reality tend to be deficient. Let us assume that Bergson's view of the world has exercised a persuasive influence on some minds. The same can be said of the view presented by Marx and Engels. But these views of reality are not the same. In some important respects they are incompatible. How are we going to distinguish between them in regard to truth except by examining arguments, if there are any to examine? Mention has indeed been made above of a cumulative argument. But how is this to be conceived? Do I mean to imply that two weak arguments somehow become strong arguments by being juxtaposed? If, for example, Bergson's argument to prove that there is an *élan vital* is insufficient to prove what he wants to prove, and his argument to show that in mystical experience the mystic is in contact with a source of life other than himself and the visible world is also insufficient to prove his thesis, are these insufficient arguments supposed to become sufficient simply by being conjoined and regarded as contributing jointly to a general view of reality? We surely have to examine the arguments separately; and if each is found wanting, the whole edifice collapses. That is to say, its truth-claims collapse, even if its persuasive force remains for people who fail to examine the arguments in a critical spirit.

Let us suppose that Tom is found dead, stabbed in such a way that he cannot have committed suicide. Bill comes under suspicion as the possible murderer, as it is known that Tom had wooed and married the girl whom he, Bill, had set his heart on marrying and that from that time Bill had nursed a grudge against Tom. The fact that Bill had a serious grudge against Tom is clearly insufficient proof that he is the murderer. After all, many people have reasons for bearing grudges against others but do not murder them. Let us suppose, however, that it is then discovered that Bill was absent from his home at the time of Tom's murder, that he is unable, or unwilling, to say where he was at the time, and that he would probably have had time to kill Tom and get back to his own house. Once again, Bill's absence from home, taken by itself, is far from being a sufficient proof that he murdered Tom. Other people may well have been absent from their homes at the relevant times without being able to prove that they had no opportunity of killing Tom. None the less, the combination of motive and opportunity increase suspicion against Bill. And if it is then found that Bill possesses a weapon with which the deed could have been performed, suspicion is further increased, even though the mere possession of the weapon is not a sufficient proof that Bill is the murderer. (I assume of course that there are no bloodstains on the weapon, corresponding to Tom's blood.) Taken by itself, each argument to show that Bill committed the murder is weak. But the factors, taken in combination, justify increasing suspicion. This does not alter the fact that each argument, taken singly, is weak. But, taken together as a cumulative argument, they are stronger than any individual member taken by itself. To be sure, the facts, as I have presented them, are not sufficient to convict Bill of murder. The possibility of his innocence remains open, even if he had both motive and opportunity to kill Tom and possessed a weapon with which the murder could have been committed. At the same time the facts justify further investigation, unless of course other facts come to light which point definitely to someone else as the murderer. My point is simply that the idea of a cumulative argument is not meaningless. One can imagine other facts being discovered which would increase justifiable suspicion of Bill.

There can, it seems to me, be something analogous of this kind in the case of world-views. Let us assume, for example, that a number of mystics belonging to different cultures and periods claim to have enjoyed experiential knowledge of a reality other than the physical world and the individual self or ego. Obviously, this does not prove that the claims are true, even if there is no reason to doubt the sincerity of the claimants. We may perhaps believe that there is no such thing as suprasensory perception or intellectual intuition, and that the mystics' claims, taken by themselves, are not sufficient to show that there is. Again, it may seem highly probable that in some cases at any rate what a mystic encountered, if he encountered anything save a blank, was his own psyche, at a level below consciousness and the subject-object distinction. And we may suspect that the same may be true in regard to other cases. If, however, a philosopher, by citing examples from a field other than mysticism, has made out a reasonable case for claiming that there can be such a thing as suprasensory perception or intuitive knowledge, we shall probably be now prepared to consider the possibility of the mystics' claims being true. Further, if the philosopher has also made out a reasonable case for believing that the world reflects the work of a creative power, the claims of the mystics, or at any rate of some of them, are likely to appear to us as less improbable than if they were taken simply by themselves. In other words, through the convergence of different lines of thought a general world-view may progressively emerge, a general picture into which religious experience in general, and mystical experience in particular, fits in an intelligible manner.

It does not follow of course that a world-view which has been developed in this way can be regarded as providing us with certainty about the nature of reality. For we have assumed that the various lines of argument are not strong enough to prove their conclusions independently and there remains the possibility that some other world-view is equally tenable or even more probable. But neither does it follow that there is no way of judging between world-views. Apart from the test of coherence, it may be possible to argue that one world-view is to be preferred to another in so far as the first both accommodates and throws light on a certain set of phenomena (ethical phenomena, for example, such as the consciousness of moral obligation) which the other world-view either passes over or cannot accommodate without distorting their nature. It must indeed be admitted that there can be differences of opinion about the real nature of the phenomena and about what constitutes distortion. If we talk about one world-view making sense of a certain set of phenomena while another does not, there may well be disagreement about what making sense in this particular context actually means. Further, even if one world-view is superior to another in one respect, it does not follow that the second world-view has no positive contribution to make to our interpretation of reality. A good many people would doubtless be prepared to claim that the picture of the world presented by Marx and Engels distorts the religious life of mankind, and that religious experience in general and mystical experience in particular fit much better into the world-picture presented by a philosopher such as Bergson. But it by no means follows that Marx did not draw attention to and throw light on phenomena which receive scant, if any, attention in some other world-view. If we talk about one world-view being superior to another, we ought to be prepared to specify in what respect or respects we judge it to be superior. My point, however, is simply that rational discussion of the comparative merits of world-views is possible. It may be said that any judgment about the superiority of one world-view in comparison with another will be made within the framework of the world-view in question, and that to make a contrary judgment one would first have to be converted to the second world-view. But even if sudden conversions of this kind are possible, it is more likely that a conversion is preceded by intellectual dissatisfaction with one's previous world-view and an increasing perception of the greater intellectual satisfactoriness of another world-view. I do not think that we can ascribe all such changes in outlook simply to wishful thinking or emotive reaction.

V

To conclude. There is obviously a great deal more which could be said about mysticism, from, for example, the psychological, ethical, social and theological points of view. It is a complex phenomenon. Phrases such as 'mystical experience' are commonly used to refer to a variety of what may very well be, and in my opinion are, experiences or states which ought to be distinguished as far as it is possible to do so. As a Christian, I certainly believe that there can be different degrees of realization or awareness of the divine presence, and that such an awareness can have a powerful effect on a person's life and can be of social value. I also believe that an awareness of this kind can occur in different religions, though interpretations are obviously likely to differ. These beliefs do not however prevent one from recognizing that there may be experiences which are commonly described as mystical but which may have little to do with religion as ordinarily understood. This constitutes a difficulty in discussing the theme which I selected, namely the value of mysticism as evidence for the existence of a transcendent reality, the One. At any rate it makes the theme more complicated. And I am aware of course that my treatment has been sketchy and inadequate. It may also seem to be inconclusive. So it is. I am doubtful, for reasons which I have mentioned, that a really convincing argument simply from the occurrence of mystical experiences to the existence of a transcendent reality is possible. What I have suggested is that any such line of thought gains in impressiveness when it figures as one strand among others in a cumulative argument. And by impressiveness I mean intellectual impressiveness, not simply the ability to evoke an emotive response.

CHAPTER 10

ETHICS, METAPHYSICS AND
SOCIAL IDEALS

*Normative ethics and metaphysics – monism, theism and social
concern – ethics as an autonomous discipline*

I

We have been considering belief in the existence of a One. If we
prescind however from certain developments in modern western
philosophy (to which reference will be made later), philosophy
in the past was generally practical as well as theoretical. That
is to say, philosophers generally included moral teaching in their
field of thought, expounding the general principles of a way of
life leading to happiness or to the full development of human
nature, or telling people, in general terms, how they ought and
ought not to act. In other words, moral philosophy usually
formed part of a greater whole, comprising metaphysics, cosmology and epistemological or psychological themes.

When moral philosophy formed part of a complex whole, a
philosophical system or a world-view, we would naturally expect
to find some interaction, or interrelations, between the different
parts. Without any such interrelations it would be a question of
a juxtaposition of separate disciplines, not of a system or of a
coherent world-view. To see what the interrelations were, we
obviously have to examine and reflect on the different philosophies. We have to avoid any exclusive concentration of attention
on a particular philosophical system.

For example, if we focus our attention on the philosophy of
Spinoza, and if we lay emphasis on the quasi-geometrical form
in which his great work, the *Ethics*, is expressed, we may conclude that he tried to deduce ethics from metaphysics. If therefore we regarded Spinoza as the model metaphysician, we might
be tempted to draw the general conclusion that constructors of
philosophical systems or world-views have tried to deduce moral
philosophy, in the sense of a normative ethics, from metaphys-

ical premises. In this case it can be objected that metaphysical theories purport to tell us how things are, and that from statements of how things are we cannot deduce how things ought to be. To take a simple example, the statement that on an average *X* number of children are killed by their parents every year tells us nothing about how parents ought to behave towards their children. From the mere fact that people behave in a certain way we cannot deduce either that they ought or that they ought not to behave in a certain way. Analogously, from the statement that all finite things depend ontologically on a One or that the empirical world is the appearance of one ultimate reality we cannot deduce how human beings ought or ought not to behave.

Given this point of view, we may conclude that it is highly desirable that ethics should be dissociated from metaphysics. There may of course be other reasons for thinking this desirable. At present however I am concerned with the particular reason mentioned. And I wish to argue that inclusion of moral philosophy in a larger organic unity, a philosophical system or world-view, does not necessarily mean that the philosopher in question is trying to deduce normative ethics simply from metaphysical premises considered as statements of fact. By arguing in this way I may perhaps lay myself open to the accusation of setting up an Aunt Sally which I then proceed to knock down. But there are some distinctions which I wish to make and which are relevant to the general line of thought in this chapter.

In the first place the relation between moral philosophy and other elements in a general world-view has not been uniform. Sometimes moral philosophy has played a subordinate role, not in the sense that it has been considered of little importance but in the sense that it has constituted one particular field for the application of certain concepts and principles which have been regarded as basic and which have contributed to giving an organic unity to the philosophy as a whole. For example, in Aristotle's teleological ethics a fundamental role was played by the concepts of potentiality and act which pervaded his whole philosophy. Obviously, his philosophy was not and could not be deduced from these concepts alone, but they helped to integrate his ethics into his thought as a whole. At other times moral philosophy has itself been basic, though in the course of time it was found necessary, or at any rate desirable, to give it a wider framework by developing or borrowing cosmological or metaphysical themes which provided a setting for teaching about human life and conduct. Confucianism, for example, was basically an ethical system, centering round the idea of the human being as a moral agent in a social context; but it came not only to incorporate within itself the ancient *Yin-yang* cosmology but also to construct for itself, though with some dependence on other schools, a metaphysics such as that expounded by the neo-Confucianist thinker Chu Hsi. In other words, some philosophers have started with reflection on the moral life with a practical end in view, such as the reform of society, though the need for a wider outlook and framework of thought came to be felt and met by their successors.

The matter is indeed much more complex than the foregoing remarks suggest. There is obviously no question of Confucian ethics having been actually deduced from metaphysics or theology. But it is true that Confucius, according to the records, maintained that the moral precepts which he accepted and taught expressed the will of Heaven. Thus the Confucianists laid themselves open to the accusation brought by the Taoists, that they attributed their own moral convictions to Heaven and then professed to derive them from Heaven. It can also be objected of course that to attribute a certain moral code to Heaven is to declare the code sacrosanct and thus to discourage critical questioning. But this does not alter the fact that the ethics of Confucius was due much more to reflection on the needs of society as he saw them than to any deduction from metaphysics. As for Aristotle, the influence of metaphysics can indeed be seen in his ethics, inasmuch as he applies certain metaphysical principles and concepts to man's moral life on the ground that the human being is part of the cosmos and therefore subject to the metaphysical truths or principles which apply throughout the world, or to being in general. It is clear however that Aristotle did not claim to be able to deduce all moral phenomena from what he described as 'first philosophy'.

In the second place we can note a distinction between philosophies which include the idea of a One, one ultimate reality. In some philosophies of this kind the One has been described in moral terms. This is notably the case in theistic thought, with its belief in a personal God. In Judaism, Christianity and Islam God is described as good, or as infinite goodness, not as bad, nor as indifferent to good and evil. The same can be said of the theistic tradition within the Vedānta school in India. Even when God has been conceived as the universal cause of all things, including human actions, attempts have been made to interpret this belief in such a way as not to entail the conclusion that God is the author of evil.[1] In some other philosophies however the One, the ultimate reality, has been conceived as transcending good and evil, in the sense that moral epithets are inapplicable to the One. In Taoist philosophy, for example, it is not a case of the One being evil or bad because it is not good. The thesis is that neither term can be applied. The language of moral distinction is inapplicable to the One. The same can be said in regard to Nirguna-Brahman in the Advaita Vedānta. In the West Spinoza refused to qualify the infinite Substance, the Absolute, as being either morally good or morally evil. Such terms cannot be meaningfully predicated of the Absolute. Again, according to F. H. Bradley, in so far as good and evil can be said to exist, they must exist in the Absolute, but they do not exist there *as* good and evil. For the Absolute transcends all relations and distinctions.

On the face of it, as the result, that is to say, of a superficial glance at philosophies of the One, we might perhaps be inclined to say that in philosophies of the second kind there can be no question of deriving a normative ethics from the metaphysics of the One, inasmuch as morality, with its distinctions, is relative to human beings, so that moral epithets cannot be meaningfully predicated of the One. Morality is a purely human phenomenon, and moral philosophy must stand on its own feet. In philosophies of the first kind however the One, conceived as personal, good and the source or cause of everything other than himself, must be regarded as the source of the moral law. Those actions are considered morally obligatory which have been commanded by God. Those actions are wrong which have been forbidden

[1] I am thinking, for example, of the contention that though God is the ultimate source of all finite being, evil as such is a privation of being and not a positive entity created by God.

by God. To be sure, it can be argued that, as in the case of Confucianism, human moral convictions are first attributed to God and are then said to have their origin in God. But as far as the formal presentation of the philosophy is concerned, a normative ethics is based on metaphysics, on philosophical theology. The objection can then be raised that the statement that God has forbidden actions of type X is a factual statement, whereas the statement that human beings ought not to perform actions of type X is a moral statement and cannot be deduced from a factual statement. Religious devotion may of course demand that God should be obeyed. But the logical point remains valid.

This reading of the situation is over-hasty and does not do justice to the historical facts. Consider Taoism, for example. Though Chuang Tzu regarded moral codes as conventional and not as emanating from or ratified by the One, the Taoist philosophers did not hesitate to draw from reflection on the Tao what can be fairly described as moral lessons. Thus the *Lao Tzu* reiterates the claim that just as the Tao or One lets things be themselves and develop spontaneously, so should rulers allow the citizens to be themselves and not try to mould them according to a uniform pattern based on moral principles which were purely conventional and inhibited spontaneity. In other words, in spite of the Taoist attitude to Confucian ethics, they can be depicted as deriving a moral theory of their own from the metaphysics of the One. When however we turn to St Thomas Aquinas, a theistic philosopher, we find him developing a moral theory according to which it is much truer to say that God forbids certain actions because they are wrong than that the actions are wrong because God forbids them. It is true that in late medieval philosophy a theologically based ethical authoritarianism became prominent, as with William of Ockham. But as far as Aquinas is concerned, he believed that the human reason itself could in principle discern the basic principles of the natural moral law, even if a person did not accept the Bible as the revealed word of God. It is true that Aquinas believed that in practice revelation was required if everyone was to know his or her moral obligations clearly and easily, but this does not alter the fact that he recognized the possibility of a normative ethics derived from reflection on human nature. It would therefore be incorrect to say that in monist philosophies, with their doctrine of a One which transcends moral distinctions, ethics is independent of metaphysics, whereas in theistic philosophies, with their conception of a personal and good God, ethics is essentially dependent on and derived from metaphysics.

It can reasonably be objected that I have been confusing several issues, which ought to be distinguished. First, there is the question of theologically based authoritarianism, the doctrine that certain actions are obligatory because God has commanded them and certain actions wrong because God has forbidden them. Authoritarianism of this kind evidently cannot be present in a philosophy which does not include the idea of a personal God and in which the One is conceived as transcending moral distinctions and as being, in some sense, indifferent to good and evil. In a theistic philosophy theologically based ethical authoritarianism can be present, and it sometimes has been present; but it need not be present. It is possible to hold, for example, that to kill one's parents is forbidden by God because it is wrong, rather than it is wrong because it is forbidden by God. All that is required is to give a meaning to the word 'wrong' which is not equivalent to 'forbidden by God'.

Secondly, there is the question of the extent to which a given system of normative ethics is dependent on metaphysical presuppositions. It might be maintained, for example, that though St Thomas Aquinas certainly did not regard the moral law as determined by an arbitrary decree, in the sense that the precepts of the moral law could have been very different from, or even the opposite of, what they actually are, his conception of the natural moral law really makes sense only in the context of a theistic and teleological view of the world. In other words, the dependence of ethics on metaphysics can take various forms. Theologically based authoritarianism is only one of them. And it should be distinguished from the other forms of dependence. One can make metaphysical presuppositions which influence one's ethical thought, even if the idea that the arbitrary will of God is the sole fount of the moral law is not one of them. If one is justified in talking at all about Taoist ethics, it was influenced by Taoist metaphysics; but there was obviously no question of a theologically based authoritarianism.

Thirdly, there is the question of the deduction of normative moral statements from factual premises. Anyone who accepts the 'no ought from an is' thesis, is committed to maintaining that a normative moral statement cannot be deduced from a set of premises which do not include at least one normative statement or judgment of value. The factual statements in question may of course be metaphysical statements, but they need not be. It is indeed difficult to find criteria enabling us to determine precisely which statements count as metaphysical and which do not. But a statement such as 'all human beings seek for pleasure' would ordinarily be regarded as a psychological, factual or empirical statement, true or false as the case may be. And the person who accepts the 'no ought from an is' thesis would maintain that no conclusion could be drawn from such empirical statements alone about the way in which human beings ought or ought not to behave. Metaphysics does not come into the matter. It is a question of logic. If in a given philosophy a normative ethics is represented as following from two premises, one of which is a metaphysical statement purporting to state how things are, as a matter of fact, while the other is a non-metaphysical statement of fact, an empirical statement, this is a ground for objection. But it is equally a ground for objection if the premises are all non-metaphysical and factual or empirical. In other words, even if it can be shown that in a given world-view a system of normative ethics is not deduced simply from the metaphysical part of the world-view, the ethical system may none the less be open to objection on the ground that it conflicts with the 'no ought from an is' thesis.

The 'no ought from an is' thesis has been challenged. It has been argued, for example, that it presupposes that a clear distinction can be made between factual statements on the one hand and value-judgments on the other, and that we cannot in fact make a sharp distinction of this kind. It has also been argued that when we are asked to justify a particular moral judgment, we often appeal to factual statements, and that the 'no ought from an is' thesis makes nonsense of our ordinary moral reasoning. Suppose, for example, that someone says that

Jane ought to leave London immediately and go to Bristol, and the speaker is asked to justify the statement. If the speaker replies, 'Jane's mother is dangerously ill in a Bristol hospital', nobody is likely to object that this is a factual statement and that a moral judgment cannot be derived from a factual statement.

In regard to the first line of objection against the 'no ought from an is' thesis, I do not think that I have any fresh light to shed upon the question of the distinction between factual statements and value-judgments. My own inclination however is to accept the distinction. I am therefore prepared to say that, on the assumption that the distinction is valid, I accept the 'no ought from an is' thesis. In regard to the second line of objection, I do not believe that it is fatal to the thesis in question. It is of course perfectly true that to justify moral judgments we often appeal to factual statements; and it is also true that such appeals are often accepted without further argument. But is not this the case because both parties take for granted a certain judgment of value or a certain normative statement, and that it is therefore not necessary to mention it? If, for instance, the statement that Jane's mother is dangerously ill in hospital at Bristol is accepted as a perfectly adequate reason for asserting that Jane ought to leave London and go to Bristol, this is surely because both parties take it for granted that children ought to show consideration for their parents when the parents are seriously ill. If something of the kind were not assumed, someone could say, 'I do not see any connection between Jane's mother being dangerously ill in Bristol and an obligation on Jane's part to leave London and go to Bristol'.

What has all this to do with the relation between normative ethics and world-views? The connection is this. It seems to me that in world-views or metaphysical systems as wholes there may be inbuilt or assumed judgments of value. If these are not mentioned but are taken for granted, it may well appear that a philosopher is trying to derive normative moral statements from what purport to be statements of fact. If however the inbuilt judgments of value are explicitly mentioned and do not function simply as tacitly assumed premises, this impression may disappear.

The point can be illustrated in this way. Let us suppose that someone claims to be a devout Christian. He tells us that he believes firmly in the doctrines of the Trinity and the Incarnation. He adds however that he does not regard love among human beings as a value. On the contrary, he hopes that they will hate one another to such an extent that the human race will be blotted out. We might well comment, 'My dear sir, you have a very odd idea of Christianity. Being a Christian is not simply a matter of accepting certain beliefs about what is the case, for example that God is three Persons in one Nature. It includes acceptance of love as a supreme value. To be sure, Christians may have often behaved in a notably unloving manner. But this does not alter the fact that acceptance of love as a supreme value is an integral part of adherence to the Christian religion. It is, so to speak, part of the package-deal.' Given this inbuilt judgment of value, it can serve as a premise, together with statements of fact, in drawing moral conclusions. It is true that there can be dispute about precisely what loving other people implies. But such disputes are in any case a familiar feature of moral reasoning. My point is simply that an argument which looks as though it infringed the 'no ought from an is' thesis may not really do so, as there may be a tacitly assumed judgment of value which functions as an unspoken premise.

A further example. Let us suppose that Śaṁkara or some other adherent of the Advaita Vedānta says to someone, 'You ought to control your sensual desires.' 'Why?' asks the person in question. 'Because,' says Śaṁkara, 'your real self is one with Brahman, and it is not possible for anyone who is a slave to the passions to realize his true self.' It may seem that Śaṁkara is trying to prove the truth of a moral judgment by deriving it from factual statements alone. But is this the case? Śaṁkara evidently presupposes that realization of the true Self in the intuitive awareness of oneness with Brahman is of supreme value for the human being. If the other person accepts this judgment of value, the reasons given by Śaṁkara for saying that sensual desires should be controlled will doubtless seem adequate.

This is all very well, someone may say, but an important issue has been evaded. From a set of premises containing a value-judgment, whether explicitly stated or tacitly assumed, we may certainly be able to deduce a more particular judgment of value. Eventually however we come up against basic judgments of value which cannot themselves be deduced from more general value-judgments. We are then faced with a choice. On the one hand we can claim to be able to derive a basic value-judgment from statements of fact. Thereby we preserve the unity of a general world-view by deriving its basic value-judgment or judgments from other elements in the complex whole. We can do this however only by denying the 'no ought from an is' thesis. On the other hand we might maintain that the truth of basic judgments of value is perceived intuitively, that they are self-evidently true. In point of fact some philosophers have maintained that there are both theoretical and practical principles which are self-evidently true. This idea does not indeed involve denial of the 'no ought from an is' thesis. Apart however from the fact that it is assumed that truth and falsity can be predicated of value-judgments, an assumption which might be questioned, it is very difficult to show that any value-judgment is self-evidently true. Many people may feel that there are such judgments. For example, many people would doubtless be prepared to claim that it is self-evidently true that love is more valuable than hatred. But if someone denies this and is prepared to accept all the consequences of the assertion that hatred is to be preferred to love, we are probably reduced to regarding him as a warped personality, which is not quite the same thing as proving that the value-judgment which we accept and he denies is self-evidently true.

There is no reason, however, why a world-view should not include basic judgments of value, even if they can neither be deduced from metaphysical premises which state simply how things are, as a matter of fact, nor be shown, to everyone's satisfaction, to be self-evidently true. If, that is to say, a given world-view includes not only an account of reality as it is or as it is thought to be but also a programme for human life or a normative ethics, it has to include judgments of value. And these judgments are not simply excrescences. If we are concerned not simply with how the world is but also with human life in the world, with the way in which human beings ought to act in this world, we cannot make the transition from the theoretical to the

practical aspects of the world-view without stating or implying
certain basic judgments of value. These, as I have maintained,
can be inbuilt into the total world-view, in the sense that the
latter cannot be accepted unless the relevant value-judgment or
judgments of value are accepted. Once this is done, we can of
course appeal to elements from the theoretical or descriptive
part of the world-view in our moral reasoning. As we have
noted, the 'no ought from an is' thesis does not state that no
factual statements should ever function as premises in moral
reasoning. What it claims is that a normative moral statement
cannot be deduced from a set of premises which contains *only*
statements of fact.

II

In the foregoing section we have been concerned primarily with
theoretical issues. I have been discussing the assumption that
the 'no ought from an is' thesis makes a valid logical point; and
I have argued that, even if this assumption is accepted, it does
not constitute a decisive objection to the construction of
world-views. It might conceivably be claimed that a world-view
should be confined to reflection on the nature of reality, to an
account of how things are. But it is difficult to see why this
should necessarily be the case. For the human being as a moral
agent, seeking the realization of values, is part of reality. We
can try to give an account of how things are. But through their
actions human beings can affect how things are. They react on
their environment in a variety of ways. And reflection on goals
and action to attain these goals inevitably arises. There is
nothing to be surprised at if philosophical systems and world-
views have generally included what an Aristotelian would describe as practical philosophy. It is obvious that the great
religions of mankind have been orientated not only to belief but
also to practice, to action in accordance with belief. And though
philosophies, by their very nature, tend to have a more restricted
practical influence, it would be quite implausible to claim that
they have never had a practical influence. Quite apart from the
'no ought from an is' thesis, from the psychological point of view

at any rate some philosophies have exercised a powerful influence with practical effects.

This thought gives rise to the following line of reflection. Nowadays we tend to attach great value to social ideals and to action directed to actualize these ideals. We do not generally look on traditional social structures, as they have come down to us, as sacrosanct, as unmodifiable in principle. And we think of human beings as capable of changing structures and institutions, of effecting social change. Needless to say, most of us do not desire change simply for the sake of change. Still less are most of us inspired by the nihilistic ideal proclaimed by Nechayev, the nineteenth-century Russian revolutionary conspirator, in his *Revolutionary Catechism*, 'total, universal and merciless destruction'. But at any rate we recognize that it is both possible and desirable for human beings to attempt to remedy social evils and injustices. Even if we do little or nothing about the matter ourselves, we pay some tribute to social ideals. Even when the tribute amounts to little more than lip service, this lip service at any rate testifies to the prevalence of social ideals. It is therefore natural that there should be a tendency to judge past philosophies (and not only past ones) in the light of these ideals. To be sure, it can be argued that philosophy is concerned with truth, and that truth is truth even if it does not contribute to the realization of social ideals. But if a past philosophy seems actually to inhibit social activism and to impede the realization of social ideals, we probably tend to think that there is something wrong with it and that it cannot serve as a philosophy for today, for our modern world. Even if we are not prepared to claim with Karl Marx that it is the business of philosophy to change the world, we are unlikely to take a rosy view of a philosophy which seems to stand in the way of social change and to discourage it.

At first sight at any rate the kind of metaphysics most likely to discourage social ideals and to inhibit social activism is the monism represented by the philosophy of non-difference in India, the Advaita Vedānta. It is not a question of making out that in this philosophy there was no ethical doctrine. In spite of the fact that the Absolute was conceived as transcending good and evil, the concept of moral purification and progress was a perfectly meaningful one for Śaṁkara and other Advaitins.

Further, though the world of plurality, the world in which moral distinctions are meaningful, was regarded as the appearance of Brahman, an appearance which was unreal in relation to Brahman in a manner analogous to that in which the world of dreams was said to be unreal in relation to the world of waking consciousness, it was none the less the world in which human beings live and act until they are fully liberated. And in this world human beings have duties. When commenting on the thirteenth verse of the fourth part or discourse of the *Bhagavad-Gītā*, Saṁkara asserted that people should not sit in idleness or renounce action. Even if a man had attained knowledge of the true self, he should continue to perform actions for the benefit of other people. In other words, Saṁkara was far from advocating a policy of complete quietism. Nor did he himself follow such a policy. At the same time the philosophy of non-difference presented as the ideal for the human being the transcending of individuality, individual personality that is to say, an ideal which might not unreasonably be described as that of transcending the human condition altogether.[2] It was not a question of the Advaitin philosophy throwing overboard the teaching of the Vedas about the hierarchy of ideals related to successive periods of life.[3] It was a question of the fourth ideal or goal, that of spiritual liberation, receiving so much emphasis that it tended to overshadow the others. It would be unfair to describe the Advaitin ethics as being simply self-centred. As all selves were regarded as ultimately one with Brahman and so with one another, benevolence towards others in the world of plurality was naturally demanded. But the orientation of the moral life to the attainment of liberation, including liberation from individuality, a liberation which, in its final form, involved passing beyond good and evil, was hardly likely to stimulate a passionate concern with social ideals in the world of appearance. Needless to say, passing beyond good and evil did not mean that the liberated self was free to perform at will those actions which in

---

[2]This description reflects of course the point of view which an Advaitin might regard as unenlightened.

[3]The Vedas recognized as values wealth or prosperity, the satisfaction of desire (stimulated by beauty), the performance of moral duties (in family life, for example) and spiritual liberation.

moral terms are described as evil. It was a question of the self realizing oneness with the Absolute which was conceived as transcending all distinctions and relations. One could not perperly speak of the Absolute, Nirguna-Brahman, as being interested in the promotion of social ends in this world. And the person who concentrates on attaining absorption in Brahman is not likely to show any great concern with this matter.

An obvious comment to make is that the primary question for the philosopher is whether Advaitin monism is true or false, not whether it is likely to encourage or discourage active concern with the realization of social ideals in this world. It is not, however, my intention to imply that the truth or falsity of a theory can be determined purely pragmatically, by showing that it tends or does not tend to produce effects which many people think desirable. I am concerned simply with discussing the sort of ethical ideals which the Advaitin metaphysics is likely to encourage. And it seems clear to me that the doctrine that the human being's real self is one with an Absolute which transcends the sphere of moral distinctions is likely to encourage an ethics in which the emphasis is laid on mural purification with a view to transcending individual personality. In other words, it is likely to encourage a turning of attention inwards or upwards, rather than outwards, in the direction, that is to say, of social activism in this world. Obviously, if one judges a past philosophy in terms of present-day preoccupations, one lays oneself open to a charge of anachronism. But it is not a question of blaming Śaṁkara and other Advaitins for not remedying what seem to us social evils but which may at the time have appeared as facts of life, as structures which had simply to be accepted, such as the Hindu caste system. It is a question of the ethical attitude likely to be encouraged by a given metaphysics. Recent Indian adherents of the Advaita Vedānta, such as Sri Aurobindo, have understandably been sensitive to claims that the philosophy of Śaṁkara encouraged a turning away from this world to an escapist mysticism and that it is therefore not what is needed either by modern India or by humanity at large. They therefore tried to reinterpret the Advaita Vedānta in such a way as to enable its adherents to rebut such claims. There is of course no reason why they should not make this attempt. But by making it they implicitly admitted that the charges were not without foundation. Besides, there are a good many Indian philosophers who certainly do not believe that the Advaita Ve-dānta is a suitable philosophy for today. It is not simply a question of thinking that the Advaitin metaphysics is largely false. It is also a question of finding it to be socially harmful. To be sure, this verdict rests on a value-judgment, which may not be universally shared. But it can hardly be described as perverse.

Those Advaitins who have tried to interpret their philosophy in such a way that it could more easily accommodate a socially oriented ethics have naturally tried to give a more dynamic character to the Advaitin metaphysics. Thus Sri Aurobindo saw the world as the self-expression of infinite Spirit, as though Brahman or the Absolute descended, as it were, into matter. In the process of evolution, however, the world ascends in the direction of spirit, in the direction of divinization, through the emergence of living organisms, of the human mind and the future development of supermind. In fact, Sri Aurobindo's in-terpretation of the Advaita philosophy bears a marked resem-blance to the picture of the world presented by Teilhard de Chardin. Whether it should be described as pantheism or pan-entheism or in some other way is not clear to me. But thinkers such as Sri Aurobindo seem at any rate to have approximated to some form of theism. And this prompts the question whether theistic philosophy does not provide a much better background or framework of thought than monism for a socially oriented ethics.

The answer would seem to be 'Yes'. If activities such as thought, volition and choice are conceived as unattributable to the Absolute, the Absolute obviously cannot be represented as creating the world for a purpose. In theistic philosophy however the world is conceived as having been created by God for an end or purpose, to be attained through or with the co-operation of human action. This idea gives rise to a number of problems, problems relating, for example, to human freedom and divine providence. At the same time the idea of a world created for a purpose, the implementation of which requires human effort within history, certainly seems to provide a better background for social activism than the conception of the world as an inexplicable and semi-real appearance of the Absolute.

It is indeed true that we can find mysticism not only in oriental religion of a non-theistic kind but also in theistic religions such as Christianity and Islam. Indeed, in the history of Christianity we can find certain movements which some would describe as world-fleeing or escapist. It is also true, as far at any rate as orthodox Christianity and Islam are concerned, that the human being's final goal is conceived as transcending this world, a belief which can of course lead to depreciation of this world. None the less, this goal has normally to be achieved through conduct and action in this world.[4] And in theistic religion we find the ideal of a unified human society to be created by man in co-operation with God, a society reflecting the divine unity. It is arguable that this ideal finds its most congenial home in Christianity, in which God himself is conceived as an identity-in-distinction, a conception which would find its created reflection in a unified society of human persons. But a social ideal is common to all the great theistic religions. In Islam we find the ideal of a unified human society in which sacred and secular would be one, undivided.

It can be argued, once again, that even if theism is more likely than monism to encourage the prosecution of social ideals in this world, the primary question for the philosopher is one of truth. I have not however been arguing that theism must be true because it is more favourable than monism to social dynamism. My approach might be explained in this way. In a well-known lecture Professor R. B. Braithwaite maintained that 'many people find it easier to resolve upon and to carry through a course of action which is contrary to their natural inclinations if their policy is associated in their minds with certain stories',[5] the relation between 'stories' and action or a way of life being 'a psychological and causal one'.[6] In terms of Braithwaite's way of speaking I have been arguing that in regard to the develop-

---

[4] I say 'normally' in order to allow for those who die in infancy.

[5] *An Empiricist's View of the Nature of Religious Belief*, p. 27 (Cambridge University Press, 1955).

[6] *Ibid.* Braithwaite does not claim that normative moral statements can be logically deduced from statements of fact or alleged fact. At the same time the latter can certainly exercise a psychological influence.

ment of social ethics and of an active prosecution of social ideals the psychological influence exercised by theistic 'stories' is likely to be much stronger than that exercised by monistic 'stories'. Other things being equal, therefore, people who attach a great value to social concern and dynamism are likely to be more favourably disposed to theistic thought than to monism.[7]

Mention of Professor Braithwaite's lecture arouses in my mind the following line of thought. The contention that beliefs, including beliefs about what is the case, can exercise a psychological influence by stimulating people to embrace a certain way of life or act in certain ways seems to me to be undoubtedly true. I should have thought however that this influence would tend to diminish and grow weaker in proportion as the beliefs are recognized as or thought to be 'stories', stories which one tells oneself. If a person has been stimulated to try to practise love towards other people by beliefs about the divine love and about what God wants, and if the person later comes to think that these beliefs are simply stories or fables, most people, it seems to me, would assume that the stimulative power of the beliefs on his mind is thereby considerably diminished, even if it does not disappear altogether. If this is the case, it does not follow that the person must abandon the policy of loving other people. He may continue to try to implement this policy. But he will do so because he has come to recognize love as a value, independently of any theological or metaphysical beliefs.

The point can be expressed in this way. If a given judgment of value could not be asserted without implying the truth of certain theological or metaphysical beliefs, the connection between them could not be broken. Anyone who accepted the value-judgment would be logically committed to recognizing the truth of the relevant beliefs. If he did not accept the beliefs, he could not, logically speaking, accept the value-judgment. If however it is a question not of logical entailment but of possible psychological influence, the connection between the beliefs and the value-judgment can be broken.

---

[7]Other things are not always equal of course. A person might value social dynamism but none the less be more favourably disposed to monism than theism on other grounds. He might regard monism as being, for example, the less given to encouraging fanaticism.

In this case it is possible to argue on the following lines. In the modern world many people do not accept traditional theological beliefs. And many people are mistrustful of metaphysics. Though however they can steer clear of theological and metaphysical beliefs,[8] they cannot live without making at any rate implied judgments of value and having some implicit maxims of conduct, even if the maxims are such that many people would disapprove of them. It is therefore important that there should be careful and systematic thought about ethical problems, in other words that moral philosophy should continue. It is also important that ethics should stand on its own feet and not be presented as dependent on metaphysics or theology. The 'no ought from an is' thesis provides a basis for this separation. It is doubtless true that in Christianity, for example, there are inbuilt judgments of value. Given however the 'no ought from an is' thesis these judgments of value can be asserted independently of the associated theological beliefs. To treat them in this way is not necessarily to assert that the beliefs are false. This is another question. The point is that even if they are true, the value-judgments can none the less be asserted independently. And in the modern world it is desirable that they should be treated in this way. As for social ethics in particular, it may well be true that theistic belief has given an impetus to social concern, but for a considerable time this concern has tended to pass into secular hands. In any case, if we attach great value to active concern with human welfare and the good of society in this world, it is highly desirable that social ethics or social philosophy should not be treated as though it were dependent on any metaphysical beliefs, whether theistic or monistic.

Nobody of course would wish to deny that as an historical fact ethical thought developed, to a very great extent, within the framework of a general philosophy, world-view or religion. It has been argued however that the separation of ethics from metaphysical and theological assumptions or beliefs represents

[8]I doubt whether one can steer clear of all metaphysical beliefs. Many people implicitly assume, for example, that to exist is to be a possible object of sense-perception. This is an ontological or metaphysical assumption. But the person who claims that we can steer clear of all metaphysical beliefs is doubtless thinking primarily of 'transcendent metaphysics', to borrow a phrase used by Professor W. H. Walsh.

an advance, and that ethics should be treated as an autonomous discipline, even though it falls under the general heading of philosophy. I now wish to discuss this idea of ethics as an autonomous or self-contained discipline.

III

In a book on Indian ethics[9] the author, Dr I. C. Sharma, notes that Jainism, Buddhism and the Vedic schools present ethico-metaphysical systems, and he expresses his belief that this combination of ethics and metaphysics exhibits the superiority of Indian to western philosophy. The author must obviously be aware that the history of western philosophy too provides us with plenty of examples of a combination of ethics and metaphysics, and that it is by no means simply a question of Indian thought. Presumably, however, the author is thinking of the tendency in modern western philosophy to detach ethics from metaphysical and theological beliefs and assumptions, a tendency of which he disapproves.

Up to a point I sympathize with Dr Sharma's general point of view (for reasons which will be explained presently), but I hardly suppose that he would deny the desirability of distinguishing between logical, psychological, ethical, aesthetic and ontological questions and of not confusing them. Philosophy has sometimes suffered from a failure to make such distinctions. When discussing, for example, the topic of universals, we ought not to muddle up psychological and logical questions. Similarly, in the interests of clarity it is desirable to distinguish carefully between an account of reality as it is or is thought to be and a normative ethics, which indicates how human beings ought or ought not to behave. I do not see how anyone can reasonably object to distinguishing, in this sense, between metaphysics and ethics.

It is not however simply a question of sorting out different kinds of questions, for the sake of clarity. If we accept the 'no ought from an is' thesis, we obviously should not present a normative ethics in such a way as to imply that it is deducible

[9]*Ethical Philosophies of India*, by I. C. Sharma, edited and revised by Stanley M. Daugert, Ph.D. (London, 1965).

simply from metaphysical beliefs or theories about what is the case. If we reject the thesis, we can of course argue that a given ethical system is logically dependent on a certain metaphysics. If, however, we allow that the thesis makes a valid logical point, this is a reason for distinguishing carefully between metaphysics and ethics.

The 'no ought from an is' thesis is not indeed (or so I have argued above) of such great practical importance as might be thought from all the fuss which has been made about it. For it does not forbid any appeal to factual premises, provided that the premises of a moral argument do not consist *only* of statements of fact. And the factual statements functioning as premises could be metaphysical or theological statements. This situation may well seem to militate against any rigid separation of ethics from a metaphysical or theological background.

At this point there intervenes a pragmatic consideration, to which reference has already been made. In the modern world belief in metaphysical theories, whether theistic or monistic, cannot simply be taken for granted. To a good many people moral arguments which appeal to metaphysical or theological premises are unconvincing. This might not matter, if moral convictions were a luxury, if it mattered little whether one had them or not, or if it were a matter of no practical importance what people's moral attitudes are. This is clearly not the case. So for practical reasons, it can be urged, ethics should be detached from metaphysics and from theological beliefs and treated as an autonomous discipline. The 'no ought from an is' thesis may not forbid appeal to factual premises, but this is not a good enough reason for including in a set of premises factual statements which a good many people believe to be false, while others think that there is no way of deciding whether they are true or false.

This line of thought may well sound sensible. But a further question arises. If we assume that basic judgments of value cannot be proved, and if we are not prepared to claim that they are self-evidently true, one may reasonably ask whether it is the business of the philosopher to promulgate value-judgments as though he were in a privileged position for doing so. He can reflect on the nature of the value-judgment, from a logical point of view; and he can examine and try to exhibit clearly the logical structure of the kinds of argument actually employed in moral reasoning. But it does not follow that it is his business, as a philosopher, to make substantive judgments of value or to tell people how they ought or ought not to act.

The matter can be expressed in this way. Both religion and morality form given phenomena, data, for the philosopher. The philosopher is entitled to examine and reflect on features of religious language, on the logic of religious discourse. But it is not his business to invent a new religion, nor even to usurp the role of the apologist and conduct propaganda on behalf of an existing religion. Analogously, it is not the philosopher's business to devise a new moral code, nor even to exhort people to follow some existing code. The Christian preacher, for example, will exhort people to live in accordance with Christian values and moral convictions, but the philosopher should confine his attention to the logic of the language of morals, to meta-ethics. To be sure, people can have personal moral problems. If they want advice, they had better turn to some wise, experienced and sympathetic person. Such a person may, of course, be a philosopher. But if a philosopher acts in this capacity, he is not acting precisely as a philosopher. The philosopher may indeed be able to clarify a person's thought if it is confused; but this is not quite the same thing as telling a person what he or she ought or ought not to do. As for social ethics and social concern, what reason is there to suppose that the philosopher is in a position to solve our social and political problems for us? There is a sense in which, as Wittgenstein remarked, philosophy leaves everything as it was before.[10]

On this view of philosophy ethics is obviously detached from metaphysical and theological beliefs and assumptions. At the same time normative ethics disappears, being left to people vaguely described as moralists, preachers and what not. Moral philosophy proper is reduced to meta-ethics, the study of the logic of moral discourse. Though however this view of the philosopher's function had a vogue for a time, it understandably came to give rise to protests from younger philosophers who had

---

[10]*Philosophical Investigations*, Part 1, Section 124.

no particular metaphysical or theological axe to grind but who felt that their colleagues who proposed and defended the view in question were neglecting the philosopher's social responsibility by refusing to address himself to substantive moral and social issues of importance. Moreover, the critics were by no means all Marxists, even if Marxists were inclined to talk about analytic philosophers fiddling while Rome burned.

The matter seems to me somewhat complex, the question, that is to say, to what extent the philosopher as such is in a position to solve our social and political problems for us. After all, even if politicians have not made a conspicuous success of solving problems of world hunger or of unemployment or of the achievement of a secure and lasting peace, there does not seem to be any good reason for thinking that philosophers would do a better job. It is, however, possible to retort, what sensible person thinks or claims that they could? As far as practical solutions are concerned, the philosopher is not in a better position than the economist to solve economic problems. Nor is he, by virtue of being a philosopher, in a better position than the politicians to solve the practical problem of securing a stable peace here and now. At the same time it is perfectly reasonable to argue that the moral philosopher can in principle contribute in a variety of ways to the solution of substantive moral issues and of social problems with moral aspects. He can, for example, draw attention to the implications of the values which a given society professes to accept, implications which can be easily overlooked. Again, as John Dewey suggested, the philosopher can draw attention to the implications of social ideals which are beginning to be accepted. There are plenty of ways in which he can help the society in which he lives to come to a decision about substantive ethical issues. One can sympathize therefore with the critics of the reduction of moral philosophy to metaethics, provided of course that they do not throw overboard any positive results achieved through the analysis and clarification of the logic of moral discourse.

Even if all this is true, it may be said, it simply reinforces the claim that ethics can be detached from any metaphysical presuppositions or assumptions. A philosopher can perfectly well set out to examine and exhibit the types of argument actually

employed in moral reasoning without presupposing some metaphysical system. Again, a philosopher need not introduce any
metaphysical theory in order to be able to draw attention to the
discrepancy between a society's practice and the implications of
its professed ideals and values. It is a matter of logic, not of
metaphysics. Nor are metaphysical presuppositions required to
draw attention to emerging values or moral convictions, such as
the conviction that war is an unjustifiable way of settling disputes among nations, and to urge that for the actualization of
emerging values new structures are needed, such as, for example, some form of world-government.

Perhaps we should make a distinction. On the one hand it is
possible for a philosopher to approach the human being's moral
and social life in the non-committal spirit which has just been
illustrated. We can note, for example, kinds of argument actually
employed in moral reasoning without committing ourselves to
any of the positions which these kinds of argument are used to
justify. We can stand on the touchline, as it were, observe what
is going on and refrain from supporting either side. On the other
hand some of the positions which fall within the field of the
philosopher's reflection obviously make metaphysical presuppositions or naturally give rise to questions of a metaphysical
nature. To take an extreme example, though Karl Marx, possibly wisely, said little about the kind of society which he envisaged as following the desired proletarian revolution,[11] it was
certainly a society in which religion had withered away or was
in process of doing so. This ideal presupposed a view of human
nature, namely that its full development required the disappearance of religion. And this in turn presupposed materialism,
in the sense of the priority of matter to spirit. The philosopher
can of course simply note such features of Marx's thought. But
if he commits himself not only to Marx's claim that it is the
philosopher's job to contribute to changing the world, as well
as to understanding it, but also to the desirability of the kind of
society envisaged by Marx, it is reasonable to claim that he

---

[11]Obviously, Marx was wise not to attempt to describe in detail a society
which did not yet exist. At the same time his vagueness on this topic made it
possible for dictators to pass off as Marxist social structures which might well
have caused a feeling of revulsion in Marx's mind.

thereby commits himself to certain theories in philosophical anthropology and to a certain conception of reality.

In general, it may seem that the philosopher is faced with a choice. If he wishes to avoid any metaphysical presuppositions, assumptions or implications, he is well advised to confine his attention to meta-ethics, though this need not be understood in so restricted a sense as to provoke the protest that he is talking 'only about words'. If, however, the philosopher commits himself to a normative ethics and to definite social ideals, questions relating to philosophical anthropology and to the nature of the universe are likely to arise. It is not so much a question of his actually assuming the truth of a particular philosophical system or world-view as of his ethical stance naturally giving rise to questions about the beings who make moral judgments and judgments of value and about the universe in which these beings live and act and about their relation to it. The moral life is lived in a wider context.

If this dichotomy is accepted, it leaves room for philosophers who wish to steer clear of ontology or metaphysics and confine their attention to meta-ethics. But is the dichotomy altogether satisfactory? I doubt it. We can hardly dispute the right of a philosopher to confine his attention to the logic (in a broad sense) of the language of morals if he wishes to do so, avoiding committing himself to any substantive normative statements or judgments of value. At the same time the language of morals, as I have already remarked, is spoken by human beings, and it cannot be adequately seen except in the light of human life as a whole. Further, human beings live and act in a universe to which they are related in a variety of ways. Even therefore if we start from the language of morals as a datum and try to confine our attention to inquiring into the logic of this language, further questions naturally arise. I do not claim that every moral philosopher should pursue them. All that I am saying is that they naturally arise. It is not so much a question of logical implication in a strict sense as of one question suggesting another. Gilbert Ryle remarked that 'philosophical problems inevitably interlock in all sorts of ways'.[12] I suggest that the language of morals

[12]Quoted from 'The Theory of Meaning' contributed to *British Philosophy in the Mid-Century*, edited by C. A. Mace (London and New York, 1957, p. 264).

needs to be seen in the light of a form of life, that reflection on this form of life leads naturally to a philosophical anthropology, and that this in turn needs to be placed in a wider context. We need not start with a metaphysical system and try to deduce an ethics. We can start with ethics. But if we do, sooner or later the horizon will broaden.

CHAPTER 11

THE SUCCESSION OF SYSTEMS
AND TRUTH

Metaphysical theories as hypotheses – criteria for assessing their cognitive value – critical discussion of these criteria – metaphysics as the basic science – critical comments – the One, religion and the plurality of philosophies

I

A recurrent theme in this book has been the need for a synthesizing world-view, a need which, as was argued in the first chapter, is not fully met by physical science, inasmuch as the scientific conception of the world forms one of the elements in a wider synthesis. The Spanish writer Ortega y Gasset emphasized the vital function of reason, reason's relation to life and action. That is to say, man, finding himself in a world, in an historical situation, seeks a clear understanding of himself and his 'circumstances', as Ortega y Gasset put it, in order to be able to live and act in accordance with knowledge. For Ortega, the development of overall world-views had this vital function.

It seems to me that there is obviously some truth in this point of view. The human being can obviously ask questions about the nature of reality and about the meaning or purpose, if any, of human life and history. To be sure, it would be a gross exaggeration to claim that all human beings spend a lot of time reflecting on such problems. But it would also be an exaggeration to claim that they occur only to a very few persons. They doubtless occur to a good many people at some time in their lives, even if they make only a fleeting appearance and are quickly dismissed as unanswerable or are pushed aside by the pressure of other interests which are, or seem to be, of more practical importance. It is true that some philosophers have maintained that the so-called ultimate questions are meaningless and that for this reason they cannot be answered. But to the ordinary man the questions are meaningful, even if he thinks that we are not in a position to answer them. The ordinary man's point of view is better represented by Kant than by the logical positivist. For though Kant did not believe that reflection on what he regarded as the basic metaphysical questions could yield theoretical knowledge of true answers, he did not deny the importance of the questions for life. On the contrary, he affirmed it.[1] World-views can be regarded as attempts to answer such questions.

It is obviously possible to admit this but at the same time to doubt whether attempts to answer the questions have been or can be successful. One of the factors which can give rise to such doubts is the succession of different systems and world-views. We have considered selected aspects of some of them in this book. For Kant, the succession of systems and world-views was a sure sign of the failure of what he called 'dogmatic' metaphysics. And in his critical philosophy he undertook to explain why the failure must occur, why dogmatic metaphysics could not yield theoretical knowledge.

Some writers have argued that questions do not in fact recur, and that what seem to be recurrent questions are really different questions. This is a matter on which I have touched elsewhere,[2] and I omit consideration of it here. On the face of it at any rate the history of philosophy seems to present us with a succession of systems, world-views and theories of various sorts, a process in which few issues can be regarded as having been settled, and certainly not metaphysical questions about reality in general. Given this impression of the situation, doubt is obviously cast on the truth-claims made on behalf of world-views.

The point can be expressed in terms of Ortega y Gasset's idea of genuine philosophy. In his view genuine philosophizing arises when the traditional beliefs which form the common presuppositions of a society or culture are subjected to criticism and doubt, thus ceasing to be presuppositions and becoming a sys-

---

[1]It is possible to argue that problems which Kant believed to be basic and important should, in view of his doctrine in the *Critique of Pure Reason*, be regarded as meaningless, in a technical sense. But I am concerned here with what Kant actually said, rather than with what might be taken to be the implications of certain features of his philosophy.

[2]*Philosophers and Philosophies*, ch. 2 (London, 1976) and *Philosophies and Cultures*, ch. 7 (London, 1980).

tem of ideas, the truth-claims of which are open to question. Philosophy arises as an attempt to overcome such doubt, and to substitute for threatened traditional beliefs a rationally grounded system of ideas. Any such system of ideas, however, the philosophy of Plato for example, will be conditioned by, and to this extent relative to, the historical situation in which it arises. Sooner or later it will itself be subjected to criticism and doubt. It does not follow that world-views have no vital function to perform. But even if a philosopher produces a world-view which satisfies the needs of his contemporaries, he can hardly produce one which will satisfy the needs of people living in another and different historical situation. We can therefore expect to find a succession of world-views.

Why ever not? someone may ask. We find a succession of scientific hypotheses. Why should we expect to find no analogous succession in the case of metaphysical theories? It was all very well for Kant to make a sharp distinction between physical science on the one hand and metaphysics on the other. The plain fact is that he had an inadequate idea of science. When Kant remarks that we cannot point to one particular book and say, 'This is metaphysics' as we can point to Euclid and say, 'Here you have geometry',[3] the modern reader is likely to comment that Euclid and geometry are not synonymous. In other words, Kant's idea of mathematics ·was defective. Similarly, Kant seems to have looked on the physical science of his time, the classical or Newtonian physics, as definitive and final, at any rate in its main lines or principles. His idea of science was not such as to be able to accommodate the changes in scientific theories and hypotheses which have taken place since his time. When therefore he disparages traditional metaphysics because of the succession of systems, he lays himself open to Whitehead's retort, that if the history of European philosophy is 'littered with metaphysical systems, abandoned and unreconciled',[4] so is the history of science littered with abandoned hypotheses. If we do not hold this against science, why should we complain that in metaphysics there is an analogous process of change? To be sure, if we recognize change as a feature of metaphysics which

[3] *Prolegomena to Any Future Metaphysics*, section 4.
[4] *Process and Reality*, p. 18 (London, 1929).

really does not stand in more need of justification than change in scientific theories and hypotheses, we shall have to disregard the more extravagant truth-claims made by some metaphysicians of the past on behalf of particular systems or theories. But most of us do this in any case.

This line of thought obviously assumes that metaphysical theories can be treated as hypotheses, assimilated to scientific hypotheses. Some philosophers are quite content to look on metaphysical theories in this way. But unless they are also content to look on them as completely unverifiable or untestable hypotheses, the question arises whether in the case of metaphysics there is anything at all which can be considered analogous to testing in science. We would not indeed get very far, if we accepted the logical positivist criterion of meaning and refused to recognize a theory as meaningful unless some way of confirming it in terms of sense-experience could be indicated. A theory of the One can hardly be confirmed simply by appeal to possible sense-experience. For sense-experience presents us with a world of plurality, and it certainly cannot reveal a transcendent One. If however metaphysical theories are to be successfully assimilated to scientific theories and hypotheses, there must be some way or ways of discriminating between them in regard to cognitive value. After all, though there is a succession of scientific theories and hypotheses, scientists are in principle prepared to say why they prefer one hypothesis to another.[5] And the idea of advance in science (in an evaluative sense of the word 'advance') is not meaningless. If there is nothing comparable in the case of metaphysics, to say that metaphysical theories are hypotheses seems to be a polite way of saying that they are devoid of cognitive value. They may have some pragmatic value. But this is a different matter.

---

[5]In practice scientific hypotheses are doubtless often accepted because the scientific community in general has accepted them. It does not follow however that no reason can be assigned why the scientific community has come to accept a given hypothesis or theory. The reason need not of course be empirical verification by sense-experience.

II

We cannot reduce discrimination between the cognitive values of different scientific theories and hypotheses to a matter of empirical verification, in the sense of an appeal to sense-experience. For example, one scientific theory may be preferred to another because of its greater coordinating power or because what are taken to be established laws can be subsumed under it, whereas the other theory is unable to accommodate them. And it might be suggested that the idea of comprehensiveness provides us with one criterion for discriminating between world-views. Comprehensiveness in a literal sense is indeed unattainable. It would require omniscience. But a world-view presumably aims at comprehensiveness in some sense. Whitehead referred to speculative philosophy as an 'endeavour to form a coherent, logical, necessary system of general ideas in terms of which every element of our experience can be interpreted'.[6] The word 'necessary' may need elucidation; but the quotation shows that Whitehead had in mind a general framework of ideas which would be comprehensive not in the sense that every item of experience, so to speak, was actually noted and described but in the sense that the different kinds or types of human experience could be coordinated and interpreted in the light of the framework. If world-views are regarded as aiming at comprehensiveness in this sense, they can be judged in terms of their success or failure in fulfilling this aim.

For example, if the system of general ideas is originally suggested by reflection on the physical world about us, taking the form of a philosophy of Nature, then to satisfy the criterion of comprehensiveness it should also be applicable to mental phenomena and be capable of accommodating and throwing light upon moral and religious experience. If a given world-view cannot accommodate moral and religious experience without distorting or caricaturing it, it is thereby shown to be inferior, in this particular respect, to a world-view which can accommodate moral and religious experience while avoiding distortion or caricature. Again, if the system of general ideas is originally suggested by reflection on the human being's aesthetic, moral

[6]*Process and Reality*, p. 3.

and religious experience but is unable to accommodate the picture of the world as presented in natural science, it must be judged to be inferior, in this respect, to a system of general ideas which can accommodate the world of physical science as well as the human being's aesthetic, moral and religious experience.

It is hardly necessary to say that comprehensiveness needs to be taken in conjunction with logical coherence. The general system of ideas must be logically coherent, as indeed the word 'system' implies. And it must enable us to give a coherent account of reality without internal contradictions. That is to say, a world-view which is free from internal contradictions is intellectually superior, in this respect, to one in which internal contradictions can be detected. It is necessary to include the phrase 'in this respect', as a world-view which contained an internal contradiction and could not be accepted as a whole might conceivably express fresh insights which were notably lacking in a world-view which was logically coherent.

As comprehensiveness in a literal sense is not attainable, and as every world-view is constructed in a definite historical situation and reflects to some degree the empirical knowledge of the time and human experience up to date, we can expect to find a succession of world-views. It is not a work which can be accomplished once and for all. At the same time world-views can approach the ideal of comprehensiveness and logical coherence in varying degrees. And we can thus discriminate between them in terms of the two criteria which have been mentioned. We can add that any inferences implied by the world-views must be logically valid.

It is also possible to discriminate between world-views from a pragmatic point of view, in terms of the kind of conduct which they tend to promote or which they encourage. The term 'world-view' might, I suppose, be understood in the sense of a purely descriptive account of reality. But what are called world-views are generally more than that – as noted in the last chapter, they can include inbuilt judgments of value, they may recommend programmes for life or policies of action, and they can sometimes exercise a psychological influence on life or conduct. We can therefore discriminate between them in terms of what we consider to be their probable practical consequences or effects. We cannot of course argue that one world-view is to be preferred to another because its likely influence on personal conduct or on society is to be preferred to the probable influence of the other world-view, without giving expression to a value-judgment on our part. But in ordinary life we often judge pro-posed policies in terms of the practical effects which we think that they are likely to show. So why should we not adopt a similar approach to world-views?

Well, there is of course one reason. Unless we accept a prag-matist definition of truth, we must allow for the possibility that a theory could be true, even if it was likely to promote or suggest a line of conduct which we consider undesirable or of which we disapprove. If we accept the correspondence theory of truth, we cannot assess the truth or falsity of theories simply in terms of possible effects, which we happen to consider desirable or un-desirable. As therefore we are concerned here primarily with criteria for assessing the truth or falsity of theories, and as I do not accept the pragmatist interpretation of truth, I do not wish to lay emphasis upon the pragmatic approach. At the same time we do not necessarily have to accept a pragmatist view of truth in order to evaluate the probable practical effects of world-views. And if we believe that a given world-view tends to produce practical effects which we consider highly undesirable, we are likely to scrutinize its truth-claims pretty closely. Besides, most philosophical world-views do not consist simply of statements about what is the case. They often include programmes of action or tell us what ought to be the case. They often include or presuppose judgments of value. So one can hardly claim that what I have described as the pragmatic approach is entirely irrelevant. If we look at some of the practical effects of Marxist doctrine and disapprove of them, this obviously does not prove the falsity of Marx's materialism (the theory that matter is prior to mind or spirit) or of his economic theory of history. But let us assume that Marx positively advocates the dictatorship of the proletariat, as distinct from claiming simply that historical laws will bring it about. If we think that the so-called dictator-ship of the proletariat means in practice a dictatorship over the proletariat, and if we disapprove of this state of affairs, we are perfectly entitled to criticize Marx's advocacy of the dictatorship

of the proletariat by appealing to what we believe to be its
probable practical consequences. If we wish to criticize his
theoretical materialism, we have of course to find other grounds
for doing so than dislike of it.

Having mentioned the pragmatic criterion, I now wish to
return to comprehensiveness and logical coherence and pursue
a brief critical discussion of these suggested criteria for discriminating between world-views in regard to their cognitive value.

III

Use of comprehensiveness and logical coherence as criteria for
assessing world-views doubtless presupposes that we attach
value to comprehensiveness and logical coherence. But I do not
think that there is much of a problem here. In evaluating scientific theories relative comprehensiveness is one of the factors
which can legitimately be taken into account. And there is no
a priori reason for prohibiting the extension of synthesis beyond
physical science. Unless therefore we are prepared to reject the
idea of synthesis altogether, it is difficult to see how we can
reasonably deny any value to comprehensiveness, provided that
it is not understood in a sense which would make it absurd to
aim at comprehensiveness. As for logical coherence, we have
indeed to remember that, as has been already noted, a theory
which tried to combine two incompatible theses might conceivably be intellectually superior, in a particular respect, to a theory
which was more logically coherent. For one of the incompatible
theses might be worked out in such a way as to express an
insight which the more logically coherent theory did not express.
In other words, we could learn something from the first theory
which we could not learn from the second. At the same time it
is improbable that anyone would seriously claim that a logically
incoherent theory, simply because of its lack of coherence, is
superior to a theory which is logically coherent. Further, even
if we have reason to believe that a theory which tries to combine
two incompatible theses is superior, in a certain specified respect, to a more logically coherent theory, we are also likely to
think that the first theory would benefit by being made more
coherent.

We are not however concerned simply with awarding good or bad marks to world-views according to the degrees in which they embody ideals of comprehensiveness and logical coherence. We are concerned with these qualities as criteria of truth, when truth is understood, in the context, as correspondence between theory and reality. And I wish to make some remarks about this topic, beginning with logical coherence.

Someone might object that we have no reason for assuming that reality is logically coherent. Apart however from the argument that in knowing anything we apprehend the intelligibility of being and that intelligibility involves logical coherence, it is not altogether clear to me precisely what is meant if it is suggested that reality may be riddled with contradictions. If there are contradictions, they must surely be in an account of reality, taking the form of contradictory or incompatible propositions. And a philosophy which is riddled with contradictions is, in this respect, bad philosophy. Our world exists for us in so far as it is conceived, and a conception which is self-contradictory is unacceptable, unless we are prepared to consign the ideal of coherent thinking to the dustbin, in which case we had better steer clear of philosophy.

Even if however any account of reality should aim at logical coherence, does it necessarily follow that a logically coherent account of reality must be true, in the sense of corresponding with reality? After all, even if an incoherent novel is, in this respect, a bad novel, it does not follow that one which is coherent and free from internal contradiction represents fact rather than fiction. It may present a logical possibility, but this does not justify our claiming that the events narrated actually occurred. Analogously, might there not be a picture or account of reality which was coherent but which did not represent reality as it really is, even if it represents a logical possibility?

It is possible however to argue that there is a way in which the criterion of logical coherence can be used to prove the truth of a metaphysical theory. Consider monism. Historically, monism has generally been expounded in such a way as not to exclude pluralism altogether. The Many have been represented, for example, as appearances of the One, as real in a relative sense, in relation to a certain level of experience. But if we are talking about ultimate reality, about the 'really real', monism and pluralism are clearly opposed, or at any rate can be opposed. If someone asserts that ultimate reality is one single being, without any internal distinction at all, and someone else asserts that ultimate reality is not one single reality without any internal distinction, the assertions are contradictory. And if we accept the principle of excluded middle, one must say that one assertion is true and the other false. But this does not tell us which is true and which false. To determine this some criterion other than the logical incompatibility of the two assertions is required. But is not the situation altered, if one makes the following addition to the situation as described? Monism, as stated, is obviously opposed to its negation. Suppose however that it can be shown that monism, as described, cannot be stated without involving oneself in a contradiction. It could be argued, for example, that I cannot assert that there is only one reality without objectifying this reality as an object of thought and reference over against myself, and that I thereby inevitably imply that there are at least two realities, the One and myself. If this argument is accepted, monism has been shown to be self-contradictory. Are we not then entitled to claim that the negation of monism must be true?

Yes, perhaps so, but to negate monism as described is not the same thing as committing oneself to any other positive view of reality. One might, for example, reject monism as stated and none the less maintain that there is a One, an identity-in-difference, a One with internal distinctions. Or we might maintain that there is no One but only the Many. And even then there are various forms of pluralism to choose from. It seems therefore that a reasonable case can be made out for claiming that the primary use of the criterion of logical coherence is to exclude theories rather than to prove the truth of any particular theory. The truth of a theory might be provable in some other way or ways. But this is another matter.

The objection can be raised that it is not really a question of using the criterion of logical coherence, taken simply by itself, to prove the truth of a world-view. Coherence must be taken together with comprehensiveness. We can recall Hegel's assertion that 'philosophy is concerned with the true and the true is the whole'.[7] If a world-view presents an account of reality which is both logically coherent and comprehensive, it must be recognized as true. This statement may seem to make unwarranted assumptions about reality. But we cannot set out to understand reality without assuming that it is intelligible. And if we develop a philosophy which shows reality to be intelligible, this confirms an initial assumption or faith, and the philosophy must be true. To put the matter in another way, if being is intelligible, the philosophy which displays its intelligibility in a comprehensive manner is the true philosophy. In virtue of its coherence and comprehensiveness the system becomes its own criterion of truth. It imposes itself on the mind.

This is all very well, but comprehensiveness is, as we have noted, relative. When Henri Bergson published his reflections on morals and religion, his philosophy became, we may say, more comprehensive than it was before, in the sense that it covered more areas than it had previously covered. Again, though Hegel's philosophy belongs to an earlier period, it was more comprehensive than Bergson's in the sense that Hegel had devoted attention to areas about which Bergson had little to say, political life for example. Though however one world-view can be more comprehensive than another, we are not in a position to give a literally comprehensive account of reality. Human history, for instance, is open-ended, not a finished product. For the matter of that, our knowledge of reality as it actually exists is limited. The criterion of comprehensiveness therefore, even when combined with that of logical coherence, cannot prove that a given world-view is true in an absolute sense, final and definitive.

Even if all this is true, it may be said, it simply reinforces the claim that world-views should be looked on as very broad hypotheses. We cannot determine the degree of probability of a given world-view in mathematical terms. But it does not follow that nothing can be done to show that one world-view is more reasonable than another. After all, I have not claimed that criteria such as comprehensiveness and logical coherence are of no use at all in evaluating metaphysical philosophies. A comprehensive world-view must find room for sense-experience; and

[7]*The Phenomenology of Mind*, translated by J. B. Baillie, p. 79 (2nd edition, London, 1931); *Werke* (edited by H. G. Glockner), Vol. 2, p. 24.

compatibility with sense-experience is a test which one can apply. Moreover, in the development of any world-view infer-ence, argument, will be employed; and argument can be evalu-ated from a logical point of view. To say that inference is employed is not inconsistent with regarding world-views as being hypothetical in nature. In the development of a scientific hypothesis inference is employed, and nobody claims that the hypothesis is not an hypothesis on this account. We cannot explain the phenomenon to which Whitehead drew attention, namely that the history of science is littered with discarded theories, unless we see scientists as proposing hypotheses which are open in principle to revision or change. Similarly, the most reasonable explanation of the succession of metaphysical phi-losophies is that they are hypotheses or sets of hypotheses. A world-view, by its very nature, may be more difficult to confirm than a scientific hypothesis. But provided that some measure or measures can be taken to test its truth-claims, it can count as a hypothesis or as analogous to a scientific theory. If we adopt this view, we would expect to find a succession of world-views, corresponding to changes in empirical knowledge, in man's ex-perience of himself and his environment and in the social and political life of mankind. Stagnation would hardly be a benefit to philosophical thought.

IV

Some philosophers would claim that the idea of metaphysics which we have been considering is a perversion of the true ideal of metaphysics. It is not a question of asserting that the concep-tion of metaphysics as presupposing the work of the particular sciences and as attempting to develop a wide synthesis has never been exemplified in the history of philosophy. The inductive approach, which is characteristic of this idea of metaphysics, can be found, for example, in the thought of Lotze and Wundt in Germany and in that of Bergson in France. Nor is it necess-arily a case of trying to prohibit people from developing world-views, in the sense in which we have been using the term, if they wish to do so. Rather is it a question of maintaining that metaphysics aims at establishing truth, the actual basic structure of reality, and that it cannot fulfil this aim if it has to assimilate itself to what it is not, namely empirical science. If inductive metaphysics bases its conclusions on science, the science of the period, these conclusions cannot be certain. Further, as metaphysical theories are not in fact scientific hypotheses and are not amenable to testing in the ways in which scientific hypotheses can be tested, they tend to become imaginative constructions, without any firm foundation. The way is then open for suggestions such as that of G. T. Fechner, who claimed that if a metaphysical hypothesis had some positive ground and does not contradict any established fact, we are entitled to adopt it all the more readily if it seems likely to make us happy. It would hardly occur to anyone to make a similar suggestion in regard to a scientific hypothesis. And if the suggestion seems sensible in regard to metaphysical hypotheses, this simply shows that the hypotheses are shaky from the cognitive point of view. It is indeed true that a philosopher may adopt an inductive approach and then develop his metaphysical theories without establishing any real connection between them and the sciences which he claims to presuppose. In this case however he probably leaves the principles and presuppositions which he employs in his metaphysics without any critical examination, possibly even without any explicit formulation. This is one of the chief objectionable features of inductive metaphysics, namely its lack of self-criticism and of a firm foundation. In brief, it is a flimsy construction; and the logical positivists were justified in taking a dim view of it, even if they went too far by claiming that metaphysical theories were meaningless.

What is the alternative? That is to say, if the philosophers of whom we are speaking criticize inductive metaphysics adversely, what is the idea of metaphysics which they wish to substitute for it? One model proposed is that of a two-phase method, comprising reduction and deduction. That is to say, there is first a movement of the mind back from the questionable to the unquestionable, from the uncertain to the certain, and then a process of deduction from the unquestionable point of departure.[8] Given an unquestionable point of departure and a system-

---

[8]See, for example, *Metaphysik. Eine methodisch-systematische Grundlegung*, by E. Coreth (Innsbruck, Vienna and Munich, 1961).

atic process of deduction, the result will be a system of certain truths, firmly established truths, not ill-founded speculations dignified by the name of hypotheses.

A natural comment to make is that we are confronted here with a recall to a rationalist idea of metaphysics, an idea which looks to mathematics as a model and which has been discredited. Surely, it may be said, Kant's criticism of dogmatism in metaphysics should be sufficient to warn us off from trying to go back to the past. It is indeed understandable that philosophers who have apologetic aims in mind and who wish to make philosophy serve the interests of religious faith and theology should not be satisfied with the interpretation of metaphysical theories as hypotheses and that they should hanker after the attainment of absolute certainty. But all attempts to construct metaphysics according to a mathematical model have failed. And it hardly seems worthwhile trying to renew such attempts. Besides, how can a modern philosopher justifiably neglect the development of the empirical sciences or proceed as though this development had never taken place?

For the moment I confine my attention to the last question, as this may help to explain what seems to be the idea of metaphysics which we are considering. The particular sciences have different formal objects, as the Scholastics would say. They deal with different kinds of beings or of the same beings considered under different aspects or from different points of view. Metaphysics however is not a particular science in this sense. It treats, in Aristotelian language, of being as being. It is concerned with the basic structure of reality. The evidence, so to speak, is always there. Obviously, metaphysics did not start with the beginning of the human race. But its relatively late arrival on the scene does not alter the fact that the evidential starting-point for metaphysical reflection was always there. Its appearance did not have to await scientific discoveries. What is required for a properly developed metaphysics is to proceed from propositions which can be questioned to a point of departure which is self-evidently true, cannot be questioned and needs no demonstration, and from this firm basis to deduce truths in a systematic manner. There is no question of metaphysics taking the place of the particular sciences. It cannot do this. It is the basic science which logically precedes all the particular sciences and does not presuppose them. At the same time it lets these sciences be themselves. There is no reason why the metaphysician should despise or belittle the particular sciences. But as he is treating of what logically precedes them, he should not represent metaphysics as dependent on them. If he does do so, we shall continue to have conflicting world-views. But if metaphysics were conceived as the basic science, and if it were developed in accordance with the model indicated, there would be a ground for hope that the succession of conflicting metaphysical systems could be brought to an end, however many changes there might continue to be in scientific hypotheses and theories. In short, what is needed is not to assimilate metaphysics to empirical science but to insist on the difference between them.

V

Let me turn to some critical discussion of this idea of metaphysics. In the first place it can be objected that though there have been several attempts in the history of philosophy to establish metaphysics on a sure and certain foundation and then to develop it deductively, all have failed, in the common estimation of philosophers that is to say. For example, Descartes believed that he had found an indubitable truth in his *Cogito, ergo sum* (I think, therefore I am), and he deduced the existence of God. 'I exist, therefore God exists.'[9] Spinoza gave a deductive form to the exposition of his philosophy in the *Ethics*. J. G. Fichte maintained that 'every science must have a fundamental proposition (*Grundsatz*)',[10] that philosophy is the basic science, and that it must therefore have a fundamental proposition from which it is deduced. But though we can doubtless learn something from all three philosophers, whether it is a question of insights or perhaps even of what to avoid or not to do, it can hardly be claimed that any of them succeeded in presenting a philosophy of such a kind as to put an end to the succession of philosophies, systems and metaphysical theories.

[9]*Rules for the Direction of the Mind*, 12. *Oeuvres*, edited by C. Adam and P. Tannery, Vol. X, p. 422 (13 vols., Paris, 1897–1913).
[10]*Werke*, edited by I. H. Fichte, Vol. 1, p. 41 (8 vols., Berlin, 1845–6).

The defender of the idea of metaphysics under discussion might reply that none of the philosophers mentioned actually exemplified in his thought the relevant model. Descartes's claim to have found an indubitable truth has been questioned, and in any case his philosophy, as it developed, was by no means simply deduced from this truth. Spinoza did not hesitate to postulate additional axioms and principles when the subject-matter of which he was about to treat seemed to require it. Fichte's alleged basic truth, that 'the ego simply posits in an original way its own being',[11] is ambiguous; and he explicitly states that no theoretical deduction of the non-ego is possible and therefore has recourse to what he calls a practical deduction. In other words, it is not so much a question of the model having failed as of its not having been exemplified.

This is a possible line of reply, but it is not a very satisfactory situation if one claims that metaphysics ought to conform to a certain model and then asserts that no example of conformity to the model can be cited. When philosophers of science discuss scientific method, they are not concerned with claiming that scientists ought to adopt a certain method which in point of fact they have never employed. They are concerned with exhibiting the method or methods which are actually exemplified in science. And we might expect the same sort of procedure in regard to metaphysics.

The upholder of the model of metaphysics in question might reply that he is not concerned with trying to impose on meta-physics an unheard-of method, an entirely new invention of his own. Metaphysics in the past has aspired to follow the method under discussion, but it has failed to do so with complete rigour and consistency. It is in this sense that the model has not been exemplified. The objection can indeed be raised that even if metaphysics has aspired to follow this method in the past, it has turned away from it, not capriciously but because it was seen that use of the method was unable to increase our positive knowledge of reality. But how can this have been seen, if the method had not been employed vigorously and consistently? It may have been believed, but it cannot have been seen.

[11]*Werke*, Vol. 1, p. 98. (See Note 7.)

However this may be, the only way in which one is likely to convince people that the reductive-deductive method in metaphysics is capable of providing certain knowledge of reality is to develop a philosophy which exemplifies the method and is seen to yield certain knowledge. I do not of course mean to imply that we can expect from metaphysics fresh empirical knowledge such as can be obtained in empirical science or through geographical exploration. Knowledge of the basic structure of reality, of the fundamental categories, if there are any, would be an example of the kind of knowledge which I have in mind.

Those philosophers who have claimed that metaphysics can be put on a firm foundation only by the use of the reductive-deductive method have in fact applied the method. I have no wish to accuse them of refusing to take any risks, of saying simply what they believe to be wrong with metaphysics and how it could be put right, without making any attempt to apply the proposed remedy. Such an accusation would be grossly unfair. But we cannot undertake to examine concrete examples here. Instead, I wish to make a few general remarks about the relevant method. For the very brief description of it which I have given prompts questions which I have made no attempt to answer. And I wish at any rate to mention some of these questions.

It has already been explained that the reductive-deductive method involves two movements of the mind, a movement to an unquestionable truth, which can serve as a point for departure, and a movement of systematic deduction from this point of departure. What sort of truth is envisaged as forming the unquestionable point of departure? Is it a formal logical principle? Fichte has sometimes been accused of trying to deduce philosophy (which was, for him, the deduction or reconstruction of consciousness) from the principle of identity stated as A = A. This accusation seems to me to be unjust and to be based on a serious misunderstanding of Fichte's view of the relation between philosophy and logic.[12] But we need not pursue this theme here. The question which I wish to ask is this. Suppose, for the sake of argument, that a philosopher deduces a system from formal logical principles. What sort of a system would it be?

[12]See my work, *A History of Philosophy*, Vol. VII, pp. 48–50.

Would it not be a system of formal logic, rather than a metaphysics of reality? Would we have any real justification for assuming that the result provided us with knowledge of reality and not simply with the implications of certain logical principles? We might perhaps appeal to Spinoza's statement that 'the order and connection of ideas is the same as the order and connection of things'.[13] But if we appeal to Spinoza's statement, the question arises whether we are not tacitly assuming a metaphysics in advance of our deduction, at any rate as a working hypothesis.

Or is the unquestionable point of departure an existential proposition? Descartes believed that he had found at least one indubitable existential proposition, the *Cogito, ergo sum*. For my own part, I think that it is self-evidently true that, as St Augustine remarked, I could not doubt unless I existed. But is this in any case a promising point of departure for the deduction of a metaphysics of reality? It might do as the starting-point for a deduction of consciousness. Fichte hoped to deduce or reconstruct consciousness using the self-positing of the ego as the point of departure, though, as we have noted, he came to the conclusion that he could give no purely theoretical deduction of the non-ego. But could we justifiably assume that a deduction of the structure of consciousness is necessarily a deduction of the structure of reality without presupposing an idealist metaphysics?

It might be said that though the ego is the condition of the possibility of 'my world', as object for me, there is no good reason to suppose that it is the source of all reality other than itself. The One however, whether conceived as personal or suprapersonal, is the source of all besides itself. A deductive metaphysics of reality should therefore start with the One, with God.

For some minds this is an attractive idea. But it is open to serious objection. Many people would refuse to admit that the existence of God can form an unquestionable and ultimate point of departure for a process of deductive reasoning. It is not simply a question of agnostics and atheists. Whether it makes sense, as

---

[13] *Ethics*, Part 2, proposition 7.

St Thomas Aquinas thought it did, to talk about a proposition which is self-evidently true in itself but not for us is open to discussion. But Aquinas refused to admit that the proposition affirming God's existence is self-evidently true, an analytically true proposition, as far as we are concerned. Hence he did not believe that the metaphysicians could legitimately start with the existence of God. As far as he was concerned, God is first in the ontological order but not in the epistemological order. And in regard to the second point at any rate most philosophers, whether theists or not, would agree with him. Further, if it is assumed that we can start from the existence of God as an unquestionable point of departure, to claim that we can deduce the world from God is presumably to claim that creation is necessary, that the world follows from God as a conclusion from its premises. And how could we justify this assumption except by maintaining, with Spinoza, that the order and connection of ideas is the same as the order and connection of things?

The idea of metaphysics as the basic science, a discipline in which the mind moves by a rigorous and systematic process of deduction from unquestionable premises to equally certain conclusions, can exercise a powerful fascination on the mind. If the method could be employed in metaphysics, we would have a metaphysics which would be in a real sense presuppositionless, in the sense, that is to say, that there would be no presuppositions which had been left uncriticized or unexamined. *Ex hypothesi*, the point of departure of the deductive process would be unquestionable. Though however I can certainly feel the fascination of this idea of metaphysics, I doubt whether employment of the method in question is capable of providing us with a basic science of reality. Even if we assume that it is possible to work out a system of propositions deduced from an unquestionable point of departure, would this system reveal to us the fundamental structure of reality? Or could we be certain that it did? Perhaps defenders of the idea of metaphysics in question can cope successfully with such questions. I cannot exclude the possibility. Until however I am convinced that they can, I continue to doubt whether the succession of metaphysical theories and interpretations of reality can be brought to an end by employing in metaphysics the method which we have been considering.

Let us assume however that it is in fact possible to develop, in the way indicated, a basic science which reveals to us the fundamental structure of reality and which is independent of the changing hypotheses and theories of empirical science.[14] There would still be room for philosophies which took into account current scientific conceptions of the world and of the human being and problems arising out of reflection on these conceptions. I do not think that one could justifiably expect to be able to divide human knowledge neatly between an invariant metaphysics on the one hand and changing scientific theories and hypotheses on the other. It is all very well to pour scorn on inductive metaphysics. It is arguable that it meets a genuine need, that of reinterpreting the world and human life in the light of the experience and knowledge of the time.

To avoid a possible misunderstanding, I had better make it clear that I have no intention of denying that there can be propositions the truth of which transcends any relation limiting it to a particular historical period or situation. Let us assume, for example, the truth of the statement that any finite thing is, by its nature, capable of change (not necessarily of any and every kind of change but of some kind). The statement can then be described as perennially true, not of course in the sense that it is a self-subsistent object out there, but in the sense that it is true whenever enunciated, whether in the fourth century B.C. or in the twentieth century A.D. The statement does not of course tell us that there are finite things. What it says is that if there is a finite thing, it is capable of some kind of change.

Given this conviction that there can be perennially true propositions in the sense mentioned, I am committed to granting that if such propositions can be so coordinated as to form what can be reasonably described as a system, there can be a perennially true system. I do not believe that it is possible to deduce all necessarily true propositions from one ultimate proposition,

---

[14]It is not simply a question of the basic science being logically prior to empirical science. According to Fichte and those who agree with him on this point, metaphysics, as the basic science, grounds logic and does not presuppose it.

the truth of which is unquestionable or self-evident. But there might be a set of propositions which could be regarded as presenting the logical scaffolding of the world, or as part of it.

What has just been said is relevant to the subject of the metaphysics of the One. If it can be shown that the existence of a plurality of things necessarily implies the existence of a One as their source, then the statement that if there is a plurality there is a One, would count as a perennially true proposition. The existence of a plurality would of course be known by experience. The point is however that the statement in question would be true in any historical period or culture or society. To be sure, every human being lives in a particular historical situation and sees the world from an historically conditioned perspective. But the statement in question could be used in any such situation to shed light on the structure of reality.

Is it clear however that the existence of a plurality necessarily implies the existence of a One as their source? Three loaves of wheat-bread are obviously all made of wheat; but it by no means follows that they all come from the same batch of flour or from the same baker. It may be objected that this is an absurd remark. When we talk about the Many and their relationship to the One, we are talking about the totality of finite things considered precisely as beings in which essence and existence are distinguishable, as the Scholastics would say, and no one of which exists by itself, in virtue of its essence. It is the ontological nature of finite beings which demands assertion of the One as their source.

In other words, we are back with some version of a traditional metaphysical argument for the existence of God. I cannot discuss these arguments here. I can only say that if one of them is accepted as a demonstrative proof, it must constitute a proof in any historical situation. For there is no good reason to suppose that the basic ontological structure of finite things changes from historical period to historical period or from one culture to another, even if there can be different ideas or interpretations of this structure. If however no version of the traditional metaphysical arguments is accepted as a demonstrative proof, it becomes a question whether a metaphysics of the One is reasonable, more reasonable than a philosophy which excludes the concept of a One.

VI

It may seem that we have strayed from the main theme of this work, religion and the metaphysics of the One. To be sure, the foregoing remarks are relevant to the metaphysics of the One. But how does religion come into the matter? The concept of the One, taken by itself, brings to mind such ideas as the nameless One of the *Lao Tzu*, the Emptiness or Void of Buddhist thinkers, H. L. Mansel's Unconditioned, Herbert Spencer's Unknowable and Karl Jaspers' Comprehensive. Such ideas may indeed appeal to mystically minded people who are fascinated by the notion of the divine darkness or of the cloud of unknowing (to borrow the title of a famous medieval mystical work). But they express a degree of agnosticism which is foreign to the Christian mind or, for the matter of that, to the mind of the devout Jew or Muslim. The God of the Bible is certainly not a being of whom nothing can be said, except that it is one. Nor is the God of the Koran. And who is going to worship Emptiness or pray to I-know-not-what? One can pray to God, but not to the Absolute; to Vishnu, but not to Nirguna-Brahman. While Allah demands of human beings certain kinds of intentions and actions, the Tao of Taoist philosophy is indifferent to good and evil. From the religious point of view was not Schelling right when he asserted that the person seeks a person, a God who acts and exercises providence? F. H. Bradley maintained, as was noted in Chapter 6, that the concept of God, if subjected to genuine philosophical reflection, is inevitably transformed into that of the Absolute. With Schelling however we find a movement in the opposite direction. When substituting what he called 'positive philosophy' for his previous 'negative philosophy', he insisted that 'without an active God . . . there can be no religion, for religion presupposes an actual, real relationship of man to God'.[15] So much not only for Schelling's earlier concept of the Absolute as the vanishing-point of all differences but also for

---

[15]*Werke*, edited by Manfred Schröter (Munich, 1927–8), V, p. 750.

Hegel's Absolute. Must not religious people, it may be asked, agree with Schelling? Among Indian thinkers Rāmānuja and Madhva would certainly agree with him. As we have seen, they criticized the monism of Saṁkara in the name of devotional religion. The Muslim thinkers who emphasized the relationship of love, between man and God that is to say, would also sympathize with Schelling's position. It seems evident that the concept of the One represents the result of a process of emptying out most of the positive content of such concepts as those of God, Allah and Vishnu or Iśvara. Further, if we regard religion as a social phenomenon, it should be obvious that the metaphysical concept of the One is quite unsuitable for the great majority of the members of a religious community.

Though this line of objection is understandable and possesses a persuasive force, it seems to me to be based on a misinterpretation of the point of view defended in this book. It is not the author's intention to reduce religion to metaphysics or the concept of God to that of the One. He has argued that the movement of the mind in metaphysics towards the One can have a religious significance; but he has also argued that the competence of metaphysics to grasp a reality which transcends the Many and to describe it is extremely limited. It is doubtless true that the concept of a mysterious, elusive One is seriously defective by the standards of orthodox Judaism, Christianity and Islam. For example, the concept of the One, taken by itself, is not the same as the concept of a loving Father. But it does not follow that the latter must be discarded. The author's thesis is that the analogy of a loving Father does not come from metaphysics but is accepted by Christians on the authority of Christ, as recorded in the gospels. In other words, it belongs to the Christian language-game and is accepted by participants in the relevant form of life. Its function in this language-game is a matter for reflection primarily by members of the Christian community. It is true of course that a given metaphysician may reject the concept of a revelation or a divine self-disclosure and insist on stopping short at what Jaspers called 'philosophic faith'. But this need not be the case. And a metaphysics which recognizes its limitations is by no means necessarily hostile to religion.

The matter is not of course as simple as the foregoing remarks may seem to imply. If metaphysics is conceived simply as an approach to the idea of a transcendent reality, an approach which respects certain limits and leaves room for a divine self-disclosure or revelation, it obviously cannot be justifiably described as hostile to theistic religion. But what if we presuppose a definite religious faith such as Christianity or Islam? If the metaphysician has stopped with the idea of a transcendent One and has refrained from attempting to describe the One in terms of language which has developed in response to the need for referring to empirical realities, is he not likely to turn a critical eye on the statements made about God by adherents of a theistic religion? F. H. Bradley, for example, thought that this was the case. Indeed, he thought of theistic philosophers as covertly undermining the faith which they professed to accept, even though this was not their conscious intention. He argued, for instance, that to satisfy the demands of the religious consciousness these philosophers undertake to show that the ultimate reality is personal. This is at any rate what they wish to show. They also wish however to avoid anthropomorphic representations of the infinite. They proceed therefore progressively to eliminate the meaning which a term such as 'personal' ordinarily has for us. At the same time they continue to use the word 'personal', thus creating a mental fog through 'the sliding extension of a word'.[16] Obviously, Bradley is not condemning the metaphysicians in question for eliminating anthropomorphic features from the concept of the ultimate reality or One. What he objects to is the way in which, as he sees it, they continue to use a descriptive epithet in spite of the fact that they have rendered it vacuous. In the present context the point is that Bradley finds an insuperable tension between the demands of metaphysical reflection and those of the religious consciousness, even if the philosophers in question try to conceal its presence.

Bradley would presumably admit that a theologian or theistic philosopher is justified in trying to make the description of God as 'personal' consistent with other statements made about God, for example that God is infinite. What he is concerned with arguing is that in the process of fulfilling this task the theologian

---

[16]*Appearance and Reality*, p. 533.

or philosopher renders the concept of personality vacuous, that it is only in the all-inclusive Absolute that contradictions are overcome, and with the transformation of the concept of a personal God into that of the Absolute the basis for theistic religion is destroyed. Since any thorough examination of this line of argument would involve one in a huge task of conceptual or linguistic analysis I must content myself here with making a few remarks about the alleged undermining of religion.[17]

A philosopher may indeed represent the concept of a personal God as an 'appearance' of a suprapersonal Absolute or One. As far as western philosophy is concerned, Bradley is an example. In India Śaṁkara provides another example. And it is certainly arguable that for those who accept this point of view much of what is ordinarily understood by religion is undermined. Śaṁkara, as noted in Chapter 4, had no desire to destroy personal religious devotion to God; but in the eyes of thinkers such as Madhva full acceptance of Śaṁkara's monism would in fact undermine the basis of *bhakti* or religious devotion to a personal God. The religious devotion in question involves thinking of God in terms of analogies, such as that of personality or, in the case of Christianity, of a loving Father. To be sure, those who think in terms of such analogies do not generally imagine that they are to be understood absolutely literally, in the sense that, when applied to God, they must retain the whole of the meaning which the relevant concepts originally had, in view of their derivation. The empirical realities which we describe as personal, namely human persons, are physical organisms, composed, as it is traditionally put, of bodies and souls; but Christians, Jews and Muslims do not generally conceive God as embodied in this way. Again, Christians do not think of the heavenly Father as performing physical procreative acts. The trouble is however that when the process of 'purifying' a concept such as that of personality is carried further and it is said for example that God understands but not in precisely the same way as a human being, the concept progressively approaches

---

[17]The topic is discussed in Chapter VII of my *Contemporary Philosophy* (second edition, London, 1972, and New York, 1979), though I do not regard myself as committed to everything I then said.

vacuity.[18] And it may very well seem that the theologian or philosopher is in effect substituting the concept of the Absolute or that of Nirguna-Brahman for the concept of God. In this case, as analogies cannot fulfil their pragmatic function of stimulating attitudes and active responses unless they retain something of their content, it seems to follow that much of what is ordinarily understood by religion is lost. The analogy of a loving Father can retain its pragmatic effectiveness even if it is separated from any sexual connotation. But it cannot very well retain its stimulative power if it has been completely deprived of content and rendered vacuous. In other words, it may seem that Bradley's account of the goings-on of theistic metaphysicians is fully justified.

There is however another way of looking at the matter. If we think of God in terms of positive concepts based on our experience, these concepts will be inadequate for describing a transcendent ultimate reality. But we have no others. To be sure, there should be some reason for selecting one analogy rather than another. But some positive concept is obviously required for religion in its devotional and social aspects. No theologian or theistic philosopher who values religion as it actually exists would try to exclude the use of analogies. At the same time the theologian or theistic philosopher may very well think it important to remind those who are capable of understanding what he is talking about that the analogies *are* analogies, not with a view to substituting another concept for that of God but to help people to remember the divine transcendence and God's incommensurability with finite things. I cannot see that this procedure is a threat to religion. Indeed, in this respect we can see philosophical reflection and religious mysticism as converging towards the same end, though by different paths. We must add however that though mystical writers have emphasized the divine transcending of our conceptual web, they have also emphasized intuitive apprehension of the divine presence, whether of the divine presence within or of God in all things and all things in God. In other words, it is not simply a question of

---

[18]In orthodox Christianity God is not conceived as 'a Person'. But I prescind here from the doctrine of the Trinity. In any case God is certainly conceived by Christians as 'personal', not as non-personal.

darkness, of the cloud of unknowing. In Christian and Sufi mysticism there is an equivalent to what the Zen Buddhists call *satori*. This sort of awareness of the divine presence, an awareness which influences life and conduct, is clearly not the same thing as assent to the conclusion of a process of philosophical reasoning. I am certainly not suggesting that metaphysics and mysticism are the same thing. If however we consider metaphysics simply as a movement towards the ultimate reality, the One, and as insisting on the limitations of language to describe the transcendent reality, we can reasonably see it as converging, in these respects and up to a certain point, with mysticism. Some philosophers might admit that this line of thought is not without historical foundation and then go on to claim that this constitutes a good reason for steering clear of the metaphysics of the One. But even if this form of metaphysics is hardly fashionable nowadays, it is premature to announce its final demise. A good deal depends on the presence or absence of a religious interest, in a broad sense of the phrase.

INDEX

Z

Zaehner, R. C., 48, 104–5, 107, 141
Zazen, 58, 64, 118

Zen Buddhism, 16, 57–67, 118, 273.
  See also Rinzai sect *and* Sōtō sect
Zoroaster, 104
Zoroastrianism, 97, 104